OPERA

OPERA

An Informal Guide

STEPHEN M. STROFF

a cappella books

Library of Congress Cataloging-in-Publication Data

Stroff, Stephen M.

    Opera : an informal guide / by Stephen M. Stroff

      p.cm.

    Discography :
    Videography :
    Includes index.
    ISBN 1-55652-170-7 : $11.95

    1. Opera. 2. Operas--Stories, plots, etc. 3. Singers.
    I. Title.

ML 1700.S94   1993   92-33208
782.1--dc20   CIP
                                                  MN

Published by a cappella books,
an imprint of Chicago Review Press, Incorporated

Printed in the United States of America

5 4 3 2 1

Editorial offices:
P.O. Box 380
Pennington, New Jersey 08534

Business/sales offices:
814 North Franklin Street
Chicago, Illinois 60610

Cover art: From *The Blue Aspic* © Edward Gorey, courtesy of Edward
Gorey and Gotham Book Mart & Gallery, Inc., New York City.

CONTENTS

INTRODUCTION

So you're interested in knowing more about opera? Good! You've come to the right place.

Maybe you've heard Luciano Pavarotti in a TV concert (he certainly gives enough of them), and liked the music you heard. Or maybe you've seen a complete opera, either on TV or in person, and were hooked by its combination of drama and melody. Perhaps you were even led to opera indirectly, through one of the various plays or books that have been transformed into librettos (the texts of operas), or had a friend play you musical excerpts that changed your mind about the supposed simplicity of the form.

Whatever the reason, I'm glad you're reading this. Even if you begin with no more knowledge than the liking of a particular voice, or a handful of "top pop" arias, you will emerge with a greater understanding of the reasons why opera has survived as a viable artform even into the era of advanced video technology.

As with my previous book, *Discovering Great Jazz* (Newmarket Press), I will take you step-by-step through the history of the music. Yet because opera is so much more complex, involving stagecraft and acting in addition to musical values, the journey will be a little different. I'll start by explaining the reasons for opera's birth, trace its declines and revivals through the centuries, and explain how voices adapted to the evolving styles of music that emerged. We'll discuss the various facets that an opera comprises—conducting, singing, ballet, choral music, acting, and direction—and evaluate their importance to the production as a whole. Then we'll run through the best operas, era by era, and recommend the best available audio and video recordings of each.

If this sounds like a lot of information, it is; but don't be scared off by that. There are certainly easier ways to learn about opera—going to a few performances, listening to Metropolitan Opera broadcasts, or just picking up recordings at random and reading the liner notes—but no other book, to my mind, ties it all together like this. Besides, this will be a relatively painless learning process, and (I think you'll find) enjoyable to boot. I remember how I started, from a position of not knowing anything about opera, and what processes led me to greater knowledge and a fuller understanding. And I know, from talking to others, that the majority (though not all) of opera buffs started much the same way I did—with the thrill that a specific voice or voices brought them. In fact, I'm willing to bet that most of you reading this started this way as well.

As for getting involved without spending a lot of money, that's easy, too. Most large public libraries are chockful of opera recordings, and the CD revolution has guaranteed that at least some of my recommended recordings will be in excellent listening condition. In addition, the proliferation of videotapes and laserdiscs means you can enjoy a wide variety of opera in your own home; and a great many of these recordings are available in public libraries, too. You'll find several of the best listed among my recommended recordings, plus a few listed as alternates. And, of course, there's always public television and cable stations, which (though uneven in quality) are certainly prolific in quantity.

As you gain understanding and appreciation of the finer points of operatic production, you'll find that you are able to determine whether a particular telecast is good, bad, or indifferent. And that's my goal: making you your own critic. For no listening experience is quite as subjective as opera. Despite certain objective points on which we must agree in order to make any headway, the bottom line is that all of us hear voices differently. There are some performers who are universally recognized as being the finest, of course, but after that you're on your own.

So, let's get started. We'll start with some basic definitions, a short history, and descriptions of the various facets that go into making an opera.

ONE

What Is Opera?

Everyone knows what opera is: a bunch of overweight people with trained voices, singing loudly in a foreign language. The plots are silly and dated, the music is complicated, and it isn't over 'til the fat lady sings. In other words, opera is a joke perpetrated on an unsuspecting public that just barely lasted until music videos came along. Right?

Well . . . not exactly.

Certainly, all opera singers (even bad ones) have trained voices, which means that they're taught to project their sound into full theaters without the aid of a microphone. When this works, however, there is no more thrilling sound in classical music than a voice that, basically, carries its own amplifying system. Some very famous singers have indeed been heavyweights; but just as many, if not more, were normal-sized folks. The only thing that all opera singers have in common is that their chests are more expanded, for their size, than those of average people; but then again, they exercise their singing-machines daily. Many (though not all) opera plots are indeed convoluted, a fact that inspired the nicknames "soap operas" for daytime radio and TV dramas and "horse operas" for long Western films. But the important thing to remember about opera is that the plot itself, and even the specific words, are not important in

1

and of themselves. Their emotional and intellectual effect on the listener is wholly dependent upon the music to which they are set.

Opera is a form of musical drama in which the emotions and situations of the protagonists are expressed through the music as played and sung. If the singers also happen to be good stage actors, and the sets are better than average, the effect can be heightened. Some operas (primarily French ones) also include ballets, but a ballet is no more a necessary part of an opera than a baseball game: it is an extra, and an occasional extra at that. The important thing to remember about opera, and the thing that sets it apart from musicals and operettas, is that the music is of an extraordinarily high caliber, and its effect on the listener depends first and foremost upon how well it is sung and played.

Let me give you one example. In the opera *Il Trovatore (The Troubadour)* by Giuseppe Verdi, the brother of a Spanish count (named di Luna) is captured by gypsies as a baby and is presumed dead. In reality, he has been raised by an old widow-gypsy (Azucena) and passed off as her son; he is now a Troubadour named Manrico, and has fallen in love with Leonora, a high-born Spanish woman who happens to be the favorite of his unknown brother, the Count. In order to trap the Troubadour and make him a captive, the Count kidnaps Manrico's "mother" just as Manrico is getting married to Leonora; the plot works, but when Manrico is put to death, the old gypsy tells the Count that he has killed his own brother.

On paper, there is nothing to admire about such a silly, convoluted plot. If it were a play, it would have died a well-deserved death about 100 years ago (and in fact, the actual play from which it was adapted has disappeared from the stage). Yet the music is superb, expressing the sorrows of Leonora, the anguish of Manrico, and the gloating triumph of Count di Luna in a *more profound and artistic way* than the lyrics that are being sung. In addition, Verdi found in this opera a perfect balance between memorable "tunes," such as one might find in an operetta or a musical, and genuinely creative music, transforming the threads of simple melody through the use of altered chords, variations on the melodies, and even counterpoint. One particularly magic moment comes at the end of the first act, when di Luna (a baritone), Leonora (a soprano), and Manrico (a tenor) interweave their separate voices into a musical tapestry that appeals to both the heart and the head. This is "music drama" at its most effective, and the greatest sets, costumes, and stage direction in the world could not improve on it. The music is the message.

Of course, there are operas in which (as already mentioned) the interaction of good singing and acting can considerably enhance your enjoyment. And this is as much true of some older works as later ones. Both Wolfgang Mozart's comedy *Le Nozze di Figaro* and Camille Saint-Saëns's biblical drama *Samson et Dalila* benefit from good actors, especially *Samson et Dalila*, which has long arias and duets that require some expressive movement. In even later operas, where the music is often more complex and less apt to capture the imagination of average listeners while they sit and watch the proceedings, the importance of good acting cannot in fact be over-stressed; yet in Alban Berg as well as Ludwig van Beethoven, Béla Bartók as well as Giacomo Puccini, it is first and foremost the musical treatment that makes an opera performance work or fail.

As musical extensions of drama, operas are generally long, averaging about two-and-a-half hours to perform. Thus, you must have a decent attention span to enjoy operas, even if you take them in one act at a time. In our highly visual age, the newcomer's enjoyment is often enhanced in the theater by the use of "supertitles," which are the translated words of the libretto placed on a screen above the stage. As you become increasingly familiar with the standard repertoire, however, you will find that supertitles are unnecessary and, sometimes, even a distraction to enjoyment. At home, of course, such devices are unnecessary; most complete opera recordings come with a libretto, printed in three to four languages, so that you can read along as you listen. Sometimes this, too, can be a distraction, though it is generally recommended that you follow the libretto the first time you hear any particular opera to familiarize yourself with the plot and to appreciate how these singing-actors accent certain words to convey an appropriate dramatic mood.

In the main body of the book that follows, we will examine fifty operas in great detail, and several more briefly. For the principal operas discussed, descriptions and plots are given, and a recommended recording is briefly described. Interspersed with these will be other aspects that pertain to opera: the development of acting, stage direction, and especially the changes that took place in singing. Because of the evolving nature of operatic music, which became gradually higher in range and pitch, more expressive, and less technical, singers had to change the ways that they sang. Naturally, we are hindered somewhat in examining these changes because sound recording technology wasn't developed until the late 1890s. As a result, we will have to (at times) approximate style changes with 20th-century artists who come the closest to our ideal. Nevertheless, it is important that you understand this facet of opera, because it will help you set your own standards when you begin to attend modern "live" performances. I have included a separate chapter on the "Golden Age of Singing," that thirty-year period between 1890 and 1920 when so many great singers were around that "name" artists were often given supporting roles just so the opera houses could use them all!

There's a lot of information to follow, but don't be daunted. If you stick with it, and take it a step at a time, I think you'll find that it all fits together and makes sense after a while. And remember, many of my recommended recordings—even some of the recital albums—can be found in most big-city libraries. Don't be shy about asking your librarian for help: you'll be surprised how much some of them know! A complete list of record and video company addresses is given at the end of the book for those who wish to order directly; all label names are spelled out, with the exception of the standard abbreviations RCA (Radio Corporation of America) and DG (Deutsche Grammophon). A good source for foreign CDs and cassettes is Chambers Record & Video Corp.; videos can be ordered from Lyric Distribution, Homevision, or Kultur. In the following cast lists of the complete operas, these standard abbreviations are used: s, soprano; ms, mezzo-soprano; c, contralto; ct, countertenor; t, tenor; br, baritone; bs, bass. All catalog information for recordings are for CD releases unless otherwise noted. Good luck, and have fun!

TWO
Early Opera

There is a tendency to think of early music as being less sophisticated and less "complete" than that which came later on. In some respects this is true; the symphony and concerto as we know them today did not develop until the mid-to-late 18th century, and the fine art of orchestration was not completely developed until the 19th century. Yet both the concerto and symphonic forms became "formulas," set ways of doing things that could not be deviated from without invoking sharp criticism from critics and audiences alike; and, by and large, music at its most creative is music that takes risks and succeeds. As a result, earlier forms of musical expression can often be as interesting as their mature brethren.

THE ORIGINS OF OPERA

"Masques," staged musical dramas based on classical Greek or Roman legends, which proliferated throughout Italy between 1580 and 1600, were the first form of sung dramas. They consisted of roughly twelve to fifteen set pieces, songs and duets, that put the dramas to music in a way not unlike that of folk or lute music—the kind of thing sung by the original troubadours (traveling singers). But masques did not have continuous plots, and were rather episodic. This led a group of Italian intellectuals, most of them from Florence, to consider expanding the format of the masques in order to present full-blown musical stage plays in which every note was played or sung. The title for this new type of sung drama, *opera*, was taken from the Italian word for "opus" or "work."

Opera is separated from earlier music by its use of richer harmonies. In the Middle Ages, the Roman Catholic Church promoted music that was simple in harmony and melody in order to appeal to the greatest number of people (especially, so they hoped, to converts). Because operas were originally written for the courts, where the intended audience was considered better educated and more musically inclined, this rule could be relaxed. Operas also used a larger number of supporting instruments to underscore the melody being sung. This, in turn, led to the melodies themselves being more varied and extended than was possible in a masque. Spoken drama lost its independent identity, but putting the words to music gave composers wonderful ideas for presenting the dramatic action through the melody line.

As a result, the simpler melodies of the 15th-century troubadours, which stayed within a five- or six-note range and had only the simplest harmony, became immediately old-fashioned. Even the first opera composers, Giulio Caccini (c. 1545–1618) and Jacopo Peri (1561–1633), attempted to match the rhythm of speech—the way syllables fell on the ear—and gave emotional climaxes to the melodies they wrote; and these *affective elements* were underscored by the use of vocal embellishments or *decorative elements*. These embellishments included items as simple as trills, grace notes (short notes from above or below that "lead in" to the main melody note), and rapidly sung scales, all of which have survived to today, as well as such now-archaic devices as staccato (short, clipped, repeated notes) sung on the same pitch (a trick also known, wrongly, as the "Baroque trill"), and flute imitations where the voice would pinprick notes softly but sharply in order to imitate the flute's sound.

From the beginning, then, composers attempted to match speech rhythms to their music. As time went on, they even became conscious of vowel-sounds of the particular language they were setting when choosing particular notes for their melodies. This is why, unlike operettas and musicals, operas usually *should not* be translated into other languages. It has nothing to do with snobbism, and everything to do with language matching notes. Even if operas were not sung, there still would be some problem: after all, Shakespeare, Goethe, and Chekhov do not translate well either. Sung drama is an even more ticklish situation, because the sound of the music and the sound of the words are supposed to match. The only opera that is immune to this sort of thing, to my knowledge, is Friedrich von Flotow's early 19th-century opera *Martha*, which was composed for texts in German, Italian, and French. Moreover, because the actual words of most operas are silly (as opposed to the music), singing them in the vernacular can actually detract from the audience's enjoyment.

EARLY OPERATIC SINGING

When opera began, there was (obviously) no such thing as an "operatic" voice. The first male opera singers were church singers, with pure tone, clean execution, and a natural, unforced sonority within their specified range. Because female concert singers, by decree of the Vatican, were not allowed to sing in churches, they too came into the operatic fold, but their voices were expected to match their male counterparts.

These early singers made their impact through what we now call *vocal coloration*: changing the timbre of the voice so that it could be melting and lyrical one moment, intensified and dramatic the next. Yet even in the most "intense" moments, the voice was still expected to respond to the demands of ornamental graces: trills, staccato, grace notes, octave leaps (going up from one note, say a C or D, to the one an octave above it), and scale runs. This style wasn't called "coloratura" back then (as it is today), simply because everyone was supposed to be able to do it. It was just plain operatic singing at that time. Most operas written between 1600 and 1700 have now completely disappeared, and with good reason: They were experiments by composers who had not found their own musical style and/or who had problems adapting their musical style to the peculiar demands of opera. In addition, this was the first great era of the "castrati," castrated male sopranos and altos, whose voices had the pure sound of boys coupled with the lung-power of adult males. The mere thought of such a perversion today raises the hackles of our enlightened psyches; but bear in mind that this, too, came about as a result of the Catholic Church's decree (based on the letters of St. Paul) that no females be allowed to raise their voices in song in churches or cathedrals. The advanced church music of Giovanni Palestrina and his contemporaries required voices with a semi-female range, and so they employed the castrati, whose condition was passed off as due to the results of "accidents" (a fall from a horse was the favorite excuse). As time went on, the castrati moved swiftly and easily into the upper echelon of opera. During the mid-to-late 17th century, many composers wrote music that was so convoluted, in order to show off the technique of the castrati, that not only is most of it unsingable today but it just isn't very interesting.

FIRST OPERA COMPOSERS

There were, however, two composers who were able to impose their mature musical style on the fledgling operatic artform, and as a result their works have survived. First and most important of these was Claudio Monteverdi (1567–1643), the "Genius of Mantua," who forbade his singers to add their own cadenzas (extra notes) or flourishes; 99 percent of his music was written out. In doing so, Monteverdi went against the grain of then-contemporary performance tradition that singers could add their own embellishments to a score. The other composer who tried to rein in the excesses of opera performers was Jean-Baptiste Lully (1632–1687). In a letter written by a zealous secretary, Lully's 1676 opera *Atys* is described as a work in which "everything has been created, calculated, measured so that the action of the drama progresses without ever weakening." Unfortunately, Lully went too far in trying to control the performers. Despite the charm of his dances and the beauty of some of his arias, his music is too restrictive and too formal for modern ears. As a result, where Monteverdi remains intriguing and inventive, Lully has the dubious distinction of being a "period" composer whose works are more museum pieces than part of the living tradition.

Monteverdi's music, like that of his contemporaries, was harmonically simple, following set patterns of major and minor chords. Yet within that framework, he worked miracles. He developed the use of "passing tones," notes that do not belong to a certain chord, but serve as transitions between chords, to give his music a dissonant feeling. He used different orchestral instruments to vary the sound of the accompaniment, a trick that gave his music great color. And he matched the words and music of his operas in such a way that they came much closer to the patterns of sung-speech, or *sprechstimme*, a technique that our modern atonal composers have revived in the 20th century. As a result, there are few extended passages in Monteverdi's operas, no arias that develop into duets or trios or larger ensembles, but short, dramatic musical fragments mixed with slightly longer lyrical ones. In the few extended arias that he wrote, one hears not the usual regular, bouncy melodies of 19th-century "bel canto," but irregular tunes, often based on only two or three chords, where he embellishes or flattens out the melody line depending on what the lyrics dictate. In other words, his music sounds different from that of any other great opera composer, and takes some time to understand, but if you follow the words of the libretto as you listen you'll be amazed at how brilliant he was at capturing the dramatic situation in music.

L'Orfeo
1607   Claudio Monteverdi

Emma Kirkby, s (Music); Nigel Rogers, t (Orfeo); Patrizia Kwella, s (Euridice); Helena Alfonso, s (A Nymph); Guillemette Laurens, s (Messenger); Catherine Denley, s (Hope); David Thomas, bs (Charon); Jennifer Smith, s (Proserpina); Stephen Varcoe, bs (Pluto); Mario Bolognesi, br (Apollo). London Baroque Opera, dir. by Charles Medlam; London Cornett and Sackbut Ensemble, dir. by Theresa Caudle; Chiaroscuro, dir. by Nigel Rogers. Angel (EMI) CDCB-47141 (two CDs).

Like the majority of operas from the 17th through the mid-18th centuries, *L'Orfeo* is based on Greek legend, in this case the story of the poet Orpheus (to use the original Greek) who goes to Hell to rescue his beloved Eurydice. Monteverdi's musical treatment is far more complicated than the later opera by Christoph Wiilibald Gluck, involving many peripheral characters (Music, Hope, Nymphs, and Shepherds) whose contributions to the drama are skillfully interwoven into the plot. It is also one of his most formal operas, which means that the music is more regular and less adventuresome than his later works; but it is still great.

Despite its brevity, the opera is divided into five acts, each of which centers around a specific scene and set of emotions. The first act, depicting the marriage of Orpheus and Eurydice, is happy; the second, centering on Eurydice's sudden death, is sad; the third, describing Orpheus's resolve to seek her in the afterworld, is tensely dramatic. The fourth act depicts the decision of Proserpina and Pluto, queen and king of the underworld, to release Eurydice to Orpheus's care, provided that he does not look back at her; when he does, she is lost forever. The final act begins with Orpheus's heartbroken lamentations, but changes to joy when Apollo, his father, descends from heaven and promises to make him immortal and reunite him with Eurydice.

Keynotes

L'Orfeo fuses many elements of popular and classical music of its time into one extended work. Chief among these is polyphony, the simultaneous use of two or more melodic parts. Also included are the rhythmic subtlety of the French *chanson* (or art song) and the then-common practice of embellishing a vocal line with short notes (staccato) and scale runs (coloratura). In this respect, listen to Orfeo's song in Act II, *Vi ricordo o boschi ombrosi* (*Do you remember, o shady groves*), which establishes his happy mood before the revelation of Eurydice's death, followed quickly by the Messenger's lament and the echoing sadness of the Shepherds. Also, in Act III, notice the clever use of an organ (that has a dark, sinister sound) to accompany Charon, the boatman of the River Styx, contrasting strongly with the gentler strings that accompany Orfeo's great aria, *Possente spirto* (*Powerful spirit*). Here, Monteverdi creates one of his most extended set pieces, reflecting the changing moods of his words with tremendous dramatic force.

The Recording

The recommended recording of this opera has a slightly cold and clinical sound quality, but this can be compensated for by boosting the midrange and bass and cutting the treble a little on your stereo. The singers, even in such supporting roles as Music, Hope, the Messenger, Shepherds, and Spirits, are all excellent, and the joint conducting of Charles Medlam and Nigel Rogers (who also sings Orfeo) is appropriately crisp and remarkably (for ancient instruments) in tune. This recording uses Monteverdi's final version of the opera, which dates from 1615, but is in most respects identical to the 1607 edition.

Follow-up Listening

The operas of Monteverdi are not everyone's cup of tea: the apparent thinness of the orchestra, the lack of regular, discernible melody, and the complexity of construction leave some listeners cold. If, however, you are struck (as I am) by the originality and freshness of this music, you will want to investigate the longer and even more brilliant *L'Incoronazione di Poppea* (*The Coronation of Poppea*, 1642) in the performance with Arleen Augér, Della Jones, and Grayson Hirst, conducted by Richard Hickox, on Veritas VCT 7-90775-2 (three CDs).

HENRY PURCELL AND CHAMBER OPERA

By the late 17th century, the rather stilted French opera of Lully had become the norm by which great operas were judged, the Italian style (after Monteverdi's death) having deteriorated into endless roulades (vocal ornaments sung to a single syllable) and cadenzas (vocal flourishes added toward the end of an aria). Then Henry Purcell (1659–1695) came along, a composer best known for his songs. He was asked to write his first opera for Mr. Josiah Priest's Boarding-School for Young Gentlewomen. Such a task could hardly have been inspiring; after all, none of Mr. Priest's "young gentlewomen" were professional singers. As a result, Purcell had to write "down" for the types of voices available to him. Also, because this was a private school for girls, all parts had to be sung by females—including that of the hero, Aeneas, who was later assigned to tenor or baritone voices. Considering all of these handicaps, it is surprising that he wrote anything good at all, let alone one of the greatest chamber-operas of all time.

Dido and Aeneas
1689 Henry Purcell

Emma Kirkby, s (Dido); Judith Nelson, s (Belinda); David Thomas, br (Aeneas); Jantina Noorman, ms (Sorceress); Emily van Evera, s (Enchantress); Tessa Bonner, s (Spirit); Rachel Bevan, s (Enchantress, Sailor). Taverner Choir and Players, cond. by Andrew Parrott. Chandos CHAN-8306.

Like Monteverdi, Purcell strove for musical and dramatic unity. He also used a small orchestra, in keeping with the limitations of Mr. Priest's school. What he did differently, however, was to abandon the semi-spoken *recitatives* of Italian opera (*recitatives* arc words spoken rapidly on one or two pitches, with one instrument, generally a harpsichord or piano, as accompaniment), instead using the *arioso*, a free-form song, to connect dramatic passages. He cleverly used related keys, such as A minor and D major, to link melodic passages, giving his music a logical sequence. These innovations, combined with his ability to mix drama and humor, had a profound effect on later Baroque composers—even those who wrote much more ornate music than this.

The end result was a short opera, in English, which begins in a lighthearted vein yet grows steadily more serious. The plot is based loosely on the Greek drama of Dido and the Trojan wars, a subject explored much more fully 150 years later by Hector Berlioz in his two-part opera, *Les Troyens* (1856–1859). Purcell ignores most of the side issues to concentrate on the love between Dido, Queen of Carthage, and Aeneas, the "Trojan guest," having his librettist (Nahum Tate) invent along the way a coven of witches who plot Dido's destruction by issuing a phony "divine command" that Aeneas must leave Carthage. When Aeneas returns, he tries to explain his hasty departure to Dido, but she shuns him and dies.

Keynotes

Unlike Monteverdi's *Orfeo*, the main attraction of which is its complexity, *Dido* succeeds by its very simplicity. The music is tuneful, even memorable—the first opera to accomplish such a feat, thus ensuring its longevity—and the witches' scene is so "mad" sounding that one hears it as it should be, which is as comic relief. Yet as the music progresses, the drama deepens; and Dido's final lament, *When I am laid in earth*, with its relentless, descending ground bass beneath a broken, minor-key melody, is one of the most poignant moments in all opera.

The Recording

There was, in the 1950s and early sixties, a tendency to cast such true "operatic" voices as Kirsten Flagstad and Elisabeth Schwarzkopf for leading roles in *Dido*, but in recent decades the pendulum has swung back in the other direction. The tendency now is toward lightweight voices, which may or may not be appropriate in some Baroque operas, but which are perfect for approximating the "young gentle-women" who first performed *Dido and Aeneas*. Emma Kirkby's pure, virginal sound is remarkably appropriate for Dido, Jantina Noorman is the best Sorceress on record, and Andrew Parrott never conducted a finer performance.

Follow-up Listening

None of Purcell's other operas are "through-composed," which means that there is dialogue between musical numbers, and there is not nearly as much dramatic continuity because these later works were written more as musical plays. But if you liked *Dido*, you may also enjoy his "semi-opera" *The Fairy Queen* (1692), especially in the performance by Elisabeth Priday, David Thomas, and the English Baroque Soloists conducted by John Eliot Gardiner on DG ARC-419221-2 AH2 (two CDs).

EARLY EIGHTEENTH-CENTURY OPERA

After the deaths of Lully and Purcell, the Italian style overtook all others. Even German composers, not yet ready to create their own operatic identity, fell under the spell of the florid Italian music; in fact, the greatest opera composer of the early-to-mid-18th century was a German, claimed equally by his native country and England, Georg Friedric (later Anglicized as George Frideric) Handel (1685–1759).

Unlike most opera composers (with the exception of the Italian Antonio Vivaldi), Handel proved himself a master of many forms: oratorio, concerto grosso, choral anthems, instrumental showpieces, ballet, and incidental music. He managed to both tame the wild, rococo fantasies of the lesser operatic composers, with works that had greater form and less disconnected vocal flourishes by the castrati, and inject a warmth and passion that made his characters less wooden. Indeed, the raw emotion of some of his dramatic scenes have led many scholars to consider him the true grandfather of the Romantic era. Certainly, both Mozart and Beethoven admired him to the point where they arranged some of his music in their own styles.

By this time, of course, the castrati had become the darlings of the opera world. Only a few female sopranos were able to compete with them, and though there were certainly tenors and basses, they always received the short end of the stick in contemporary scores. With their unnaturally short vocal cords and man-sized lungs, the castrati were able to perform feats of vocal gymnastics that are all but impossible today: long-winded phrases full of crescendos (gradually getting louder), decrescendos (gradually getting softer), trills, roulades, runs, and held high notes. This type of vocal virtuosity was just the ticket for the Baroque era. The frills, furbelows, and curlicues that you see in Baroque design found their musical expression in the feats of the castrati.

Unfortunately, only one castrato was recorded (Alessandro Moreschi in 1902–04; these recordings are available on Opal CD-9823), but his voice was past its prime, and as chief singer and choir-director of the Vatican his repertoire was limited to religious music. Today, castrato parts are sung either by females or "counter-tenors," adult males with a highly trained falsetto. In general the white-sounding "hoot" of a falsetto, however well trained, is not the same thing as a true castrato, but since it is all we have we must rely on it. American countertenor Drew Minter is recommended for his excellent album of Handel arias (Harmonia Mundi HMC-905183/405183 [CD/cassette]) written for the famous castrato "Senesino" (Francesco Bernardi), including excerpts from the operas *Giulio Cesare, Rodelinda, Tolomeo, Riccardo Primo, Orlando,* and *Flavio.* Especially recommended are *Fammi combattere* from *Orlando* (a melody also used later in England by Handel for his aria *Let the bright Seraphim*), *Vivi, tiranno* from *Rodelinda,* and—especially insofar as the next opera is concerned—his versions of the two arias from *Giulio Cesare*.

Giulio Cesare in Egitto
(Julius Caesar in Egypt)
1724–1730 George Frideric Handel

Janet Baker, c (Caesar); Valerie Masterson, s (Cleopatra); Sarah Walker, ms (Cornelia); Della Jones, ms (Sextus); James Bowman, ct (Ptolemy); John Tomlinson, bs (Achillas); John Kitchiner, bs (Curio). English National Opera Chorus and Orch., cond. by Sir Charles Mackerras. Thorn-EMI video HTVE-3558 (two tapes).

The general tendency in Italian-styled music of the early 18th century was to convey the drama solely through vocal shadings and flashy technique; the music itself was often of little interest harmonically and often unrelated to the text. Handel changed all that by charging his arias with emotionally strong tremolos (shakes), irregular rhythms, and instrumental comments played behind the singers, depending on the dramatic situation. This is one reason why his best operas remain fascinating today; and of all of them, the 1724 version of *Giulio Cesare in Egitto* is the most unified and cogent.

Caesar sends his general to enlist the support of the Egyptian ruling siblings Ptolemy and Cleopatra, who respond by beheading the general. Caesar goes to their court and chastises them for this vicious action; Cleopatra, in disguise, intends to seduce him. Sextus, the beheaded general's son, plans to assassinate Ptolemy, but is stopped by Achillas who claims that Caesar has drowned when he leapt into the harbor during battle. Cleopatra raises her troops against Ptolemy to avenge Caesar's death. Achillas, who was refused the hand of the general's widow (Cornelia) in marriage, defects to Cleopatra's side; Caesar reappears, describes his escape, and leads the troops to victory. Ptolemy is killed in a duel with Sextus, Caesar and Cleopatra march off into the sunset, and all is well again.

Keynotes

The arias and ensemble scenes of *Giulio Cesare* are very much tied into the drama. Especially notable are Sextus's vengeance aria in Act

I, the "hunting" aria for Caesar (with French horn obbligato), Cleopatra's song at the beginning of Act II, and the arias for Caesar and Cleopatra in Act III. All of these require the greatest concentration by the singers, because Handel plays steady rhythms against syncopations (yes, there were syncopations in music before jazz!), takes the vocalists through difficult coloratura passages (including variations on the first part of the aria, a form that became known as a "da capo" aria because the singer returned "to the beginning" to repeat the melody), and requires them to interpret the music dramatically as well.

The Recording

The present version has the handicap of being in English, but the conducting of Sir Charles Mackerras and the sensitive, dramatically incisive singing of Janet Baker, Valerie Masterson, Sarah Walker, and Della Jones make for a gripping performance. In addition, it has the advantage of being a video production, and the sets and costumes—while not really authentic Roman-cum-18th century—are quite good. Note especially how Baker has mastered the not-so-easy art of walking like a man, giving the illusion of a masculine Caesar despite her being a contralto.

La Serva Padrona
1733   Giovanni Battista Pergolesi

Paolo Montarsolo, br (Uberto); Anna Moffo, s (Serpina); Giancarlo Cobelli (Vespone) Rome Philharmonic Orch., cond. by Franco Ferrara. V.I.E.W. Video 1411.

Giovanni Battista Pergolesi (1710–1736) was a prolific composer of chamber and sacred music, including a well-known *Stabat Mater* (1729), as well as such full-length serious operas as *Adriano in Seria* (1734). In 1733 he was asked to provide an intermission feature for a full-length performance of his opera *Il Prigioner Superbo* (1732); he responded with the small-scale bagatelle *La Serva Padrona* (*The Servant Mistress*), and—just like that—the genre of "opera buffa" (or "comic opera") was born.

Opera buffa appealed greatly to those in French society who detested the outmoded complexity of Lully's and Jean Philippe

Rameau's operas, and in fact inspired a left-wing artistic movement called the "Guerre des Bouffons" ("War of the Clowns"), headed by Jean Jacques Rousseau. As a result, Pergolesi's work was given an astonishing 100 performances between 1752 and 1753 at the Paris Opéra. In 1753 it was moved to the Comédie Française, where it received ninety-six more!

The plot concerns Serpina, a rebellious maid, who is sick of her master's (Uberto's) orders. Uberto, in turn, is tired of her impertinence, and asks his manservant Vespone (a mute role) to find him a wife. Of course, Serpina overhears this conversation and plans to be that person herself. She pretends to have found a husband of her own, an ill-tempered soldier named "Captain Tempest" (Vespone in disguise), and brings him around to badger the old man much the same way Count Almaviva was later to do to Dr. Bartolo in *Il Barbiere di Siviglia*. Uberto is alarmed at Tempest's behavior. Serpina claims that the Captain requires a large dowry; if it is not forthcoming, he will insist that she marry Uberto; and, as soon as Uberto gives her the money, Vespone whips off the false mustache and military disguise. Uberto admits that he loves Serpina, and as the curtain falls she seems certain to be installed as mistress of the house.

Keynotes

Pergolesi's arias are in a simplified Italian style. They have the sprightly pace and follow the *da capo* form, but are less technically demanding than Handel's. Uberto's first aria is especially fine, being less formal than the others, and the concluding duet, with its drum imitations, sets a pattern for all future operas in this genre.

The Recording

Because of the mute acting role of Vespone, strictly audio recordings of *Padrona* are never quite satisfactory, even when the opera's only two singers (Uberto and Serpina) interpret the music to the fullest. Here, despite the lack of subtitles, all is made clear in the juicy singing of Paolo Montarsolo and Anna Moffo, and the clever combination of 18th-century opera buffa and 20th-century slapstick (not too heavily applied, thank goodness). The camera work is also surprisingly good, adding an extra dimension not normally found in theatrical productions.

You Can't Tell the Players Without a Scorecard

Though the earliest opera composers, like Monteverdi, basically adapted Greek and Roman dramas as the basis for their operas, by the early Baroque period composers began to "gussy up" these plots in order to make them different and/or more attractive. As a result, librettos became so complicated that audiences began ignoring them completely, concentrating more on the magnificent singing that they paid their money for in the first place.

Probably the best (worst?) example of this sort of thing was Johann Hasse's (1699–1783) 1731 opera *Cleofide* (musically a very good work, by the way, and available on Capriccio 10193/96, four CDs). In this gem, the army of Indian King Poros has been badly beaten by Alexander's troops. Poros contemplates suicide, but is deterred by his beloved Cleophis, queen of another part of India. She assures him of her love, but he accuses her of being Alexander's mistress. Meanwhile, having given up on suicide, Poros trades his crown for the helmet of his general Gandartes to deceive the conqueror, and is so convincing in the part that he receives a special present for Poros from Alexander. After Poros (in disguise) leaves, his kidnaped sister Eryxene is brought in to Alexander as a form of "tribute"; Alexander's general Timagenes declares his love for her, but Alexander—without knowing it—has already won her heart, and lets her go.

But that's just the half of it! Later in the same act, Cleophis admits that she was flirting with Alexander, but claims it was just to convince him to spare India. The Macedonians reclaim Eryxene, and return her to her brother; Eryxene tells him of Alexander's generosity, and Cleophis hurries to the conqueror to lay her kingdom at his feet. Timagenes, jealous and angry at Alexander's gesture, shows up looking to revenge himself by revealing a traitorous scheme to Poros—but instead he does so to the disguised Gandartes, who is still wearing Poros's crown! Meanwhile, the real Poros shows up at Alexander's camp (still disguised as the general) and maliciously tells him that Cleophis's vows of fidelity are worthless. By Act III things are so mixed up that Cleophis believes that Poros has drowned in battle, but Eryxene is told the truth. When, still believing Poros to be dead, Cleophis agrees to marry Alexander, Eryxene (who doesn't know that Cleophis hasn't been told the truth), believes that Cleophis is unfaithful. In Hasse's version, the usual "Greek tragedy" is averted in favor of a happy ending: no one dies, Poros and Cleophis are reunited, and Alexander winds up with Eryxene.

And you thought "Dynasty" was confusing?!?

THREE

The Classic Era

After the death of Handel, opera found itself at a crossroads. The Italian style continued to dominate, yet there emerged a field of talented young German composers who were determined to expand Handel's innovations into something more dramatically expressive. The most influential of these composers were Wolfgang Amadeus Mozart (1756–1791), who worked his revolutions within the operatic conventions of his time, and Christoph Willibald Gluck (1714–1787), who sought to erase the conventional forms of aria and duet to produce works of lesser melodic appeal but greater dramatic force. Naturally, Mozart found greater sympathy for his works in Italy, because his style was still recognizably Italianate, as well as in Germany where Handel's influence was still strong. Gluck, conversely, found a more receptive audience in France, where he settled permanently in 1773. Both streams of thought had a profound influence on all opera that followed, and in fact were combined in the only opera written by Ludwig van Beethoven (1770–1827).

GLUCK

Gluck's operatic reforms did not extend to the introduction of more contemporary plots; on the contrary, he followed his predecessors' pattern of using ancient Greek plays and Roman legends for his stories. However, he eliminated the florid style of the Italians as being inappropriate for such elemental drama. He also sought and wrote for larger, more expressive voices, the kind we today consider essentially "operatic." His music also combined melody and dramatic thrust with the musical cohesion sought by Monteverdi, Lully, and Purcell. As a result, he rarely stopped the action for arias or duets, and was even less patient with singers who introduced unwritten variations into his music, instead writing continuous streams of music in which arias and duets were way stations in the pursuit of drama.

Alceste
1776   Christoph Willibald Gluck

Jessye Norman, s (Alceste); Nicolai Gedda, t (Admète); Tom Krause, br (High Priest); Siegmund Nimsgern, br (Hercules); Robert Gambill, t (Evander); Kurt Rydl, bs (God of the Underworld); Bernd Weikl, br (Apollo). Bavarian Radio Symphony Orch. and Chorus, cond. by Serge Baudo. Orfeo S/C-027823-F (three LPs/CDs).

Alceste, originally performed in German in 1767 but later revised in French for the Paris Opéra, is perhaps the summit of Gluck's achievement. It concerns the dying king Admète and his saddened queen Alceste; an oracle reveals that the king must die unless a friend can be found to die in his place. Alceste volunteers to substitute for him, invoking the gods of the underworld and defying them to do their worst. Admète miraculously recovers; he learns that a substitute has agreed to die in his place, but he is not told the victim's name. He is horrified at such a prospect, but is soon joined by Alceste in a rapturous love duet. As the music continues, Alceste is unable to hide her impending grief at leaving her husband and children. Both die; but Hercules, learning their fate, travels to the gates of Hell, where he performs his famous "seven labors" in order to save both their souls and his own. Admète and Alceste return to their people while Hercules, as a result of his heroic struggle, earned the right to become a god.

Keynotes

The High Priest's invocation in Act I is an excellent example of how Gluck was able to "build" a scene dramatically, gaining a power and momentum equal to the best work of Verdi and Wagner nearly 100 years later. Alceste's aria *Divinités du Styx*, where she invokes the demons of hell, has become a standard concert piece for dramatic sopranos, while the Act II duet of Alceste and Admète, and Admète's aria *Bannis la crainte et les alarmes*, reveal the tender side of Gluck's musical personality. In short, this is one of the most engrossing of the pre-1780 operas, as well as one of the most influential works ever written.

The Recording

Serge Baudo's conducting is not the most propulsive or exciting that you would care to hear, though he does a competent job. On the other hand, the voices of Jessye Norman, Tom Krause, and Siegmund Nimsgern are perfect for their respective roles (having both drama and full, unforced tones), and Nicolai Gedda sings better here than on any of his post-1975 recordings. In addition, the sonics are spectacular, giving solidity to the solo voices and transparency to the chorus and orchestra; and (thankfully) the work is sung in French rather than in the Italian translation.

Follow-up Listening

Those interested in other Gluck operas will enjoy the performance of *Orfeo et Eurydice* with Elisabeth Speiser, Janet Baker, and Raymond Leppard on Music & Arts Programs CD-295 (two CDs), and *Iphigénie en Aulide* with Lynne Dawson, Anne Sofie von Otter, John Aler, José van Dam, and John Eliot Gardiner on Erato/Musifrance 45003-2-ZA (two CDs).

MOZART

Where Gluck reformed opera by introducing a dramatic style practically unknown at the time, Mozart cut some of the extraneous embellishments of the Venetian school, but basically maintained its florid melodic style. On the other hand, after an early flirtation with Greek drama that ended with *Idomeneo* in 1781, he spent the last decade of his brief life writing operas based on contemporary dramas and comedies. This led to his great popularity in Austria, Germany, and later Italy. Though Gluck eventually had the most lasting influence on the direction of opera, Mozart was one of its most popular contemporary composers.

Le Nozze di Figaro
(The Marriage of Figaro)
1786　Wolfgang Amadeus Mozart

Samuel Ramey, bs (Figaro); Lucia Popp, s (Susanna); Kurt Moll, bs (Dr. Bartolo); Jane Berbié, ms (Marcellina); Frederica von Stade, ms (Cherubino); Thomas Allen, br (Count Almaviva); Kiri te Kanawa, s (Countess Almaviva); Robert Tear, t (Don Basilio). London Opera Chorus; London Philharmonic Orch., cond. by Sir Georg Solti. London 410 150-2/4-LH3 (three CDs/cassettes).

Le Nozze di Figaro is one of Mozart's greatest and most popular works. Its plot was based on a then-famous comedy by Pierre Augustin Caron de Beaumarchais, the second part of a trilogy that began with *Il Barbiere di Siviglia*, which was banned because it portrayed a lecherous nobleman.

The Barber of Seville, named Figaro, has been hired as a manservant to Count Almaviva. He is engaged to marry the Countess Rosina's maid, named Susanna, who the Count secretly lusts after. Meanwhile, Dr. Bartolo arrives to remind Figaro that he has previously promised to marry Marcellina, the doctor's elderly housekeeper, in lieu of paying off a debt to her.

Cherubino, who was once the Count's page, comes to Susanna and begs her to use her influence to get him reinstated into the Count's good graces. Hearing the Count approach, the young boy hides; the Count begins to woo Susanna. When the Count discovers that the boy has witnessed his dalliances, he arranges for him to be enlisted into the army.

A series of farcical situations follow. The Countess and Figaro make a plan to fool the Count by having Cherubino dress as a woman and pretend to be Susanna. They hope to catch the Count wooing the false Susanna, and shame him into returning to his wife.

This plot fails when the Count enters the chamber and Cherubino, narrowly escaping detection, jumps from the window. Meanwhile, Bartolo and Marcellina present their case to the Count against Figaro, and he is glad to help them to eliminate his rival for Susanna's affections.

Finally, the plot begins to unravel: Marcellina turns out to be Figaro's mother, so this impediment against his marrying Susanna is lifted. Susanna and the Countess switch clothing so that the Countess (dressed as Susanna) can confront her amorous husband. While this plot is effective, it further complicates matters because Figaro is unaware of the switch. Once this final deception is revealed, all is forgiven.

Keynotes

Le Nozze di Figaro is not only one of the most musical and cleverly wrought operas ever written, but one of the first "greatest hits" operas—a major reason why it was performed at a time when the play itself was still banned. Memorable tunes abound: Figaro's *Se vuol ballare* and *Non piu andrai*, Cherubino's *Voi che sapete* and *Non sò piu*, Bartolo's *La vendetta*, the Countess's *Porgi amor* and *Dove sono*, Susanna's *Deh vieni non tardar*, and the Count's *Vedrò mentr'io*. Yet it is the marvelous quality of Mozart's ensembles that grab us, especially the finale that begins with the Count begging his wife for forgiveness. Indeed, it is so rich in melody that Marcellina's and Don Basilio's arias are usually cut in performance.

The Recording

Despite its popularity, *Figaro* is quite difficult to cast well: even in the so-called "Golden Age of Singing," few casts for this work were thought effective. One must have a rich-voiced baritone with an exceptional upper and lower range, a lyric baritone with dramatic ability, a soubrette soprano with a silvery timbre, a lyric soprano with richness and depth to her tone, a bright coloratura mezzo with both flexibility and charm, and a competent supporting cast. In addition to all this, you must find a conductor who can both support the singers and propel the comedy. As a result, few recordings capture both the depth and quicksilver quality of the opera, but the present version is exceptional in every way. Solti propels the opera with finesse and style, has wisely chosen contrasting soprano timbres for Susanna and the Countess, and cast the flexible lyric bass of Samuel Ramey as Figaro.

Don Giovanni
1787   Wolfgang Amadeus Mozart

Giuseppe Taddei, br (Leporello); Eberhard Wächter, br (Don Giovanni); Joan Sutherland, s (Donna Anna); Gottlob Frick, bs (Commendatore); Luigi Alva, t (Don Ottavio); Elisabeth Schwarzkopf, s (Donna Elvira); Graziella Sciutti, s (Zerlina); Piero Cappuccilli, br (Masetto). Philharmonia Orch. and Chorus, cond. by Carlo Maria Giulini. Angel CDCC-47260 (three CDs). *Video alternate*: Ferruccio Furcanetto, Samuel Ramey, Anna Tomowa-Sintow, Gösta Winbergh, Julia Varady, Kathleen Battle, cond. by Herbert von Karajan. SONY/CBS S2LV-46383 (2 video discs).

As a result of *Figaro*'s popularity, Mozart was commissioned to write works for the Prague Opera. Because the former opera was a comedy, he decided to include some comic elements in his next work; yet the depth of expression that he reached in *Don Giovanni* eclipsed that of all operas before it, even the dramatic creations of Gluck. Indeed, in its rare combination of comedy and terror, melody and drama, complex musicality and memorable tunes, it has achieved status as one of the most perfect of all operas, exceeded only by Verdi's *Otello*. Yet it was performed only sporadically during the 19th century, disappeared from many opera houses in the early part of our century, and has only reclaimed its stature since the now-legendary Glyndebourne Festival performances of the mid-1930s.

Mozart and his librettist, Lorenzo da Ponte, took the legend of Don Juan Tenorio and imbued it with the quality of Greek drama. No longer is this just the story of a shameless libertine whose sexual exploits make all others seem tame, but a struggle between good and evil ending with a classic confrontation in which the Don is given two choices: repent or burn in hell, starting immediately. At the start of the opera, the Don, always successful in his amorous exploits, is losing his touch. When he tries to seduce Donna Anna, she fights him off and screams for help. When the Don kills her father, the Commendatore, it is the beginning of the end for him; he has crossed the line from seduction to murder with no thought whatsoever as to the moral implications. A former lover, Donna Elvira, appears out of nowhere to denounce him and spoil his present plans. His advances on the peasant girl, Zerlina, are rebuffed, and when he tries forcing himself on her he is exposed and chased. Mozart and da Ponte have also introduced a thinly veiled class struggle to the plot by contrasting the libertine Don, whose title makes him a nobleman despite his lack of morals, and his servant Leporello, who is morally sound and loathes his master's exploits.

In such a work, the characters become more allegorical than real: Donna Elvira a symbol for all abused women, Donna Anna (who recognizes the Don's voice as the one she heard the night of her father's murder) the symbol of human revenge, her fiancé Don Ottavio the hopeful paragon of virtue who cannot act on his indignation, and the ghost of the Commendatore (represented by a statue) the symbol of divine revenge. This in itself makes *Don Giovanni* a superb work of art, because it lifts it from the mundane world of reality and places it in the sphere of pure theatre. But add to that Mozart's music, with its chameleon-like change of mood and character, and you have an opera that renews itself with each hearing.

Keynotes

Don Giovanni, like its predecessor, abounds with memorable melodies, including Leporello's *Madamina*, the Don's *Deh vieni alla finestra* and *Finch' han dal vino*, Zerlina's *Batti, batti o bel Masetto*, and Ottavio's *Dalla sua pace* and *Il mio tesoro*, the latter being a test of the tenor's technique. On the opposite end of the spectrum are such gut-wrenching dramatic outbursts as Elvira's *Ah, chi mi dice mai quel barbaro dov'è* (*Where will I find the traitor who took my heart?*) and Anna's *Or sai chi l'onore*, at which point she realizes for certain that the Don is her father's assassin. And then there is the Act I finale, during which Leporello entertains the Don's guests while his master tries to seduce Zerlina offstage. When her cries for help are heard, Giovanni enters and blames Leporello for the disturbance. His two ex-lovers condemn his actions. Mozart portrays these multiple occurrences with a musical complexity that can only be called astounding in a composer just turned thirty-one.

The Recording

Don Giovanni is not only fiendishly difficult to cast but also to perform properly. Most recordings of the opera, in my experience, suffer from weak casting somewhere along the line (in some cases, all the way down the line) or from the choice of a conductor who sees it not as an organic whole but as a disconnected series of events. In this 1959 version, Eberhard Wächter's baritone is sometimes hard and harsh, but just as often lyrical and mellifluous; Giuseppe Taddei sings a couple of rough notes in his aria (*Madamina*), but is otherwise excellent; and the rest of the cast is superb, better both vocally and dramatically than any other. Elisabeth Schwarzkopf practically owned the role of Donna Elvira, Joan Sutherland sings with a surprising amount of dramatic conviction (and lack of "scooping," or sliding up and down in pitch), and both Luigi Alva and Graziella Sciutti turn in their finest work on record here. Moreover, Carlo Maria Giulini is one of only a handful of conductors who not only start and sustain good tempos but pull the tricky ensemble scenes together.

The video performance is not quite as well sung, Samuel Ramey being rather gruff of voice and Anna Tomowa-Sintow displaying occasional wobble. Yet, the sets and acting are first-rate, especially the climatic scene where the Commendatore's statue drags the Don to hell: The back wall "opens up" into the cosmos, into which both figures are sucked into oblivion. In addition, Herbert von Karajan conducts with an excellent combination of tautness and breadth.

Die Zauberflöte
(The Magic Flute)
1791 Wolfgang Amadeus Mozart

Jerry Hadley, t (Tamino); Thomas Allen, br (Papageno); June Anderson, s (Queen of the Night); Barbara Hendricks, s (Pamina); Robert Lloyd, bs (Zarastro); Ulrike Steinsky, s (Papagena). Scottish Chamber Orch. and Chorus, cond. by Sir Charles Mackerras. Telarc CD-80302 (two CDs).

After the brilliance of *Figaro* and the virtuosic complexity of *Don Giovanni*, the slight comic plot of *Die Zauberflöte* seems unworthy of

Mozart's attention. However, he was at the height of his powers as a composer, and lavished on *Zauberflöte* the full range of those powers. The last act includes references to the mystical beliefs of freemasonry, a secret society that counted Mozart among its members. In addition, he used this opera to enhance the German style of *singspiel*, combining spoken and sung passages in the vernacular. This was the final break in Germany from the Italian style that had dominated German opera since the days of Handel.

The plot of *Zauberflöte* is often considered confused and silly; those who do not like fairy tales will undoubtedly be put off by it. Prince Tamino, chased by a huge dragon, is saved by three ladies, servants of Astrofiammante, the Queen of the Night. The ladies slay the dragon; but Tamino has passed out, and the bird-man Papageno arrives before Tamino wakes up and claims credit for the kill. The ladies return, catch Papageno in his lies, and shut up his mouth with a padlock. The Queen appears and asks Tamino to help save her daughter Pamina, who was kidnaped by the supposedly evil Zarastro. She releases Papageno from his padlock; he joins Tamino on his quest, armed only with a picture of Pamina and a magic flute that calls the beasts of the wood to their aid whenever they need them.

In the second act, however, everything is turned upside-down. The Queen is shown to be an evil witch and Zarastro the high priest of a temple dedicated to truth and justice. Tamino goes through their entrance rites while Papageno finds his true love, Papagena, who is a bird-woman. Pamina renounces her mother's tyranny and marries Tamino; they all live happily ever after, fairy-tale style, except for (one suspects) the Queen and her ladies.

Keynotes

Because of its *singspiel* nature, *Die Zauberflöte* has more of a stop-start feel to it than any of Mozart's other famous operas (except *The Abduction from the Seraglio* [1782], which is also a *singspiel*). Nevertheless, it includes some of his finest and most famous music; Beethoven was fascinated by Mozart's use of every vocal convention of the day, from popular songs to arias and even *lieders*, or art songs. Tamino's aria *Dies bildnis ist bezaubernd* and Pamina's *Ach, ich fuhls* are art songs, while Papageno's arias and duets draw on folk and popular sources. Mozart chose his song types to complement his characters; thus, it is not surprising that the lowly Papageno's repertory is drawn primarily from German folksongs. The Queen's first aria, *O zittre nicht*, is a sort of mini-concerto, starting with a sung recitative, going into a lyric aria, and ending with the type of fast "tag" ending that became known as a *cabaletta* many years later. Zarastro's aria to the ancient gods of Egypt, *O Isis und Osiris*, has long been a test piece for basso profundos the world over, and the Queen's second aria, *Der holle Rache*, is a tour de force often unwisely sung by fledgling coloraturas in auditions because of its repeated high Fs and difficult triplets.

The Recording

During the first half of our century, this opera was so ridiculed that it was seldom performed, let alone recorded; but in recent decades it has become possibly Mozart's most popular opera, replacing *Figaro*. Most versions feature either solid but uninteresting voices with solid conducting (Sir Georg Solti, Sir Thomas Beecham, Karl Böhm), great conducting with mediocre or defective voices (James Levine, Colin Davis, Bernard Haitink), or a mix of some good singing and some good conducting (George Szell, Herbert von Karajan, Neville Marriner). In this 1991 recording, Robert Lloyd (Zarastro) is a bit off his best form, and June Anderson (Queen) is a little unsteady in her first aria (*O zittre nicht*), but otherwise all sing exceedingly well, imparting a life and zest to the music that most others lack. In addition, Sir Charles Mackerras's conducting is nothing short of spectacular, and the sound quality is also superb.

Follow-up Listening

Mozart's earlier *singspiel*, *The Abduction from the Seraglio* (1782), is given a competent performance by Arleen Augér, Reri Grist, Peter Schreier, Kurt Moll, and Karl Böhm on DG 435 395-2 GX5 (five CDs–also look for the out-of-print two-CD version, 423 459-2); and his brilliant 1790 comedy *Cosi Fan Tutte* (*So Do They All*), in which the singers' voices are used more like instruments than as a means of personal expression, is given a joyously high-strung performance by Rachel Yakar, Alicia Nafé, Gösta Winbergh, Tom Krause, and Arnold Östman on L'Oiseau-Lyre 414 316-2 OH3 (three CDs).

BEETHOVEN

Fidelio
1806   Ludwig van Beethoven

Gerhard Unger, t (Jacquino); Ingeborg Halstein, s (Marzel-
line); Christa Ludwig, ms (Leonore [Fidelio]); Gottlob
Frick, bs (Rocco); Walter Berry, br (Don Pizarro); Franz
Crass, bs (Don Fernando); Jon Vickers, t (Florestan).
Philharmonia Orch. and Chorus, cond. by Otto Klemperer.
Angel CDMB-69324 (two CDs).

Beethoven's only opera is often called a freak. So much attention was
given to the music, and the extension of the drama through it, that
there is little if anything left for the performers to do on stage; and,
even at this early stage in opera history, patrons had come to expect
more than that from the recent works of Gluck and Mozart. In its
original form, as *Leonore* (1805), it was even flawed musically; but
Beethoven kept working at it, on and off, for another nine years, and
in its final version it met with success. The text comes from a book
by Frenchman Jean Nicolas Bouilly, and had been previously used as
a libretto by three other composers (Pierre Gaveaux, Johann Simon
Mayr, and Ferdinando Paër).

The plot concerns a Spanish nobleman, Florestan, who was unfairly arrested and held as a political prisoner by his enemy Don
Pizarro. Florestan languishes in the darkest dungeon while Pizarro
spreads rumors of his death. But the prisoner's wife, Leonore, suspects the truth; and so she disguises herself as a man, uses the name
of "Fidelio," and obtains a job as assistant to Rocco, the chief jailer.
A complication arises in that Rocco's daughter Marzelline has a
crush on Fidelio and has rebuffed her former boyfriend, Jacquino
the turnkey. Pizarro asks Rocco to kill Florestan before the arrival of
Don Fernando, the King's minister. He refuses, but consents to dig
the grave if Pizarro will kill Florestan himself. Leonore, overhearing
the plot, resolves to save her husband at any cost. She helps Rocco
dig the grave, brings food and water to the condemned man, and
throws herself before Pizarro when he comes to kill Florestan. Don

Fernando arrives in the nick of time, recognizes his old friend in the starving prisoner, and has Pizarro arrested.

There is no question that *Fidelio*'s libretto was the finest contemporary drama of its time. Gluck exploited Greek drama to good effect, and Mozart did wonders with Don Juan's legend, but the story of Florestan and Leonore has a timeless quality of its own. Even in our day, political prisoners are held and tortured unfairly; in fact, when soprano Kirsten Flagstad sang the part of Leonore in 1950 her husband was undergoing a similar incarceration simply because he was a food-taster for the rightwing Quisling party. The dramatic situations are almost unbearably tense, with the exception of the lighthearted mock romance between Fidelio and Marzelline. Beethoven, the master of dramatic music, exploited this intense plot to the utmost.

Keynotes

As I mentioned, Beethoven combined the best qualities of Gluck and Mozart in his only opera. From Gluck, he took the use of heavier, dramatic voices rather than high, agile ones; from Mozart, he learned the art of writing theatrically effective ensembles, arias that are mini-concertos, and dramatic *singspiel*. Note, for example, the Gluck-like thrust of Pizarro's aria of hate, *Ha! Welch' ein Augenblick!*, and the well-balanced (if action-stopping) arias for Leonore and Florestan, *Abscheulischer! Wo eilst du hin?* and *Gott! Welch dunkel hier*. The first-act quartet, *Mir ist so wunderbar*, is one of the most beautiful and clever pieces ever written, and the second-act duet, *O namenlose Freude*, has an ecstatic quality echoing Mozart at his most inspired. What's more, the clarion trumpet call announcing Fernando's arrival is one of the most dramatically effective moments in all opera.

The Recording

Otto Klemperer was one of the great conductors of the 1930s and forties; a series of mishaps left him, by 1960, a crippled man in a wheelchair, beating out time with one fist. As a result, some of his recordings (including this one) are slower and a bit more ponderous than was his wont twenty years earlier, but the cast assembled here is almost perfect. Christa Ludwig strains a bit for her highest notes, but the secure middle and low ranges convey Leonore's music with great emphasis; Ingeborg Halstein, Gottlob Frick, and Walter Berry are superb; and the work of Jon Vickers as Florestan is in a class by itself.

Follow-up Listening

Another opera from this period in the same vein as *Alceste* and *Fidelio*, and which had a significant influence on Bellini's *Norma*, is Gaspare Spontini's 1807 *La Vestale*. Although Italian by birth, Spontini dropped his earlier light-hearted style to create this dramatic work that was hugely popular in Napoleonic France. He later served for twenty years as opera director in Berlin, greatly influencing the growth of German opera. The recording with Maria Callas, Ebe Stignani, and Franco Corelli, on Melodram MEL-26008 (two CDs), is particularly effective.

Fidelio She Wasn't

German soprano Wilhelmina Schröder-Devrient (1804–1860), the most famous Leonore in the final (1814) version of Beethoven's opera (and also the first soprano soloist in his Ninth Symphony), scarcely presented the image of a chaste maiden in real life. In fact, she was known as a sensuous libertine who could rival Xaviera Hollander, the "Happy Hooker" of the 1970s, in her numerous affairs and sexual escapades.

In 1868, a few years after her death, a most remarkable two-volume set was published surreptitiously in Berlin: *Aus den Memoiren einer Sängerin*, or *Memoirs of a Singer* by "Madame S.," claimed to be Schröder-Devrient's "autobiography." It was written in the form of letters addressed to an old friend, a doctor, among whose papers they were supposedly found at his death and edited by his nephew. Authentic or not, *Memoirs of a Singer* is one of the hottest classics of blue literature, a book so unbelievably explicit that even today it is rarely if ever seen in the complete, unexpurgated edition (it was last published in this form, in English, by Collectors Publications of California, a sex-book specialist, in 1969). Let's put it this way: if this book is to be believed, she went after anything that moved short of the animal kingdom. Perhaps her last name should have been "Schröder-Deviant"; in any case, it certainly wasn't Fidelio, which is German for "fidelity"!

FOUR

Bel Canto
Operas

As a result of the popularity of Mozart's comedies and the dramas of Gluck and Beethoven, Italian opera composers began to show a strong Germanic influence in the early 19th century. Though not sacrificing their gift for melody, Italians began to use many elements introduced by German composers for their own means. Chief among these was the use of embellishments (trills, staccato, runs, and so forth) for a specific dramatic or comedic purpose, and the use of more contemporary plots in place of stories from Greek mythology. This break with their own traditions was not altogether final or always successful; but in the generation that followed Mozart, Spontini, and Beethoven, three names rose to the top, defining a new movement that consolidated these innovations and then created new breakthroughs of their own: Gioacchino Rossini (1792–1868), Vincenzo Bellini (1801–1835), and Gaetano Donizetti (1797–1848). Their combined output came to be known as the bel canto school, taken from the Italian words for beautiful singing.

The greatest innovation of the bel canto composers was in their expanding the tenor's range, placing him squarely in competition with the soprano (or, in some cases, the mezzo-soprano). Even Mozart kept his tenor arias in a workable range, seldom if ever ascending beyond high B-flat, but by the 1820s tenors had found various means of singing beyond that range. Audiences encouraged the high notes, and, before long, high Cs became more common. Rossini and Donizetti even went beyond that, asking their tenors to reach for the stratosphere. Yet it must be remembered that, in those days, most tenors used the head-voice as a method of reaching these notes; not until the late 1830s did tenors begin to consistently reach for the skies by pushing from the chest.

These composers, and operas, introduced three new types of singers to the world: the "coloratura" soprano, the "tenore leggero," and the dramatic-coloratura mezzo. The coloratura soprano, originally known as "soprano leggero," is a light, airy voice. Most of these singers can go up to the F above high C, and a few—such as Mado Robin (1918–1960)—climbed upward to the A or even the B above that. A typical example of the breed was Lily Pons (1904–1976), darling of the Metropolitan Opera in the 1930s and forties. Her recital on Sony MPK-45694 features arias from *Il Barbiere di Siviglia*, *I Puritani*, and related operas by Giacomo Meyerbeer (see Chapter 5), Léo Delibes (1836–1891), and Ambroise Thomas (1811–1896). Though this is Pons slightly past her prime, and her singing is occasionally breathy, she displays the full arsenal of technical "fireworks" that all such singers are supposed to have: scale runs, trills, grace notes, and staccato (separated notes sung in a lightly accented, detached style).

The "tenore leggero," or coloratura tenor, also has a light, airy voice able to create a fusillade of effects. One excellent modern example is Raúl Giménez (b. 1952), whose recital of Rossini arias on Nimbus NI-5106 gives a good example of the style in a number of interesting excerpts. Obviously, it follows that the dramatic coloratura mezzo should also have a flexible voice; but because it was this female range of voice that closest resembled the castrati, mezzos were also called upon to be more dramatic than the tenors. They sang men's parts in several of the bel canto operas. The best of these in recent years has been Marilyn Horne (b. 1929); London 421306-2-LA showcases her range in several exciting excerpts from Rossini's *L'Assedio di Corinto*, *Otello*, *Tancredi*, and *La Donna del Lago* (*The Lady of the Lake*).

Rossini

L'Italiana in Algeri
(The Italian Girl in Algiers)
1813   Gioacchino Antonio Rossini

Ruggero Raimondi, bs (Mustafá, Bey of Algiers); Patrizia Pace, s (Elvira); Alessandro Corbelli, br (Haly); Frank Lopardo, t (Lindoro); Agnes Baltsa, ms (Isabella); Enza Dara, br (Taddeo). Vienna Philharmonic Orch. and State Opera Chorus, cond. by Claudio Abbado. DG 427 331-2-GH2 (two CDs).

Unlike most buffo operas written before it, *L'Italiana in Algeri* owed its structure to the Italian tradition of *commedia dell'arte*, a broad kind of farce not too far removed from the Marx Brothers. In *commedia dell'arte*, the plot is a loose sketch, not a well-constructed play, and the comedians were expected to improvise bits. Once music entered the picture, of course, the improvisation was meant to be kept within its bounds, but a good performance of this opera should still have its spontaneous moments.

The Bey of Algiers, a humorously pompous ass, no longer loves his wife Elvira. He has heard from his servant, Lindoro, that Italian girls are zesty and fun, and so instructs his servant Haly to watch for Italian ships coming to his shores. Conveniently, one such vessel is wrecked in a storm; on board are Isabella, looking for her lost love Lindoro, and her aged admirer Taddeo, who came along for the ride. Isabella recognizes Lindoro and cooks up a plan. She presents Taddeo as her uncle, and the old man offers his "niece" to the Bey as a wife. In return for this favor, the Bey bestows upon him the title Grand Kaimakan of Algeria. To compensate, Taddeo tells the Bey he can win Isabella easily once he joins the ancient order of "Pappatacci" (literally, "eat and shut up"). To do so, the Bey must continually eat and drink while pretending not to see anything that goes on around him. While he feasts, Isabella, Lindoro, and Taddeo board a boat to leave; finally the Bey wises up, but decides that Italian women are too much for him, returning to his true love Elvira.

Rossini, who was only twenty-one when he wrote this opera, finished it in twenty-seven days. Its loose structure is unusual for him; so too is his inclusion of both a coloratura soprano and a mezzo, which makes it impossible to perform in higher keys (as is the case, for instance, with *Il Barbiere di Siviglia*). Nevertheless, the unceasing inventiveness of the music, and its clever mix of memorable melody with counterpoint, have reserved for it a place of honor among his works.

Keynotes

Because this opera is more or less a succession of arias, duets, and ensembles, it is difficult to point out any one of them as superior to the others. Yet the first-act arias for Lindoro (*Languir per una bella*), Isabella (*Cruda sorte!*), and Mustafá (*Già d'insolito ardore*) are justly famous, and the duets between Lindoro and Mustafá and Isabella and Taddeo are test pieces for coloratura singers. Most striking of all, however, is the Act I finale, *Viva il flagel delle donne*, a quartet that turns into a septet, which set the style of the "Rossini crescendo"—a rhythmic figure that starts softly, then builds to a furious conclusion.

The Recording

L'Italiana is so difficult to sing, calling for the perfect blend of great voices, florid technique, and interpretive humor, that few performances do it justice; yet conductor Claudio Abbado has assembled a very good cast that works as an ensemble to perform their music with aplomb. Tenor Frank Lopardo has an unusual Rossini tenor voice, being dark in timbre rather than bright, but his coloratura singing is the best I've heard since the old days of Alessandro Bonci and John McCormack; Enzo Dara is competent, Ruggero Raimondi stunning, and Agnes Baltsa without peer in this role today.

Il Barbiere di Siviglia
(The Barber of Seville)
1816 Gioacchino Antonio Rossini

Dino Borgioli, t (Count Almaviva); Riccardo Stracciari, br (Figaro); Salvatore Baccaloni, bs (Dr. Bartolo); Mercedes Capsir, s (Rosina); Vincenzo Bettoni, bs (Don Basilio). La Scala Chorus and Orch., cond. by Cav. Lorenzo Molajoli. Music Memoria 30276/77 (two CDs).

If *L'Italiana in Algeri* was a miracle for so young a composer, *Il Barbiere di Siviglia* was a tour de force of unprecedented magnitude. Based on the first of Beaumarchais's plays (of which the second was *Le Nozze di Figaro*), the "barber" had already been turned into an opera by Giovanni Paisiello, a composer in the Venetian style, back in 1782. The Paisiello *Barbiere* was not only extremely popular but still in circulation; thus, when the twenty-four-year-old Rossini presented his version at the Teatro Argentina in Rome in 1816, it was booed lustily by the pro-Paisiello audience on general principle. This, however, did not last long: once audiences stopped booing and started listening, they made *Il Barbiere* the single most successful Italian comic opera of all time. Indeed, it is the oldest Italian opera by any composer to remain in the standard repertoire today.

Unlike *Le Nozze di Figaro*, which explores the more touchy subject of infidelity, *Il Barbiere* concerns the efforts of young Count Almaviva to wrest his beloved Rosina away from the clutches of her ward, the arrogant, rather dense Dr. Bartolo. Bartolo has on his side Rosina's governess, Berta; the scurrilous singing teacher, Don Basilio, whose favorite method of dealing with a problem is to slander the opposition; and the entire Spanish police. Almaviva, on the other hand, has the services of his beloved Rosina, as cunning a woman who ever lived, and the town barber, Figaro, whose ingenuity as a con man could put Groucho Marx to shame. First, Almaviva is dressed up as a drunken soldier with papers stating that he is to be interred with the good doctor (whom he drunkenly refers to as "Bardolo" and "Barbaro"); their argument is so loud that it wakes the town up. Almaviva reveals his true identity to the sergeant of police, and makes his escape. Then Almaviva takes the disguise of

Rosina's singing teacher; Bartolo is told that Don Basilio is home sick, and can't come. In an ironic reversal, Almaviva pretends to be helping the Doctor keep that scoundrel Almaviva away! Basilio shows up, looking fit, but Figaro, Rosina, and the disguised Almaviva convince him that he is sick, after all, and should get some bed rest. Figaro shaves Bartolo while the lovers plan their elopement; but Bartolo, overhearing the plan, shows Rosina a glimpse of a letter she wrote to Almaviva, claiming it to be from another woman. Rosina raves in jealousy, but the reappearance of Almaviva and Figaro clears the air; the lovers get married, and Bartolo gets the equivalent of her dowry from the generous Count.

The role of Rosina in *Il Barbiere* was originally written for a mezzo-soprano, but by the mid-19th century this most popular of female comic roles was appropriated by coloratura sopranos. This tradition stayed in place, even under Arturo Toscanini, until the mid-1920s when Conchita Supervia began revivals of the original version. Critics and musicologists have fought for the original, but audiences tend to prefer a soprano; the decision is up to you. The recommended recording uses the soprano version, the alternate is in the mezzo key.

Keynotes

The fast-paced *recitatives* of the librettist, Cesare Sterbini, have a rhythm and momentum all their own—but only when sung by native Italians. On the other hand, the arias, each and every one of which is famous, have been performed by singers of various nationalities. These include Almaviva's *Ecco ridente in cielo*, Rosina's *Una voce poco fa*, Basilio's *La calunnia*, and Figaro's *Largo al factotum*, which probably ranks as the most famous and instantly recognizable opera aria ever written (it is certainly the most famous *baritone* aria ever written). In addition, the more convoluted plot of *Il Barbiere* brought out the best in Rossini's creative powers, the finales of both acts being (if anything) even more cleverly wrought than the Act I finale of *L'Italiana*. Beethoven told Rossini, after reading the score of *Il Barbiere*, that he was both a great composer and a comic genius; he was right on both counts.

The Recording

Versions of *Il Barbiere* have come and gone (mostly gone) since this recording was etched in 1929, yet there is no complete performance that so completely captures the essence of the work's humor (or, in the case of Almaviva's music, its elegance). Note, however, that Dr. Bartolo's aria *Un dottor della mia sorte* is replaced here by another composer's *Manca al foglio*; and Rossini's lesson-scene aria, *Contra il cor*, is replaced by an original song written by the soprano, Mercedes Capsir. Interpolations of this sort were common throughout the 19th century. I recommend that you take a libretto out of your local library, because this issue provides none.

Video supplement: The 1947 film of this opera, with Nelly Corradi, Ferruccio Tagliavini, and Tito Gobbi, is badly cut (about one-quarter of the opera was excised), but what is left is superbly performed and it does contain *Un dottor* (Lyric Distribution 1537).

Stereo alternative: The recording with Agnes Baltsa, Francisco Araiza, Thomas Allen, and Neville Marriner on Philips 411 058-2 PH3 (three CDs) is not as well articulated or sung, nor as much fun to hear as either of the previous versions; but it is the original mezzo-soprano version, is both complete and correct, and is far and away the best version made since the '29 classic.

William Tell
1829   Gioacchino Antonio Rossini

Cesar Antonio Suarez, t (Fisherman); Sherrill Milnes, br (William Tell); Luciano Pavarotti, t (Arnold); John Tomlinson, bs (Melcthal); Della Jones, s (Jemmy, Tell's son); Mirella Freni, s (Mathilde); Ferruccio Mazzoli, bs (Gessler); Piero de Palma, t (Rodolfo). Ambrosian Opera Chorus; National Philharmonic Orch., cond. by Riccardo Chailly. London 417 154-2/4-LH4 (four CDs/cassettes).

After Beethoven told Rossini that *Il Barbiere* was a work of comic genius, he advised him never to write anything serious. Rossini paid him no heed; he wrote several "dramas" in the Venetian style, few of which survive today, and a plainly bad version of Shakespeare's *Othello*. Toward the end of his composing days, however, he was commissioned to write a truly "grand" opera for Paris; the plot he chose was the story of William Tell's insurrection against his Austrian oppressors, and he lavished on it the full measure of his genius, turning a potentially maudlin story into a vast canvas on which every emotion and dramatic scene possible was re-enacted.

The opera opens with the Shepherd's Festival; a fisherman sings an aria, and the aged, blind Melcthal blesses the loving couples among them. Yet his son Arnold does not ask for a blessing; he is torn by his love for Mathilde, the daughter of the hated Austrian governor Gessler, and his patriotic feelings for his native Switzerland. The festival is interrupted by the sound of horns, announcing Gessler's impending arrival. Leuthold, a shepherd, runs in to announce that he has killed an Austrian soldier who was forcing himself on his daughter. He flees with Tell's help; Gessler's guards arrive too late to catch him, but arrest old Melcthal in retaliation. Arnold and Mathilde meet and pledge their love, but he learns that his father was killed by Gessler's order. At a gathering honoring the 100th anniversary of Austrian rule in Switzerland, Gessler demands that the people honor his hat placed on a pole. Tell refuses to do this, and is ordered to shoot an apple from his son's head. Tell succeeds, then kills Gessler; the Swiss revolt and overthrow the Austrians, while Mathilde finds refuge in Arnold's arms.

Rossini took his libretto from Johann Christoph von Schiller, but added the characters of Mathilde and Arnold. Tell, assigned to the baritone, has some of the noblest and most interesting music written for that vocal range up to that time; yet it is the melting lyric music of Mathilde, the fiery ensemble passages by Jemmy, and the alternately suave and martial music of the tenor, Arnold, that dominate the proceedings. This was, perhaps, a mistake on Rossini's part. He himself preferred tenors with a melting head-tone to sing Arnold, but since this role became the prototype for every *lyric spinto* hero thereafter, to do so sounds ludicrous today. In addition, the conflict between a tenor-hero and a bass-villain, with a soprano-heroine caught in between, became the nucleus of many Italian operas henceforth.

Keynotes

The overture to *Tell* is the most famous ever written but, strangely, bears no resemblance to any of the music of the opera. Particularly outstanding are the fisherman's aria, the Arnold-Tell duet *Ah, Mathilde!*, Mathilde's aria *Sombre forêts* (known in Italian as *Selva opaca*), Tell's lyric scena *Resta immobile*, and Arnold's call to arms (that heavily influenced Giuseppe Verdi). Yet what strikes the listener is how cleverly Rossini reworked here the formerly comic feeling of his famous "crescendos" to dramatic purposes, especially in the Act I finale where Jemmy's voice rises, like a laser beam, over the massed ensemble.

The Recording

This performance of *Tell* is slightly cut, and is in Italian instead of the original French, but the singing of Luciano Pavarotti (with the help of a microphone-boost) is spectacular. Sherrill Milnes and Mirella Freni are excellent as well; Della Jones's Jemmy is outstanding; and Riccardo Chailly conducts very well. The sum total is a performance that may never be duplicated in our century, which certainly conveys the lyric and dramatic elements of the score with aplomb.

Follow-up Listening

Rossini's comic opera *La Cenerentola* (1817), based on the Cinderella story, is given a fine performance by Teresa Berganza, Luigi Alva, Renato Capecchi, and Claudio Abbado on DG 423 861-2 GH2 (two CDs); and his dramatic work *Semiramide* (1823), one of his few successes in the Venetian style, is sung with accuracy and brio by Joan Sutherland, Marilyn Horne, and Joseph Rouleau, with fine conducting by Richard Bonynge, on London 425 481-2 LM3 (three CDs).

BELLINI

Norma
1831 Vincenzo Bellini

Gina Cigna, s (Norma); Ebe Stignani, ms (Adalgisa); Giovanni Breviario, t (Pollione); Tancredi Pasero, bs (Oroveso). E.I.A.R. Orchestra and Chorus, Turin, cond. by Vittorio Gui. Pearl GEMM-CDS-9422 (two CDs).

By the time of the bel canto composers, the concept of opera built around tragic Greco-Roman figures was becoming a thing of the past. Part of the new modernity was to select plots that were, if not exactly contemporary, at least concerned with ideas that could be applied to contemporary life. As a result, *Norma* must be seen as an anachronism, a work out of its time, though musically it is in the style of the more recent composers Gluck and Spontini rather than the antiquated one of Handel and Hasse.

Bellini was considered the most lyrical opera composer who ever lived; indeed, he had a gift for long, extended melodies that seemed to hang suspended in midair. His style embodied all that was to become the Romantic era: delicate, wistful harmonies, tragic figures caught up in situations they cannot resolve, and an orchestra that, though larger than in the past, could be used in full or in small groupings to suggest wistful sighs and intimate moments. *Norma* was heavily influenced by Spontini's *La Vestale*, the great opera that just preceded the bel canto era by about a decade, and as a result both *Norma*'s plot and its music are similar to *Vestale*.

Norma, the high priestess of the Druid temple, has broken her vows of chastity with the Roman proconsul Pollione, who is one of the oppressors of her people. Pollione is no longer in love with her, having been enraptured by the young Druid virgin Adalgisa; Norma, who doesn't know this, tries to persuade her people to make peace with the Romans. Adalgisa confesses to Norma that she has denied her faith by falling in love. Norma is about to forgive her when she suddenly discovers Adalgisa's lover is Pollione. Adalgisa decides to remain true to her mistress and reject Pollione's advances. Norma considers suicide, then resolves to renounce her love so that Adalgisa can be free. By this time, however, Pollione has rejected Adalgisa as well; enraged, Norma spurs her people on to war. Pollione is captured in the sacred temple, but Norma intercedes and offers herself for the death penalty in his place. A funeral pyre is erected; at the last moment, Pollione joins Norma on it as a penance for his offenses before God.

Keynotes

Unlike most bel canto operas, the role of Pollione requires a lower-voiced dramatic tenor rather than the high coloratura sounds preferred by Rossini; yet it is the two women who capture all our attention. Most famous of all is Norma's aria *Casta diva* and its follow-up cabaletta, *Bello a me ritorna*, but Adalgisa's aria, the Adalgisa-Pollione duet (*Va crudele al dio spietato*), and the Norma-Adalgisa duet (*Mira, o Norma*) are all worthy of note. The musical role of Oroveso, Norma's father, is not terribly rewarding, though his opening aria (*Ite sul colle, Druidi*) has long been a test-piece for basses.

The Recording

In our time, the two most famous Normas have been Maria Callas and Joan Sutherland—the first more dramatic, the second more lyrical—but the recordings of each leave much to be desired. This 1937 recording, though slightly abridged, is the most exciting and accurately sung version ever released. Gina Cigna's voluminous soprano makes the perfect Norma, Ebe Stignani practically "owned" the role of Adalgisa during her long career, and the little-known Giovanni Breviario reveals a cutting spinto tenor voice that revels in the high tessitura of Pollione's opening aria. Vittorio Gui conducts with passion; the performance never flags, and Tancredi Pasero is an imposing Oroveso.

I Puritani (The Puritans)
1835 Vincenzo Bellini

Maria Callas, s (Elvira); Giuseppe di Stefano, t (Arturo); Rolando Panerai, br (Riccardo); Nicola Rossi-Lemeni, bs (Giorgio); Aurora Cattelani, ms (Enrichetta). La Scala Orch. and Chorus, cond. by Tullio Serafin. Angel CDCB-47308/4AVB-34065 (two CDs/cassettes).

If *Norma* represented a perfect balance between lyric and dramatic elements, *I Puritani* represented a breaking away, like Rossini's *William Tell,* from the more graceful style toward something more inherently dramatic. This is not to say that *I Puritani* does not have its lyric moments, but merely to emphasize that the extended upper range of the duets creates a greater dramatic tension, and the coloratura given to the soprano has a distinct function in promoting the plot rather than interfering with it. It was Bellini's great swan song; the composer died shortly after its premiere.

I Puritani tells the story of Elvira, daughter of Lord Walton, who is a follower of Oliver Cromwell, the puritanical political revolutionary who led the rebellion against the English crown. She loves Lord Arthur Talbot, but he is a follower of the royal Stuarts, so her father has promised her hand to Sir Richard Forth who—like himself—follows Cromwell. Surprisingly, Walton relents, and Elvira prepares to marry Arthur. Meanwhile, the Puritans have taken the Stuart Queen Henrietta prisoner. Arthur rescues her by disguising her in a bridal veil and leading her past her guards. He is accosted by his rival, Sir Richard, but when Richard lifts the veil he sees that it is not Elvira and so lets him pass. Elvira is told that Arthur has eloped with another woman, and goes mad. Richard and Elvira's uncle, Sir George, prepare to meet Arthur in battle because he has abandoned Elvira. Arthur secretly visits Elvira; her sanity is temporarily restored, but signs of her unbalanced mind disturb him. Arthur is captured and is about to be executed when a messenger arrives and explains that the Stuarts have been defeated and all prisoners are to be pardoned. With Arthur freed, Elvira's reason returns for good, and they live happily ever after.

Keynotes

Sir Richard's Act I aria, *Ah, per sempre*, and its ensuing *cabaletta* are test pieces for baritones; Arthur's aria, *A te, or cara*, requires both a melting legato and a stirring high D-flat; and the George-Richard duet *Suoni la tromba* inspired no less a composer than Franz Liszt to commission a string of variations by himself and other pianist-composers for his massive work, *Hexameron*. Yet, again, it is the soprano's music that is the centerpiece of the opera. Elvira has four outstanding moments: the first-act *cabaletta*, *Son vergin vezzosa*; the second-act "mad scene," *Qui la voce*; the third-act aria, *A una fonte afflitto*; and the Arthur-Elvira duet that follows, *Vieni fra questa braccia*.

The Recording

This is, unfortunately, an imperfect rendering of the score. Some music is cut, other sections are shortened or transposed down, and neither Rolando Panerai nor Nicola Rossi-Lemeni are in their best voice. Yet Maria Callas's portrayal of Elvira dominates the proceedings, Giuseppe di Stefano sings reasonably well if at times overloud, and in toto this is a better representation of *I Puritani* than any other version.

Follow-up Listening

Bellini's gentle fantasy *La Sonnambula* (*The Sleepwalker*, 1831) is not as dramatic as his other operas, but contains some lovely music exquisitely sung by Maria Callas, Fiorenza Cossotto, Nicola Monti, and Nicola Zaccaria, and ably conducted by Antonino Votto, on Angel CDCB-47377 (two CDs).

DONIZETTI

After Rossini's retirement from opera in 1829, it seemed as though the tradition of opera buffo would come to a grinding halt; but the emergence of a young composer from Bergamo named Gaetano Donizetti assured its continuance for a while. Like Rossini, Donizetti was a well-grounded musician with a gift for melody. Though he could write wholly original tunes, he was not a revolutionary, but was perfectly content to work in the same idiom (and within the same rules) set down by his predecessors and contemporaries. Yet his wit could be so sparkling and his sense of construction so sound that he almost effortlessly turned out *L'Elisir d'Amore*, which has proved to be as durable in its own way as Rossini's *Il Barbiere di Siviglia*.

L'Elisir d'Amore (The Elixir of Love)
1832   Gaetano Donizetti

Luciano Pavarotti, t (Nemorino); Dawn Upshaw, s (Giannetta); Kathleen Battle, s (Adina); Leo Nucci, br (Belcore); Enzo Dara, bs (Dr. Dulcamara). Metropolitan Opera Chorus and Orch., cond. by James Levine. DG 429 744-2/4 (two CDs/cassettes).

Adina, a rich and pretty landowner, is courted by the bumbling peasant Nemorino. Sergeant Belcore, who enters their village with a troop of soldiers, tries to win Adina's heart with his good looks and military bearing. Nemorino, jealous, buys a flask of cheap Bordeaux wine from "Dr." Dulcamara, a traveling quack, who assures him that it is a love potion that will make Adina his within twenty-four hours. This sets the stage for various comic situations: Nemorino's embarrassing drunkenness; Belcore's pressing Adina into a quick marriage; and Nemorino's enlistment into Belcore's army so he can earn the money to buy another flask of "love elixir." Nemorino's rich uncle dies, leaving him his only heir, but Nemorino mistakes the villagers' sudden deference to him to the influence of the magic brew. Adina spots Nemorino's enlistment paper and buys it back from Belcore; not knowing this either, Nemorino makes an ass of himself by swearing to die in battle for her, and then passes out in her arms. Sobering, Nemorino is sure that he has lost his love, but Adina rebuffs Belcore and marries him instead. Everybody is happy; even Dulcamara ends up selling his Bordeaux at good prices to villagers who think it was responsible for the marriage!

One of the keys to *L'Elisir*'s success is the fact that, despite florid passages, staccato effects, and other vocal embellishments, it is not particularly difficult to sing. The music is so cleverly written that it scarcely calls for any extra interpretation at all, and those florid passages that sound so hard are actually pretty easy for a well-trained voice. Unlike *Il Barbiere*, which calls for five outstanding singers, *L'Elisir* needs but four steady voices with competent techniques. Small wonder, then, that even in provincial opera houses one will find this a recurring staple of the repertoire.

Keynotes

Like *Il Barbiere di Siviglia*, excellent melodies abound in *L'Elisir d'Amore*, though they are not as well known to the opera outsider as Rossini's music, with the exception of Nemorino's lyric aria, *Una furtiva lagrima*. Just as captivating (if, perhaps, less memorable) is his first-act arioso, *Quanto e bella*, plus his buffo duets with Dulcamara (*Obbligato, Obbligato!*) and Belcore (*Venti scudi*). Adina is also given some charming music, particularly her duets with Nemorino (*Esulti pur la barbara*) and Dulcamara (*Quanto amore*).

The Recording

None of the current versions of *L'Elisir* are really bad (except, perhaps, the one on CBS/Sony), but this performance has an extra sparkle that makes it irresistible. Luciano Pavarotti greatly improves his performance over the one he gave with Joan Sutherland twenty years earlier, in both interpretation and technical finish, and Kathleen Battle is (as usual) pearly and fluid. Leo Nucci's entrance is marred by vocal strain and a spreading tone, but he improves through the performance; and Enzo Dara, though not generously endowed of voice, imparts a real buffo quality to the role of Dulcamara. James Levine conducts with brio and energy, and the orchestra sounds uncommonly full.

Lucia di Lammermoor
1838 Gaetano Donizetti

Mario Sereni, br (Enrico Ashton); Ezio Flagello, bs (Raimondo); Anna Moffo, s (Lucia); Corinna Vozza, ms (Alisa); Carlo Bergonzi, t (Edgardo); Pierre Duval, t (Arturo). RCA Italiana Opera Orch. and Chorus, cond. by Georges Prêtre. RCA 6504-2-RG (two CDs).

Perhaps no other Italian opera has been so much a symbol of good and bad as *Lucia di Lammermoor*, a Scottish drama set in 1700, taken from the novel by Sir Walter Scott. Extremely popular from the time of its debut, it has served as a showpiece for sopranos and tenors ever since; yet many of them twist around the music to suit their own purposes, seldom giving it the dramatic thrust it needs to lift it above the mundane, and transforming it into a personal show-case for virtuosity and brilliance of voice. In this regard, *Lucia* is a throwback to the times when the castrati (and their female soprano rivals) would "stop the show" to interpolate cadenzas and high notes. In recent years, an opposite tendency has predominated, which is to strip the opera of all cadenzas, even those in the score, because they are "undramatic." This has led to recordings and performances that seem almost schizophrenic, trying desperately (and, for the most part, unsuccessfully) to combine musical "correct-ness" with a dramatic thrust more appropriate to *Salome* than to anything from the bel canto school.

The plot is remarkably similar to *I Puritani*, which, perhaps not coincidentally, premiered just eight months earlier. The heroine's brother, Lord Henry Ashton, is trying to recoup his fortune and avoid a political *faux pas* by marrying his sister to Lord Arthur Bucklaw. Lucy, knowing nothing of this, is in love with Edgar of Ravenswood; when her brother discovers this, he uses the most underhanded methods to break off their affair. While in France on a mission of political importance, Edgar sends letters to Lucy that Henry intercepts. Thinking herself abandoned by Edgar, Lucy agrees to marry Arthur and signs the wedding contract. Edgar bursts into the wedding scene, claiming Lucy for his own, but when he is shown the signed contract he assumes that she has scorned him. Enraged, he throws the ring she gave him at her feet and leaves.

Lucy goes mad; she stabs her new husband to death on their wedding night, then dies herself; Edgar, learning what has happened, goes to the tomb of his ancestors and stabs himself.

One of the reasons why it is difficult to take *Lucia* seriously today is the very mad scene that was once prized so highly. Rather than exploring the character's anger as Mozart did in *Idomeneo*, or composing a plaintive chant as Bellini did in *I Puritani*, Donizetti instead wrote a long, drawn-out *scena* in which the soprano is required to do but one thing: sing. Trying to interpret this music dramatically is not merely difficult but impossible, as Maria Callas and Beverly Sills both learned to their grief. On the other hand, there are many excellent dramatic moments for Lucy earlier on, some of them quite melodic and most of them memorable.

Keynotes

Henry's first-act aria, *Cruda, funesta smania*, is one of those pieces that had a profound effect on Italian baritone roles henceforth, largely due to a melodic line that cuts and thrusts rather than caresses. Lucia's aria *Regnava nel silenzio*, its cabaletta *Quando rapita in estasi*, and the ensuing duet with Edgardo, *Verrano a te*, make up one of the most perfectly constructed and memorable scenes in all of opera. The more dramatic Lucia-Enrico duet, *Soffriva nel pianto*, is dramatically effective if less memorable; the famous sextet, *Chi mi frena in tal momento*, is melodically and harmonically spectacular; and the sextet that immediately follows is even more dramatic. The music that follows the "mad scene" and concludes the opera is anticlimactic, though Edgar's final aria (*Tu che a Dio spiegasti l'ali*) is quite beautiful when sung well.

The Recording

Though the mad scene is more of a vocal than a dramatic display, there is enough drama in *Lucia* to require that most difficult of marriages, perfect voices and skilled interpretation. In addition, the work needs a great conductor who can tie the various elements together, so that the performance has an organic unity rather than a stop-start feeling. No other recording of Lucia meets these requirements as well as the present version. Anna Moffo may indeed have been a "microphone singer," but before the mike in these sessions she was perfection; Carlo Bergonzi and Mario Sereni were never better recorded nor as involved with their characters; and the written high F/high D combination near the end of *Verrano a te* is only sung in this performance (although, in the score, it is the tenor who has the high F, not the soprano).

La Favorita
1840   Gaetano Donizetti

Nicolai Ghiaurov, bs (Baldassare); Luciano Pavarotti, t (Fernando); Fiorenzo Cossotto, c (Leonora); Ileana Cotrubas, s (Ines); Gabriel Bacquier, br (King Alfonso XI); Piero de Palma, t (Don Gasparo). Teatro Communale di Bologna Orch. and Chorus, cond. by Richard Bonynge. London 430 038-2-LM3 (three CDs).

By 1840, Donizetti was so popular a composer that the Paris Opéra commissioned him to write an opera for them. He responded, as Rossini did, with the greatest work of his career: *La Favorita*, based on a drama by Baculard d'Arnaud, which deals with the psychological conflict between sacred and profane love. Donizetti was forced to add a ballet to an opera that didn't need one, but he also found the right balance between lyrical elegance and passionate outpourings. The coloratura element, so integral a part of *Lucia*, is almost entirely missing here, and when it does appear it intensifies the situation or probes the character's motivation to greater depth. In short, *La Favorita* is Donizetti's masterpiece, its relatively few performances resulting from the fact that, like the original version of *Il Barbiere di Siviglia*, its heroine is a contralto rather than a soprano.

Baldassare, superior of the cloisters of St. James, asks the young novice Fernando why he seems disturbed. Fernando confesses that he loves a strange woman he has seen in church; he leaves the monastery and tracks her to Lion Island off the coast of Portugal. Meeting her secretly, he learns nothing, but assumes her to be a noblewoman; he offers marriage, but she spurns him. Fernando mistakenly assumes that this is because he is not worthy of her, so he joins the army to prove himself in battle against the invading Moors. Meanwhile, we learn that his love is Leonora di Gusman, mistress of King Alfonso, who has pushed aside his Queen for her, and a person of questionable moral stock.

Fernando returns a hero, and the King offers to grant him any favor he wishes. Fernando asks for the hand of Leonora; the King agrees. While Fernando is making ready for the wedding, Leonora sends her servant Ines with a note explaining who she is, but Ines is arrested before delivering it. Fernando only discovers after the ceremony that he has married a strumpet; he casts his medals back at the King, denounces her, and returns to the cloister. The deposed Queen dies. As Fernando is about to take his final vows, Leonora comes to him begging forgiveness and explaining the mix-up. Fernando first spurns her, then decides to leave once again for love's sake. But it is too late: Leonora, worn out by starvation and fatigue, dies in his arms.

Two years after the opera's debut, Donizctti was forced by Italian censors to change the plot. In the new version, Baldassare is supposedly the father of both the Queen and Fernando, a ludicrous situation that removes any possibility of Fernando's ignorance of the goings on at the court. But he did not change the music, which remains the most moving and expressive he ever wrote.

Keynotes

There are many moments of beauty sprinkled throughout the score, among them Fernando's aria *Una vergine, un angel di Dio*, Ines's *Bei raggi lucenti*, Alfonso's *Vieni, amor* and *A tanto amor*, and the Alfonso-Leonora duet, *Ah! l'alto ardor*. The most famous excerpts, however, are Leonora's scena *O mio Fernando* and Fernando's *Spirto gentil*, both of which test a singer's expressive qualities. Note, too, that Donizetti made Alfonso an elegant rather than an evil figure, a fact that adds a disturbing element to his cold-hearted attitude toward his Queen. In addition, the marvelous conclusion of Act III ranks with the best work of Verdi.

The Recording

Though this is the Italian rather than the French version, the singing of Fiorenza Cossotto and Nicolai Ghiaurov is excellent. Gabriel Bacquier, though somewhat defective of voice, manages to capture the lyrical qualities of his music splendidly, and this elegance seems to rub off on Luciano Pavarotti as well; this is his finest achievement in an opera recording. More importantly, Richard Bonynge holds the many-colored threads of the drama together, creating a cohesive whole spoiled only by the intrusion of the twenty-minute ballet (which can be skipped).

Follow-up Listening

Donizetti's second-most-popular comic opera, the 1843 *Don Pasquale*, contains some beautiful and moving music. It is given an excellent performance by Lucia Popp, Francisco Araiza, Bernd Weikl, and Evgeny Nesterenko on Eurodisc 7790-2-RG (two CDs).

Name That Composer

The bel canto era became so famed for its virtuoso singers that, as in the operas of the Baroque era, audiences eventually came to hear the variations that different singers put into the music rather than a dramatic presentation of music-drama. This process was one of the things that sickened Berlioz and Wagner, who made a concerted effort to limit their singers to just performing the notes as written. The one Italian composer who found the whole process amusing, if frustrating, was Gioacchino Rossini.

Ten years after the premiere of his opera *William Tell*, opera houses were so concerned with the work's length that they took to presenting it piecemeal. Sometimes each of the acts would be truncated beyond recognition; even more often, they would present an abridged version of one act only on "Gala" evenings. Once the composer was told by a friend that he had heard Act One of his *Tell* at the Paris Opéra, to which Rossini responded, incredulously, "What—the WHOLE ACT?!?"

Toward the end of his life, Rossini was presented at his sumptuous home with Adelina Patti, the sensational teenaged Queen of Song. She thought to delight the aged maestro with a performance of *Una voce poco fa*, the soprano aria from his famed *Il Barbiere di Siviglia*. Like most other virtuosi of the time, Patti generously embellished the music with cadenzas, high notes, staccato, and trills galore. Rossini listened in rapt silence, enchanted by the display. "Wonderful!" he said when it was finished. "Superb! Magnificent! A finer piece of singing I have never heard! But tell me—who was the composer?"

FIVE

German and French Opera

While the Italians were building a timeless repertoire from the remains of the old Venetian style, the French and Germans were creating new works as well. Both were influenced by the Italians, but this influence worked in different ways. The French were more impressed by the dramatic style of Rossini and Donizetti (in addition to their own hero, Gluck), while the Germans gave more emphasis to the comic element (influenced, of course, by Mozart). The result was a body of work that includes several masterpieces, some of which are still heard today, though by and large these operas are not quite as popular as the models they copied.

The French and German styles also bred a new type of tenor, one who could reach into the high range with the elegance of the bel canto singers but with even greater power. Gilbert Duprez (1806–1896), the first tenor to sing high Cs from the chest, was instrumental in developing this new style. One modern tenor whose voice and style comes close to his is Nicolai Gedda (b. 1925), who sang both lyrical and dramatic music. In his recital on Myto Records MCD-91646, he performs arias from *Les Huguenots*, *Le Prophète*, *Faust*, and *La Dame Blanche*, all from this period and style. In later years, the constant pushing of the voice destroyed much of Gedda's lyric grace; these recordings, however, were made in his prime, when the forcing was minimal and his interpretive skill without peer (See also Appendix B for a videotape of Gedda).

Les Huguenots
1836   Giacomo Meyerbeer

Martina Arroyo, s (Valentine); Joan Sutherland, s (Marguerite); Huguette Tourangeau, c (Urbain); Gabriel Bacquier, br (Count de St. Bris); Dominic Cossa, br (de Nevers); Anastasios Vrenios, t (Raoul); Nicolai Ghiuselev, bs (Marcel); John Wakefield, t (Tavannes). Ambrosian Opera Chorus; New Philharmonia Orch., cond. by Richard Bonynge. London 430 549-2 LM4 (four CDs).

Giacomo Meyerbeer (1791–1864) was one of the most eclectic composers of all time; this was hardly surprising, considering that he was an Italian-German Jew working in France. After the retirement of Rossini and the mental collapse of Donizetti, he became their heir apparent in writing large-scale grand operas, full of melody, battle scenes, and stentorian voices. Many critics consider Meyerbeer a bit of a charlatan; they think him too contrived, too lacking in spontaneity (a similar critique is leveled against Jean Baptiste Lully), but this is an unfair assessment. If Meyerbeer lacked some subtlety and continuity, he possessed a gift for theatricality second to none. Most of the blame for the failure of modern Meyerbeer performances must be given to the singers, who generally fail to meet the vocal, technical, and dramatic demands of his music. When performed properly, Meyerbeer's operas are a treat to the ear.

Les Huguenots is a perfect example of Meyerbeer's talents. Based on the 16th-century battles between French Catholics and Protestant Huguenots, the top seven roles call for outstanding singers capable of high notes, vocal shading, and full-throated coloratura. In the late 19th century, performances of *Huguenots* were referred to as "the night of the Seven Stars," recognizing the fact that it takes seven great singers to perform this work, and featured such legendary names as Nellie Melba, Pol Plançon, and the de Reszke brothers (Jean and Edouard, tenor and bass). When the supply of great voices dried up, *Huguenots* performances began to disappear. In recent years there have been revivals in France, but with defective vocalists incapable of projecting the opera's excitement.

Count de Nevers, a Catholic leader, is hosting a banquet; among the invited guests are the Huguenot Raoul and his aged servant, Marcel. Raoul sings of his love for an unknown lady whom he rescued from a gang of rowdy students. He recognizes her in the garden with Nevers; soon afterward Urbain, the page, conducts a blindfolded Raoul to a meeting with a "noble lady." This turns out to be Queen Marguerite, who plans to end the religious feud between the Catholics and Huguenots by having Raoul marry Valentine, daughter of the Catholic Count St. Bris and fiancée of Nevers. Raoul recognizes Valentine as the "mysterious lady," and refuses her hand. This incites the Catholics to ambush him; Valentine, overhearing the plot, warns Marcel. A battle between rival gangs seems imminent, but the Queen intercedes. Later, Raoul enters the home of Valentine, now married to Nevers, and learns that she intended to break off her engagement for him. He overhears the Catholics' plot to massacre the Huguenots; only Nevers refuses to take part. Raoul rushes to aid the Protestant Huguenots, as does Nevers who dies in the attempt. Valentine pleads with Raoul to convert to Catholicism and marry her. When he refuses, she agrees to die with him as a Huguenot. They are both killed by St. Bris, who doesn't know that Valentine is with Raoul; he discovers to his horror that he has killed his own daughter.

Keynotes

The score of *Huguenots* fairly brims over with excellent music. Among the highlights are Raoul's two first-act arias, Marcel's battle song *Piff, paff!*, Urbain's *Nobles seigneurs*, Marguerite's *O beau pays*, and no less than three superb duets (Marguerite-Raoul, Valentine-Marcel, and Valentine-Raoul). The latter, in fact, was the origin of the anything-you-can-sing-I-can-sing-higher concept that influenced French and Italian opera throughout the rest of the century. This duet is sometimes credited to Adolphe Nourrit, the first Raoul, rather than Meyerbeer. In any case, it is undoubtedly one of the great musical highlights of pre-1850 opera.

The Recording

No complete recording of *Huguenots* is flawless, including this one, because latter-day singers often lack either the proper voice or style.

Here, instead of seven stars, we have but five: Joan Sutherland, Martina Arroyo, Huguette Tourangeau, Gabriel Bacquier, and Nicolai Ghiuselev. Dominic Cossa possessed a competent baritone voice, but lacked the dramatic sweep necessary for Nevers, and Anastasios Vrenios (this is his only recording) had a light, thin tenor voice, not quite adequate for Raoul's more dramatic moments. Yet Vrenios made up in elegance what he lacked in volume, including some dazzling double-coloratura singing in his duets with Sutherland, trills included. (Other performers omit these duets that feature richly ornamented scale runs.) He was also helped by the engineers who balanced the voices; and, best of all, the score is presented complete.

Martha
1847 Friedrich von Flotow

Lucia Popp, s (Lady Harriet, known as Martha); Doris Soffel, ms (Nancy); Sigmund Nimsgern, bs (Lord Tristan); Siegfried Jerusalem, t (Lionel); Karl Ridderbusch, bs (Plunkett). Bavarian Radio Orch. and Chorus, cond. by Heinz Wallberg. Eurodisc 7789-2-RG (two CDs).

Friedrich von Flotow (1812–1883) was a one-hit composer, but in *Martha* he found a goldmine that paid dividends to the end of his days. Originally trained in France, he brought a very Franco-Italian lyricism to his work, unusual in a German composer. He is also unique in being the only composer (to my knowledge) to write his music to librettos in three different languages: German, French, and Italian (there is also an English translation that he approved before his death). By a strange twist of fate, it was as an Italian opera that *Martha* gained international celebrity, but since 1950 it is performed as a repertoire piece only in Germany. This is a puzzle, because its music is not only highly melodic but easily accessible, even to a first-time listener.

A bored Lady Harriet is unimpressed by any of her suitors, despite her desire to fall in love. She travels to Richmond Fair with her lady's maid, Nancy, disguised as peasant girls named Martha (Harriet) and Julia (Nancy). The pair are hired as servants by the rich tenant-farmer Plunkett and his foster-brother Lionel. It soon turns out that the farmers' new charges aren't suited for farm or household work—they can't even spin!—but Plunkett falls in love with "Julia" and Lionel with "Martha." Lady Harriet's cousin, Sir Tristan, has followed them and helps them to escape.

The next day, the farmers recognize their "servants" among the nobles in the hunting party of Queen Anne, and try to hold them to their contracts; but Harriet, afraid of scandal, denies everything while Sir Tristan has Lionel arrested. Before going to jail, Lionel gives Plunkett a ring that was left to him by his father, to show to the Queen. It turns out that Lionel is the son of the innocently banned Earl of Derby; a contrite Lady Harriet offers her hand, but Lionel rejects it. Plunkett and Nancy, having kissed and made up, plot to have Lionel come upon Harriet in her "Martha" outfit. This does the trick, and she ends up in his arms.

Keynotes

Martha has so much catchy music in it that it often resembles an operetta; yet the music is not really easy to sing, and calls for virtuoso voices in the four principal roles. Undoubtedly, the two most famous arias are Lionel's *Ach, so fromm* (known in Italian as *M'appari*) and Martha's *The Last Rose of Summer*, which was actually taken from an old English folksong. Also of note is Plunkett's drinking song, the spinning quartet and "midnight" quartet in Act II (the latter sung as the clock strikes that hour), and the Act III quartet, which is one of the most inspired moments in the entire opera, musically and dramatically. Lovers of the "Rossini crescendo" will also appreciate Flotow's adaptation of this device in the Richmond Fair scene, when the Judge introduces the girls to be hired as servants.

The Recording

This performance of *Martha* is not the most exciting or complete version you could hope for, but the singers are all quite good and what they sing is, for the most part, accurate. Lucia Popp and Siegfried Jerusalem are especially fine, though Doris Soffel and Karl Ridderbusch also have their moments. Heinz Wallberg conducts with lightness and fluidity, though his interpretation occasionally lacks momentum.

The Merry Wives of Windsor
1849 Otto Nicolai

Ruth-Margret Pütz, s (Frau Fluth [Ford]); Gisela Litz, ms (Frau Reich [Page]); Friedrich Lenz, t (Junker Spärlich [Slender]); Fritz Wunderlich, t (Fenton); Ernst Gutstein, br (Herr Fluth [Ford]); Kieth Engen, bs (Herr Reich [Page]); Edith Mathis, s (Anna Reich [Ann Page]); Gottlob Frick, bs (Sir John Falstaff). Bavarian State Opera Orch. and Chorus, cond. by Robert Heger. Angel CMS-69348-2 (two CDs).

Otto Nicolai (1810–1849) was yet another one-hit opera composer, and was also one of the finest musicians of his time. He was the first to champion Beethoven's Ninth Symphony, and held various important positions, including organist in Rome, kapellmeister in Vienna, and founder and conductor of the Berlin Philharmonic. His contention that "German operatic music contains enough philosophy, but not enough music" was sneered at by serious-minded critics of his day, yet this opera vindicates him splendidly. Based on a translation of Shakespeare's comedy by Schlegel and Tieck, it is one of the few post-Mozartian German operas to combine the German style of composition with the Italian bel canto style and the gallantry of French opera. More importantly, it is far more successful than Verdi's *Falstaff* at conveying the story's humor.

The opera follows the original play but Germanizes some names. Mistresses Fluth and Reich (Ford and Page) compare love letters they have both received from the seedy old knight Sir John Falstaff. Meanwhile, we learn that Herr Reich has promised the hand of his daughter Anna to Slender, considering the poor Fenton an unsuitable bridegroom. These two situations form the basis for various comic adventures, including Frau Fluth hiding the amorous Falstaff in a laundry basket when her husband comes in; Herr Fluth, disguising himself as "Mr. Brook," pumping Falstaff on his romance with his wife; the rivalry of Anna's three suitors, with Fenton winning out; and Falstaff dressing as an old woman to escape from Herr Fluth's home. The climax comes in the Windsor Forest scene, germanized as "Herne the Hunter's Oak," where Falstaff is tormented by Anna and Fenton, dressed as the fairy royalty Titania and Oberon, along with a group of children pretending to be giant gnats and the burghers of Windsor dressed as demons and gnomes.

Keynotes

The music of *Die Lustigen Weiber von Windsor* (to give it its German name) is witty, charming, and beautifully written; a shame, then, that in the end only a little of it is as memorable as *Martha* or *Il Barbiere di Siviglia*. Yet one should not bypass this comic gem by any means. Listen particularly to the opening duet, Frau Fluth's incredibly difficult aria *Nun eilt herbei, Witz*, Falstaff's boisterous drinking song *Als Büblein klein*, Fenton's gorgeous aria *Horch die Lerche singt im Hain*, and especially the witty (and memorable) buffo duet *In einem Waschkorb*.

The Recording

This 1963 version of the opera features two legendary German singers—the tenor Fritz Wunderlich and the bass Gottlob Frick—as well as some excellent singing from such secondary performers as Edith Mathis, Gisela Litz, and Kieth Engen, and a surprisingly dazzling portrayal of Frau Fluth by Ruth-Margret Pütz.

Faust
1859   Charles Gounod

Alfredo Kraus, t (Faust); Nicolai Ghiaurov, bs (Mephistopheles); Lorenzo Saccomani, br (Valentin); Renata Scotto, s (Marguerite); Mirella dal Piva, ms (Siebel); Anna di Stasio, c (Marthe Schwerlein). NHK Symphony Orch. and Chorus, cond. by Paul Ethuin. Lyric Distribution videotape 1724.

Unlike Flotow and Nicolai, Charles Gounod (1818–1893) was not a one-hit composer, his operas *Mireille* (1864) and *Roméo et Juliette* (1867) remaining fairly popular to this day. But in one sense he may well have been: in the seventy years after its premiere, *Faust* was the single most popular opera ever written, outdistancing *Aida* and *Carmen* by more than 1,000 performances and completely swamping the works of Mozart.

To many opera fans, critics, and performers, this seems far out of proportion to the work's actual merit. Gounod and his librettists, Barbier and Carré, watered down the original Johann Wolfgang von Goethe play so much that there was no philosophy left at all; it became a simplistic, black-and-white tale of Faust's lust, Marguerite's gullibility, and Mephistopheles's treachery. But such detractors fail to realize that, on its own merits, it is a rousingly tuneful opera, and that moreover the music is well developed and appropriate to each situation. More important from a practical point of view, there are good arias and ensembles for every one of its principals, and each of these arias is effective without being very hard to sing.

Faust, an old philosopher, is bitter because life has passed him by. He offers to sell his soul for the chance to relive his youth, which is Mephistopheles's cue to appear. The devil conjures a vision of a beautiful woman to entice Faust into signing the contract to relinquish his soul; she turns out to be Marguerite, sister of the soldier Valentin and friend of the young boy Siebel who worships her from afar. Mephistopheles gives Marguerite a box of jewels to break the ice, then sidetracks her neighbor Marthe so that Faust can have easy access to her. Faust loves her and leaves her; pregnant and afraid, she prays for forgiveness in the cathedral, but Mephistopheles arrives to predict her doom. When her brother, Valentin, and his fellow soldiers return from the war, he is insulted by Mephisto and killed by Faust with the devil's help. The two escape to the Hartz Mountains on Walpurgis Night, where Mephistopheles tempts Faust further with beautiful women; but Faust's conscience is bothering him. He demands to be taken to Marguerite, who is now in prison for killing their child. Her mind is going, but the sight of the devil returns her to sanity. She prays for redemption and dies; Mephistopheles condemns her, but a choir of angels take her spirit to heaven.

Keynotes

There are numerous musical highlights in *Faust*. The most popular are the first-act duet *A moi les plaisirs*, Valentin's *Avant de quitter*, Mephistopheles's *Le veau d'or* and the serenade *Vous qui faites l'endormie*, Siebel's *Faites-lui mes aveux*, Faust's *Salut demeure chaste et pure*, Marguerite's "jewel song" (*Ah! je ris de me voir*), and the final trio. Even better musically are the second-act scene where Faust and Marguerite first meet, the third-act quartet, the duel trio, and Valentin's death scene.

The Recording

Despite the fact that this music is not hard to sing, it requires a combination of panache and lightness that it does not always receive. In the present version, all requirements are met. Renata Scotto's jewel song is a particular delight, the music dancing and floating above the beat (though her first trill is a little lazy), and the relatively unknown Lorenzo Saccomani provides a splendid account of Valentin's music. Paul Ethuin's conducting has a drive often lacking in *Faust* recordings. (Note: Since this videotape does not come with a libretto, you may wish to make a trip to your local library to follow along.) The same performance is also available on CD as Standing Room Only SRO-811-3 (three CDs).

Les Troyens
1863   Hector Berlioz

Jessye Norman, ms (Cassandre); Barbara Conrad, c (Hécube); Jocelyne Taillon, c (Anna); Jean Kraft, ms (Cassandre's Ghost); Claudia Catania, s (Ascagne); Placido Domingo, t (Enée [Aeneas]); Allan Monk, br (Chorèbe); Morley Meredith, bs (Hector's ghost); John Macurdy, bs (King Priam); Tatiana Troyanos, ms (Didon [Dido]); Douglas Ahlstedt, t (Iopas); Paul Plishka, bs (Narbal). Metropolitan Opera Chorus and Orch., cond. by James Levine. Bel Canto/Paramount Video 12509 (two tapes, VHS).

In the realm of pre-1870 opera, Hector Berlioz (1803–1869) was a maverick. Where other composers sought simple or rousing plots, he worked with complex librettos that plumbed psychological depths; where other composers wrote simple, tuneful music, Berlioz drew attention to the dramatic situation by conspicuously avoiding regular melodies and martial airs. As a result, his work was unpopular in its day, and *Les Troyens*, his masterpiece, suffered the further indignity of being split up and performed piecemeal; and, even when both parts were performed, music was often cut. This situation continued until the 1960s, when a revival of interest in Berlioz's music led to complete performances of the opera.

In Part 1, *The Capture of Troy*, the people rejoice that their years of confinement by the Greeks are over; but Cassandre, a prophet, warns that doom is near. Even her lover, Chorèbe, thinks she is wrong, and tries to console her. Aeneas arrives with the disturbing news that Troy's high priest has been devoured by serpents after he threw a javelin into the side of a wooden horse; Aeneas claims that the goddess Pallas Athena was offended, and insists that she be placated by bringing the horse, which was dedicated to her, to her temple. While sleeping, Aeneas is visited by the ghost of Hector, who tells him that Troy has fallen. Aeneas is told to take his son Ascagne and images of the gods to found a new empire in Italy but, before he can leave, Panthée tells him that the Trojans were slaughtered during the night by Greek soldiers hidden inside the wooden horse. Aeneas rushes off to battle. In the temple of Vesta, Cassandre relates that Chorèbe was killed but Aeneas has escaped; she and a good portion of the Trojan women commit suicide rather than become Greek slaves.

In Part 2, *The Trojans at Carthage*, a festival is given to celebrate the rebuilding of Carthage. The widowed Queen Dido is hailed by the crowd while her sister Anna encourages her to remarry. Iopas reports that a foreign fleet has anchored in the harbor. Dido receives the sailors as guests; they turn out to be Aeneas and Ascagne. Narbal, her minister, informs the Queen that Numidians are invading the country and threatening Carthage itself. Aeneas leads the Carthaginian troops into battle while Ascagne remains behind to guard Dido. Afterward, Narbal confides to Anna that Aeneas's arrival may not be altogether beneficial: already Dido is neglecting the affairs of state. Anna replies that they are in love, and that Aeneas will make a splendid king. Aeneas, planning a return to Troy, is held back by his love for Dido; the ghosts of his father, Priam, as well as Chorèbe, Cassandre, and Hector, persuade him to leave. Dido begs him to stay, but to no avail. She asks Anna to intercede for her, but when Iopas sees the ships leave, Dido becomes furious, ordering her people to pursue and destroy them. She decides to burn on a funeral pyre, hoping Aeneas will see the flames and realize what he has done. Anna tries to dissuade her, but Dido stabs herself with a sword; as the fire blazes, a vision of eternal Rome rises behind the pyre.

Part of the problem with many *Troyens* performances nowadays is that some conductors approach it as a lyrical work. This smooths out the jolting rhythmic quality of the music, which was specifically designed to match the French text. In fact, Berlioz left us timings for each act, and when they are followed (as they seldom are) the music has a momentum all its own. Once you realize that Berlioz created a different approach to the problem of opera as drama, *Troyens* can be enjoyed as much as any work in its class—which, unfortunately, does not contain many operas.

Keynotes

Despite the lack of conventional melody, *Troyens* contains many interesting dramatic moments. Chief among these is the Trojan March in Act I, where Cassandre's vocal part runs opposite the jaunty rhythms, and the love duet *Nuit d'ivresse et d'extase infinie* in Act IV. Also of interest are the marvelous octet *Châtiment effroyable* in Act I, the arias of Dido and Iopas in Act III, Aeneas's aria *Inutiles regrets* in Act V, and the great finale in which Dido plots her own immolation.

The Recording

Few performances of *Troyens* come within Berlioz's timings, probably because it's so difficult to find great singers who can interpret the music dramatically and handle the difficult rhythms at the same time, but this recording comes very close. James Levine's conducting is a marvel, never allowing the pace to slacken. It was also a stroke of genius to cast the lush-voiced Jessye Norman as Cassandre and the more dramatic Tatiana Troyanos as Dido, rather than the other way around. Placido Domingo is quite good as Aeneas, Paul Plishka is excellent as Narbal, and Jocelyne Taillon is competent as Anna.

An excellent alternate version is available on Melodram MEL-37060 (three CDs). The singing of Marilyn Horne (Cassandre), Shirley Verrett (Dido), and Nicolai Gedda (Aeneas) is equal to that in the Levine video; the supporting singers are even better than Levine's; and the conducting of Georges Prêtre, though omitting the "Royal Hunt and Storm Music" that introduces Act IV, is even terser and closer to Berlioz's timings. The libretto, however, is only in French, so you may wish to visit the library for a translation.

Follow-up Listening

Weber's 1821 opera *Der Freischutz*, which set the pace for German *singspiels*, is given a good performance by Elisabeth Grümmer, Rita Streich, Hans Hopf, Kurt Böhme, and Wilhelm Furtwängler on Hunt Productions CDWFE-302 (one double-sided CD); and Jacques Halevy's dramatic *La Juive* (1835), which influenced Verdi and Wagner, is performed well by Julia Varady, June Anderson, José Carreras, Ferruccio Furlanetto, and Antonio de Almeida on Philips 420 190-1/2/4 (three LPs/CDs/cassettes).

The Trio That Isn't Always a Trio

Few ensembles in opera history are as famous as the final trio from Gounod's *Faust*; opera audiences have been thrilling to it for 130 years, and they will probably thrill to it for 130 more. But, unique among famous ensembles in the opera world, the final trio of *Faust* doesn't always come out that way.

The problem is that, for four minutes, each of the three principals—soprano, tenor, and bass—do not consciously blend together but belt out their parts at top volume. Unfortunately, because not all operatic voices are created equal, the end result depends on whether the impresario has hired three singers of equal caliber. Some basses are marvelously subtle in their presentation of Mephistopheles, but just don't have the lung power to compete with the soprano and tenor in this scene. Some tenors can produce an ear-ravishing *O merveille* and *Salut! demeure*, but fade from view when they have to project ringing high note after ringing high note. Some sopranos can sing the trills in the "jewel song" to perfection, and float beautifully in the love duet with the tenor, but peter out while the bass and tenor are going full steam. As a result, I have heard trios that were tenor-bass duets, trios that were soprano-tenor duets, and—worst of all—trios that end up as soprano solos with "noise obbligato."

Undoubtedly the funniest trio, however, took place in Stockholm, Sweden, in 1931, when the great Feodor Chaliapin appeared as a guest artist singing Mephistopheles. The tenor on this occasion was the legendary Jussi Björling, then at the beginning of his career; throughout the performance, Chaliapin noticed that the young tenor had a splendid voice and might provide too much competition for him in this crucial final scene. When the time came for them all to belt it out, Chaliapin simply removed his competition by swirling his cape around the young tenor and covering him from the sight (and sound) of the audience!

SIX

Verdi and Wagner

As the 19th century passed its midpoint, opera was in its most popular phase. Though still clinging to the patronage of the aristocracy, the fortunes of composers were determined more by box-office receipts than the nod of an intellectual archduke; and the "nouveau riche" created by the Industrial Revolution ensured the presence of common folk, or at least people who came from common stock, in the opera audience. In this fertile soil grew the talents of two composers, born in the same year, who had a far-reaching effect on both opera's present evolution and its future: Giuseppe Verdi (1813–1901) and Richard Wagner (1813–1883), the yin and yang of opera.

On the surface, it would seem that they had nothing in common. Verdi, the musical heir of Rossini and Donizetti, wrote tuneful melodies that became "pop hits," while Wagner, an innovative and explorative mind, sought to expand Beethoven's musical language and Gluck's concept of music-drama. Yet they both worked toward a view of opera as a cohesive whole; they were both profoundly influenced by Mozart and Meyerbeer, and their talents were so great that they virtually eliminated competition in their respective countries.

Because they comprise not merely the centerpiece of the 19th century, but the very center of the operatic world, we will devote more space to their works than those of any other composer, and we will consider each separately.

VERDI

Verdi approached opera more from the heart than from the head. A well-trained musician, he was the only Italian composer after Rossini capable of creating and sustaining long arias and scenes in Mozart's manner; and his melodies, though certainly regular and memorable enough, had a wonderful way of developing or overlapping so that one had the impression of continuous creation rather than the "stop-start" effect of lesser Italian composers. Yet in the end, Verdi always allowed his emotions to control the content and direction of his music. He was also an avowed patriot who fought against repression in any form; the battles he had with censors over his operatic plots usually had something to do with their inflammatory political or religious content. In his early years Verdi led a miserable life, struggling to sell his operas to theaters for minimum pay. His first two children died, followed by the death of his wife. This experience never left him; it made him a cynic who believed that fate controls your life despite anything you can do to change it. This philosophy is reflected in practically every plot he considered, especially in such later works as *La Forza del Destino* and *Don Carlos*.

Musically, Verdi was also a continuation of that "ingenious but conservative" tendency exhibited by Mozart and the bel canto composers. He wrote regular, identifiable tunes, but somehow managed to come up with just the *right* tune to describe a dramatic situation. He also emphasized the upper vocal ranges: most of his music has a high, bright sound, exploiting his singers' upper ranges (the top third of their ranges) where the notes are the "prettiest." In doing so, he created or exaggerated four categories of singers.

The lyric spinto soprano is a lyric soprano with the ability to "burst" high notes with explosive force. (Spinto is the Italian word for "push" or "thrust.") In earlier times they were expected to achieve a certain amount of technical flexibility (to perform scale runs and trills), but as time has passed we may consider ourselves lucky to find any spinto sopranos at all. One excellent example, who also was able to sing much bel canto music, was Maria Callas (1923–1977). Her recital of Verdi arias on Angel CDC-47730 includes excerpts from *Macbeth*, *Don Carlos*, *I Vespri Siciliani*, and *Aida*. The "dramatic" mezzo-soprano is, likewise, an extension of Rossini's "dramatic-coloratura" mezzo, with less flexibility but, like her soprano counterpart, she has the ability to excite audiences with bright, ringing high notes. One of the best of these was Ebe Stignani (1903–1974), who combined a smooth, velvety sound with the metallic "ring" demanded in Verdi's operas. Her recital on Preiser 89014 shows off her style in arias from *Un Ballo in Maschera*, *Don Carlos*, *La Forza del Destino*, and *Il Trovatore*; note, also, how Verdi's dramatic mezzo relates to Gluck's dramatic soprano in the aria from *Alceste*.

The lyric spinto tenor was the counterpart of the spinto soprano: he, too, had to "push" high notes out, in a forceful, piercing manner, to compete with Verdi's heroines. The most famous spinto tenor of our century was Jussi Björling (1911–1960; on some recordings, the spelling of his name was Americanized as Bjoerling). RCA 7799-2-RG features him in duets from *Aida* (with Zinka Milanov, another lyric spinto soprano) as well as *Don Carlos*, *La Forza del Destino*, and *Otello* with baritone Robert Merrill.

Though Merrill sang a lot of Verdi in his later years, he was not really the kind of piercing dramatic baritone that Verdi created. The best example of that is Lawrence Tibbett (1896–1960), who really threw the chest voice into his singing, and created a very physical, "ringing" sound. His recital on RCA Victor 7808-2-RG includes outstanding excerpts from *Un Ballo in Maschera*, *Simon Boccanegra*, and *Falstaff*; but note how his *Largo al factotum* from *Il Barbiere di Siviglia*, though exciting, lacks the easy flexibility of Stracciari or Tito Gobbi in the complete recordings of this work (see Chapter 4). For the best sound reproduction, be sure to boost the treble when playing this recording.

Rigoletto
1851   Giuseppe Verdi

Robert Bruni, t (Borsa); Mario Filippeschi, t (Duke of Mantua); Tito Gobbi, br (Rigoletto); Lina Pagliughi, s (Gilda, his daughter); Giulio Neri, bs (Sparafucile); Anna Maria Canali, c (Maddalena). Teatro dell'Opera Chorus and Orch., cond. by Tullio Serafin. Lyric Distribution videotape 1530.

Victor Hugo's play *Le Roi s'amuse* would scarcely seem to have been an ideal subject for an opera, let alone one of enduring popularity. Its plot, the dark struggle between a lecherous Duke and those who resented his attentions toward their wives and daughters, would furthermore seem to be a variation on the *Don Giovanni* theme; but Verdi surprised everyone by making the hunchbacked jester, Rigoletto, the central character, and assigning that role to the baritone. Few if any Italian operas after 1830 featured the baritone as chief protagonist; as a result, the role of Rigoletto is considered a pearl of great value.

Everyone hates the libertine Duke of Mantua except his aging court jester, Rigoletto, who mocks the Duke's victims until a curse is put on him by Monterone, father of the Duke's latest conquest. Later, Rigoletto worries about the curse; he is approached by Sparafucile, an assassin for hire, who offers his services. Rigoletto hurries to meet his daughter, Gilda, who is kept guarded by her maid Giovanna. But Gilda has met a young stranger at church and, after Rigoletto leaves, the stranger pays Giovanna to let him see her. It is the Duke in disguise; his nobles and courtiers, seeking revenge on Rigoletto, abduct Gilda, who they think is his mistress. Rigoletto pleads with them to let her go. When they are reunited, Gilda tells him about the stranger, then explains she has just come from his bedroom—in the palace. Rigoletto knows the Duke has had his way with her, and vows revenge. He takes Gilda to the ramshackle inn where Sparafucile and his sister, Maddalena, a prostitute, lure men to be robbed and/or killed. The Duke is with Maddalena; Gilda sees his unfaithfulness; and Rigoletto pays Sparafucile to kill him. But Maddalena is fond of the Duke's good looks, and convinces Sparafucile to kill the first man who comes to the inn that night. In the midst of a terrible storm, Gilda arrives, dressed as a man; she is stabbed, shoved in a sack, and presented by Sparafucile to Rigoletto. They sing a plaintive duet as she dies. Rigoletto blames Monterone's curse for his misfortune.

The one flaw in *Rigoletto* is the insipid character of Gilda; yet one can understand, if not condone, her being taken in by the only love she has ever known. Yet Verdi more than makes up for this in his portrayal of Rigoletto, who emerges as one of the most complex characters in any opera. He realizes that his actions at court are despicable, yet justifies them by the fact that his life, too, has been miserable. As for the Duke, the lighthearted quality of his music depicts a man even shallower than Don Giovanni; and the fact that he is allowed to keep his life at the end of the opera reflects Verdi's own dim view of humankind in general.

Keynotes

Rigoletto abounds with favorite melodies, none more so than the Duke's *La donna e mobile*. Others include the Duke's first-act aria, *Questa o quella*, Gilda's reflective scene *Caro nome*, the Gilda-Duke duet *E il sol dell'anima*, and the famous quartet in the last act that ranks in popularity, as an operatic ensemble, with the *Lucia* sextet. Even more skillfully wrought are Rigoletto's two big scenes, *Pari siamo* and *Cortigianni, vil razza dannata*; the Gilda-Rigoletto duet *Si, vendetta*; and the court scene in Act I, where brilliant melodic lines are played against off-beat counterpoint to create a wonderful effect.

The Recording

I have heard every complete recording of *Rigoletto* made between 1928 and 1990, and none conveys the elegance and excitement of the opera better than this one. Tito Gobbi's Rigoletto was justly famous, and in 1947 it was vocally as well as histrionically unsurpassed; Mario Filippeschi is lyrical and ardent; and Lina Pagliughi, who unfortunately is replaced onscreen by an actress, sings with superb intonation and style. In addition, the visual production is excellent, conveying the feeling of a stage performance rather than a film. This video does not, however, come with a libretto, so you'll have to trot down to the library to find one.

Il Trovatore
1853   Giuseppe Verdi

Plinio Clabassi, bs (Ferrando); Leyla Gencer, s (Leonora); Laura Londi, ms (Inez); Ettore Bastianini, br (Count di Luna); Mario del Monaco, t (Manrico); Fedora Barbieri, ms (Azucena); Athos Cesarini, t (Ruiz). RAI Rome Opera Chorus and Orch., cond. by Fernando Previtali. Lyric Distribution videotape 1961.

For his second great opera of the 1850s, Verdi turned to a melodrama by Spanish writer Antonio Garcia Gutiérrez; but unlike other composers, who wrote brutal, tawdry music for their melodramatic plots, Verdi's music combines sensitivity and passion in equal measure. In addition, *Il Trovatore* is a formal anachronism, returning to the styles and modes of bel canto more than any of his operas after

Nabucco (1842). As a result, his singers are called on not only to emote but to sing softly, execute shakes, trills, and roulades, and in general balance decorative and affective elements in a constant juggling act. Small wonder, then, that *Il Trovatore* is so difficult to sing.

The plot is also somewhat difficult to figure out, partly because much of the action has already taken place before the curtain goes up. These events are narrated by Ferrando, the old captain of the guards, in the first scene, but most non-Italian-speaking audiences pay scant attention to the words. In brief, Ferrando tells how the two younger sons of the old Count di Luna (long since dead) were killed by gypsy women—the first, Garzia, by an old gypsy hag who supposedly put a "curse" on the infant for which crime she was burned at the stake, and the second was thrown into a fire by the gypsy hag's daughter, Azucena. But, according to legend, Azucena accidentally threw her own son into the flames, keeping and raising as her own the actual Count, who passes as a gypsy troubadour named Manrico. This is where the opera begins.

Verdi gave a title to each of the four acts, a formality not usually employed by the composer. In Act I, "The Duel," we learn that the present Count di Luna (the old Count's eldest son) is in love with the Duchess Leonora, lady-in-waiting to the Princess of Aragon, but that Leonora is in love with Manrico. She sings of her sadness while waiting for her lover to appear. Count di Luna is in the shadow of the trees; she mistakes him for Manrico. Manrico then arrives, and the three of them sing a remarkable trio that balances passion with intelligent musicality (the curtain falling as "the duel" between Manrico and di Luna over who shall claim the Princess is about to begin).

In Act II, "The Gypsy," we meet the crazed Azucena. Manrico tells her that he overcame Count di Luna in the duel, but spared his life because a "voice from heaven" told him to do so; Azucena stokes the fires of vengeance, and prods him not to give in so easily in the future. In the second scene, Manrico takes charge of the gypsy forces defending the stronghold of Castellor, but rushes away when he is told that Leonora is about to take holy orders at a nearby convent because she thinks he is dead. The Count also learns about her plans, and rushes to carry Leonora away before she becomes a nun; but once again, he is foiled by the presence of Manrico.

In Act III, "The Gypsy's Son," the Count is attacking Castellor when his soldiers drag in a prisoner. It is Azucena, recognized by

Ferrando as the gypsy woman who supposedly burned the Count's brother. Azucena calls out to Manrico for help; the Count orders her to be burned at the stake. Meanwhile, Leonora and Manrico are being married, but just as their vows are being exchanged his servant Ruiz rushes in with news of Azucena's capture. Manrico goes off to battle the Count's forces and reclaim her.

In Act IV, "The Penalty," we learn that he has failed, and in fact has been captured and condemned to death with his "mother." Leonora sings of her sadness in losing Manrico again; then, as the monks chant their evening prayers, she becomes more agitated, only to be answered by Manrico's voice from the tower where he is a prisoner. The Count enters; she promises to marry him if he frees Manrico. The Count is so ecstatic that he agrees to do so. In Scene 2, Manrico and Azucena sing a mournful duet; Leonora enters and begs him to escape, but he suspects the price she has paid for his freedom, and suspicion becomes certainty when the poison she has taken kills her. Di Luna enters, finds Leonora dead, and furiously orders Manrico to be killed at once. He drags Azucena to the window to witness the death of her "son"; she waits until he is executed, then cries out, "The victim was your brother! My mother is avenged!"

Keynotes

Even when all is explained, the plot of *Trovatore* is still rather silly (though not as confusing), but the music has made it immortal. Leonora's two arias, *Tacea la notte placida* and *D'amor sull'ali rosee*, are cornerstones of the repertoires of every Verdi soprano worth her salt; and the two Act IV duets, the *Miserere* and *Mira d'accerbe lagrime*, are not far behind. Di Luna is both a lyric baritone's dream and a nightmare: the part is full of beautiful music, especially the bel canto aria *Il balen del suo sorriso*, yet requires a technique and power that few lyric baritones possess. Azucena is possibly the most difficult contralto role of all time, demanding a singing actress who can declaim brilliantly in her Act II duet with Manrico, sing softly and accurately in *Ai nostri monti*, and balance forte high notes with no less than twenty trills (!) in *Stride la vampa*. And Manrico is no picnic either, demanding a pure legato in *Ah si ben mio* and *Ai nostri monti*, in addition to truly heroic declamation in *Di geloso amor*, *Mal reggendo*, and especially *Di quella pira*. In short, this opera is practically a string of "greatest hits," all of them difficult to sing properly.

The Recording

This 1957 film performance, though requiring a treble boost to improve the sound, is surprisingly excellent, although Fedora Barbieri sings only a few of her twenty trills in *Stride la vampa* and Leyla Gencer omits the *cabaletta* to the *Miserere*. Those wishing an even better and more accurate performance can obtain the classic recording by Rosalind Plowright, Brigitte Fassbaender, Placido Domingo, Giorgio Zancanaro, Evgeny Nesterenko, and Carlo Maria Giulini on DG 423 858-2 GH2 (two CDs).

La Traviata
1853   Giuseppe Verdi

Anna Moffo, s (Violetta); Franco Bonisolli, t (Alfredo); Gino Bechi, br (Giorgio Germont); Mafalda Micheluzzi, ms (Flora); Glauco Scarlini, t (Gastone); Arturo LaPorta, br (Barone Douphol); Afro Poli, bs (Dr. Grenvil). Rome Opera Chorus and Orch., cond. by Giuseppe Patané. VAI videotape 69069 (VHS)/29069 (Beta).

The last great work of Verdi's famed "triumvirate" is *La Traviata*, based on Alexander Dumas's novel *La Dame aux Camélias*. Considering the moral Puritanism of the Victorian era, it is surprising that Verdi could get away with this "beautiful-prostitute-with-a-heart-of-gold" story. In addition, he committed the unpardonable sin of dressing his characters in contemporary fashion; as a result, *Traviata*'s first performance was a fiasco. It was only when the characters were dressed in the style of twenty years earlier that the work was successful. The bottom line is no audience really cares to see opera in contemporary dress, especially if the subject matter is morally questionable.

There is really not much to the plot of *Traviata*. Violetta, a high-class hooker, is throwing an extravagant party; one of her guests, Alfredo Germont, is chided by his fellows for loving a woman that anyone can have for a few francs. In their first duet together, Violetta learns that Alfredo is serious and wants to set up house with her. Fighting her better instincts, she gives in to her feelings. In the midst of their happiness, Alfredo's father intrudes. He tells Violetta she must give up Alfredo so his sister can marry without having the "taint" of her brother "living in sin" to ruin her happiness. Violetta reluctantly agrees; she writes a note to Alfredo, telling him that she has returned to her former life; heartbroken, he is consoled by his father.

At a gambling party in the house of Flora Bervoix, Alfredo gets into an argument with Baron Douphol, who arrives with Violetta; in anger, Alfredo summons the guests and announces that she has squandered all her money on him. He "pays her back" by throwing his winnings at her feet. In a moment of high irony, the elder Germont comes out of the back room, where he has been gambling and whoring, to console his son once again. Later, dying of tuberculosis, Violetta receives a letter from Germont; Alfredo, who survived a duel with the Baron, has been told of her sacrifice. Both father and son are coming to ask her forgiveness. Alfredo's love for Violetta is rekindled, but she knows it's too late; as Germont begs her to live so that his son can be happy, she feels her spasms stop—then sinks back onto her bed, dead.

As I said, the plot of *Traviata* is not important; what is important is that Verdi has drawn this musical portrait of Violetta (based on a real woman, Marie Duplessis) with sensitivity and care. She is far more human and feminine than any of his previous female characters; her motives are real, her choices are moral, and her suffering and death more keenly felt than those of any other Verdi "heroine." As a result, Violetta dominates this opera in a way that Verdi would never repeat. Even though the presence of a good tenor and baritone are essential, their contributions are not as pivotal as that of the soprano.

Keynotes

Both Alfredo and Giorgio Germont get only one opportunity to shine in this opera: the former's *De' miei bollenti spiriti*, and the latter's *Di provenza il mar*. Otherwise, their best moments revolve around scenes including Violetta. For the tenor, these include the first-act *Un di felice eterea*, the second-act "denunciation scene," and the third-act *Parigi o cara*; for the baritone, it is the long duet that begins with the elder Germont's words, "Mademoiselle Valery?," ends with Violetta's heartbreaking decision to leave Alfredo, and along the way includes such magic moments as *Pura siccome un angelo*, *Dite alla giovine*, and *Imponete*. As for Violetta, so much attention has been spent on her first-act scene, *Ah fors e lui* . . .

Sempre libera (although it is a superb piece of vocal-dramatic writing), that listeners tend to forget that the height of her feelings is better delineated in the long duet just mentioned, her gut-wrenching farewell to her life with Alfredo, and the abandonment of *Addio del passato*. Except for each character's solo arias, the melodies in *Traviata* are less regular and less memorable than in *Trovatore*, yet the reality of the situation is all the more touching because of this.

The Recording

No complete *Traviata* is really perfect. The role of Violetta calls for a soprano who can phrase musically, negotiate the coloratura passages, and combine melting lyricism with dramatic fire. During her brief prime (1957–68), Anna Moffo was such an artist, and this 1968 film captures her interpretation in all of its splendor, and includes partners from the operatic past and future. Franco Bonisolli, seen here as an "unknown" at the beginning of his career, is no John McCormack or Tito Schipa but sings reasonably well; and forties star Gino Bechi, though fifty-five at the time of this film (and somewhat past his prime), is still resonant and authoritative. Conductor Giuseppe Patané omits some music, notably the *cabaletta* to Alfredo's aria and the responses of Germont and the doctor when Violetta dies, but by and large gives a solid, likeable performance. The film work is excellent and Mario Lanfranchi's direction reasonably good; the only debits are a few pops and ticks in the remastered soundtrack. The best CD alternate, which includes all the music (though some quirky tempos), features Montserrat Caballé, Carlo Bergonzi, Sherrill Milnes, and conductor Georges Prêtre on RCA 6180-2-RC (two CDs).

La Forza del Destino (The Force of Destiny)
1862   Giuseppe Verdi

Silvio Maionica, bs (Marquise); Renata Tebaldi, s (Donna Leonora); Ettore Bastianini, br (Don Carlo); Mario del Monaco, t (Don Alvaro); Giulietta Simionato, ms (Preziosilla); Cesare Siepi, bs (Padre Guardiano); Fernando Corena, bs (Fra Melitone). St. Cecilia Academy Chorus and Orch., cond. by Francesco Molinari-Pradelli. London 421 598-2 LM3 (three CDs).

Like *Trovatore*, *Forza* tends to be criticized for its rambling libretto, and its music is less conventional and less tuneful than the earlier opera. But Verdi was moving forward in his style and was unswayed by public preferences; as a result, *Forza* dropped in and out of the repertoire until about 1918, when it established itself as one of his most powerful and gripping operas.

The plot concerns Don Alvaro, the lover of Donna Leonora di Vargas. They plan to elope, but their nocturnal meeting is interrupted by the appearance of Leonora's father. Alvaro denies that he has seduced her and throws down his pistol as a token of surrender; ironically, it goes off and fatally wounds the old Marchese. Alvaro and Leonora flee in different directions. Each believes that the other is dead, but Don Carlo, Leonora's brother, knows Alvaro to be alive and searches for him to revenge the murder of his father. In a boisterous inn scene, the gypsy Preziosilla tells the guests (one of whom is Don Carlo) that war has broken out between the Italians and Germans. Leonora, meanwhile, travels to a monastery to avoid capture; she is well received by Fra Melitone and the Father Superior, Guardiano, who take her in.

Meanwhile, Alvaro and Carlo, each fighting under an assumed name and unknown to each other by sight, are in Italy with the same Spanish contingent. Alvaro saves Carlo from death at the hands of ruffians; later, in battle, Alvaro is badly wounded. Thinking himself dying, he gives Carlo a small casket that he asks him to burn unopened after his death. As soon as Alvaro is gone, however, Carlo's curiosity gets the better of him; he opens the casket, and finds a portrait of Leonora inside. He swears vengeance. After Alvaro has recovered, he is accosted by Carlo and challenged to a duel. Alvaro agrees, but then flees to a monastery, taking the name of Padré Raffaello. In a scene meant to lighten the proceedings, Preziosilla and Fra Melitone join a company of soldiers who sing and dance a spirited "rataplan." Later, Melitone becomes annoyed by the persistence of beggars who flock to the monastery for their customary free soup; Guardiano reminds him that part of their mission is to serve the poor.

Carlo comes to the monastery seeking "Padré Raffaello"; Melitone says there are two monks of that name, but recognizes the disguised Alvaro from Carlo's description. When they meet Carlo again challenges him to a duel, but Alvaro declines. Carlo keeps insulting Alvaro, and slaps him across the face, until Alvaro finally gives in. Leonora, meanwhile, is praying in the grotto for peace when she overhears the sounds of fighting. Alvaro, who has mortally wounded Carlo, bangs on the door of Leonora's cell and asks absolution for the dying man. Leonora and Alvaro recognize each other immediately. She rushes to the spot where Carlo is dying; Padré Guardiano comes out to see what all the commotion is about. Carlo stabs Leonora; she dies in Guardiano's arms.

Keynotes

Despite the darkness of plot and music, and the rather forced intrusion of comic elements, *Forza* remains a powerful drama. Most of the first-act music is sung declamation, Verdi's way of updating the *recitatives* of Monteverdi. The pilgrim's chorus, the soprano-bass duet *La Vergine degli angeli*, and Alvaro's aria, *O tu che in seno*, are all great moments; the three tenor-baritone duets, *Solenne in quest'ora*, *Sleale! Il segreto*, and *Invano, Alvaro* rank among the finest pages in Verdi's output; and the entire final scene, starting with Leonora's aria *Pace, mio Dio* and ending with the soprano-tenor-bass trio, is a masterstroke equaled only by Act III of *Aida*. More interesting, however, is the music written for Fra Melitone. Its broken rhythms and orchestral accompaniment suggest an entirely new type of musical style for Verdi, one which he was to fulfill in his last opera, *Falstaff*.

The Recording

Versions of *Forza* have come and gone since this performance was etched in 1955, yet no other complete recording better captures the opera's essence. For the last time in his career, Mario del Monaco eschews his normal stentorian style in favor of a more elegant line, especially in his aria; Ettore Bastianini is a splendidly resonant Carlo; and Renata Tebaldi, whose complete recordings are often unworthy of her, sings with a freshness and delicacy unmatched in our day. Francesco Molinari-Pradelli's conducting is not the most exciting in the world, but he matches the alternating moods of brute power and ethereal elegance quite well.

Aida
1871   Giuseppe Verdi

Carlo Zardo, bs (Ramfis); Nicola Martinucci, t (Rhadames); Fiorenza Cossotto, c (Amneris); Maria Chiara, s (Aida); Giuseppe Scandola, br (Amonasro); Alfredo Zanazzo, bs (King of Egypt); Maria Gabriella Onesti, s (High Priestess). Arena di Verona Chorus and Orch., cond. by Anton Guadagno. Thorn-EMI videotape HTVE-2790.

After 120 years, *Aida* remains Verdi's most popular opera, and indeed one of the most popular operas of all time. Written on commission from Ismail Pasha, Khedive of Egypt, to celebrate the opening of the Suez Canal, it contains all the elements of Grand Opera at its grandest: big arias and duets for big-scale voices, exquisite lyric passages that alternate with moments of almost brutal drama, a ballet, and the memorable "Triumphal Scene" in which many opera houses to this day employ the services of exotic zoo animals, including elephants and camels. And yet, strictly as a work of art, *Aida* is a flawed masterpiece, utilizing pseudo-Arabic musical themes and motifs that now have a strikingly unreal sound. Verdi lapses into his earlier habit of writing self-contained scenes, producing a detached quality. In addition, the opera is fiendishly difficult to cast, with the result that its popularity often overrides the fact that there are few sopranos, contraltos, tenors, and baritones who sound really comfortable in their roles.

Unlike those of *Trovatore* and *Forza*, the plot of *Aida* is rather straightforward and simple. Rhadames, a captain in the Egyptian army, has returned triumphant from a battle with the Ethiopians; among his captives is the beautiful princess Aida, with whom he has fallen in love. Amneris, daughter of the Egyptian King, is secretly in love with him. The remainder of the plot revolves around this uneasy love triangle, the crux of the drama coming in the third act when, during their impassioned love duet, Rhadames inadvertently reveals his battle plans to Aida. Her father Amonasro, the King of Ethiopia who is disguised as a simple slave, overhears his plans; so too has Amneris, who has Rhadames arrested as a traitor. The sentence is death by suffocation: Rhadames is to be walled up in one of the pyramids. Thinking he is alone, he broods over his loss of Aida's love, but she has hidden in the pyramid and joins him in a farewell to life. Amneris, in the temple above them, sings a prayer to the gods that they may see Rhadames safely into heaven.

Keynotes

The most famous arias come in the first act: Rhadames's *Celeste Aida* and Aida's *Ritorna vincitor*. The second act contains the famous Aida-Amneris duet, the chorus *Gloria all'Egitto*, and the "Triumphal Scene." Despite the imperfections of the score, the third act is one of the most perfect Verdi ever wrote, starting softly with high strings and the voice of the High Priestess. Following this is Aida's second (and much better) aria, *O patria mia*; the long, exquisite love duet that includes *Fuggiam gli ardori* and *Là tra foreste vergini*; and Rhadames's final, dramatic realization of his treachery, *Tu! Amonasro!* The fourth act begins with the dramatic Amneris-Rhadames duet, *Già i sacerdoti adunasi*, follows through the condemnation of Rhadames, and ends with the famous "tomb scene."

The Recording

Only a sparse handful of *Aida* recordings fully capture the splendor of this opera; of these, the 1949 Arturo Toscanini performance (RCA 60251-2/4-RG, CD/cassettes) is the best conducted and the 1955 Zinka Milanov-Jussi Björling recording (RCA 6652-2-RG/ALK3-5380, CD/cassettes) the best sung. This performance, however, represents an effective compromise between the two approaches. Maria Chiara is a touching Aida, Fiorenza Cossotto a resplendent Amneris, and the little-known Nicola Martinucci a ringing, sonorous Rhadames. In addition, the conducting of Anton Guadagno is musical and dramatically experienced, and the added visual dimension of video enhances your enjoyment.

Otello
1887   Giuseppe Verdi

Virginio Assandri, t (Cassio); Leslie Chabay, t (Roderigo); Giuseppe Valdengo, br (Iago); Ramon Vinay, t (Otello); Herva Nelli, s (Desdemona); Nan Merriman, ms (Emilia); Nicola Moscona, bs (Lodovico). NBC Symphony Chorus and Orch., cond. by Arturo Toscanini. RCA Victor 60302-2-4RG (two CDs/cassettes).

In 1887, when Verdi was seventy-four years old, he premiered his next-to-last opera, *Otello*. Those who were expecting "just" another Verdi opera were stunned into silence by its dramatic sweep and power; for whereas all his previous operas, even such successes as *Rigoletto*, *Forza*, *Aida*, and *Don Carlos*, were written specifically with audiences in mind, Verdi wrote *Otello* for himself. He was no longer concerned with composing sweet, lyrical melodies that the public could hum, or inserting applause-breaks in what should be a dramatic entity. Throwing all caution to the winds, he put his entire heart and soul into the delineation of a powerful dramatic story through powerfully dramatic music. If the situation called for "regular" melodies, fine; but if it called for dramatic *recitative* set over a harmonically restless orchestral background (as in the aria *Dio! Mi potevi scagliar*), or the transformation of lyrical melody into terse dramatic outbursts (as in *Dio ti giocondi*), he would not hesitate to use all of the skill and inspiration at his disposal. Of course, it also didn't hurt that Arrigo Boito's libretto was a masterful conversion of the five-act Shakespeare tragedy into a four-act opera. In any event, *Otello* was the crowning achievement of Verdi's career and one of the few perfect operas ever written.

Anyone familiar with the Shakespeare original will have little trouble following Boito's adaptation; the only scene specifically created for the opera was Iago's "Credo" to the cruelty of God and the futility of life. The opera begins with a raging storm; the Venetian general Otello and his men are caught in the midst of it as they travel on ship to Cyprus. They arrive on the island, and Otello retires in triumph to his quarters. Iago, his ensign, plots with another officer, Roderigo, to get Otello's lieutenant Cassio drunk; Roderigo provokes Cassio to a fight, which awakens Otello, who strips Cassio of

his position. Iago advises Cassio to seek reinstatement by befriend-
ing Otello's wife, Desdemona. Later, Desdemona drops her handkerchief (personalized by an embroidered strawberry); her hand-
maiden Emilia finds it and gives it to her husband—Iago. With this
precious prop in his possession, Iago confidently pretends to soothe
Otello's nerves, while suggesting that Cassio and Desdemona are
sleeping together. In a fit of rage, Otello swears Iago to join him in
vengeance.

The ambassadors from Venice arrive to see the triumphant general. Meanwhile, Otello asks Desdemona for her handkerchief; she
stalls him, making him angry, and he finally insults her and then
curses himself for his jealousy. Immediately after, however, he sees
Iago and Cassio together. Iago hands Cassio the handkerchief,
which he innocently plays with while telling Iago of his sexual
exploits. Cassio is actually talking about his lover, Bianca, but Otello
assumes that the subject of their conversation is Desdemona. At
Otello's reception for the Venetian ambassadors, he insults
Desdemona, then falls to the ground in a petit mal epileptic seizure;
as the ambassadors leave in disgust, Iago puts his foot on Otello's
chest and crows his triumph over the fallen "lion of Venice."

In the last act, Desdemona has a premonition of death as she says
her nightly prayers; Otello comes in and, without giving her a
chance to explain, strangles her. A group of people, including Iago
and Emilia, hear the screams and rush in, but they are too late.
Emilia reveals that it was Iago, not Cassio, who took possession of
the handkerchief; Otello, understanding all, stabs himself, sings *Let
No One Fear Me*, and dies over Desdemona's corpse.

As with *Don Giovanni*, there are several levels to this opera, not the
least of which is the interesting premise that Otello's madness results
not so much from the supposed betrayal of Desdemona as from his
implicit faith in Iago. What makes this more interesting is that, even
in Shakespeare's original, Iago is not exactly the most subtle of
traitors; Roderigo sees through him in the very first act, and one
presumes that most "men of the world" could spot this type of
character a mile away. And yet, Otello is not the only one who
believes Iago—so does Cassio. Yet Cassio is a little stupid, and Otello
is (presumably) not, so that in the end one must conclude that Otello
is an intelligent, powerful, yet naïve individual, whose reluctance to
take Desdemona's word over Iago's comes from an elemental form of

chauvinism; and, therefore, he would probably have come to mistrust Desdemona, sooner or later, even without Iago's prodding.

Keynotes

As the most complex and interrelated of all Verdi's dramas, *Otello* does not lend itself to "spotlighting" nearly as well as, say, *Trovatore* or *Aida*. One could certainly point to such outstanding moments as Iago's first-act aria *Brindisi* and second-act *Credo*, Otello's *Ora e per sempre addio* and *Niun mi tema*, the second-act duet *Si, pel ciel*, the third-act duet *Dio ti giocondi*, and the scintillating Otello-Iago-Cassio trio. But all of these moments, and more, are so skillfully woven into the surrounding music and plot that they gain in power when heard as part of the cohesive whole rather than as set pieces. Indeed, only Desdemona's fourth-act *Ave Maria* and *Willow Song* stand apart as arias somewhat divorced from the whole; yet, as a self-contained unit, that scene, too, is a gem.

The Recording

Since the opera premiered in 1887, only six tenors have really proved themselves great Otellos: Francesco Tamagno, who created the role; Leo Slezak, who succeeded him as the international favorite; Lauritz Melchior, whose interpretation was surprisingly intense and musical; Ramon Vinay, who practically "owned" the role in the 1940s and early fifties; Mario del Monaco, who succeeded him; and Jon Vickers, the last great exponent of the part. Of these, only the last three made complete recordings of the opera, but the versions of del Monaco and Vickers were marred by indifferent conducting (in their first tries) and completely incompetent Iagos (in their second versions). As a result, one must turn to the classic 1946 account by Arturo Toscanini and a near-perfect cast for the best overall representation of the work, even though the first-act love duet is a little choppy and does not "flow" as smoothly as you would ideally like. It should also be mentioned that, though incomplete (it lacks the second-act aria *Ora e per sempre addio*), the video version on Lyric Distribution 1439 is the best of del Monaco's recordings, featuring Gabrielle Tucci's silvery soprano, Tito Gobbi's Iago (the greatest contemporary exponent of this role), and surprisingly exciting conducting from Alberto Erede. Indeed, one might want to do what I did, which was to splice into the tape the missing aria from one of del Monaco's commercial recordings of the opera. Though the screen is blank, it gives you a complete performance of stunning vitality and musical conviction.

Follow-up Listening

If you become enamored of Verdi, you will also want to hear his excellent 1855 opera *Les Vêpres Siciliennes*, in the performance by Jacqueline Brumaire, Jean Bonhomme, Ayhan Baran, and Mario Rossi on Arkadia CDMP-456.3 (three CDs; check your library for a libretto). *Un Ballo in Maschera* (1859) is also rather popular, and the recording by Margaret Price, Luciano Pavarotti, Renato Bruson, and Sir Georg Solti is superb (London 410 210-2 LH2, two CDs); and the sprawling but exquisite *Don Carlos* (1867) is best served in the French-language original with Katia Ricciarelli, Lucia Valentini-Terrani, Placido Domingo, Leo Nucci, Ruggero Raimondi, and Claudio Abbado on DG 415 316-2 GH4 (four CDs).

WAGNER

Where Verdi's aesthetic was ruled by the heart, Wagner's was more intellectual. This is not to say that there are no moments of great emotional beauty in Wagner's music—far from it—merely that, like Spontini, Gluck, and Berlioz, he tempered his emotionality with daring harmonies and complex structures. In the beginning he was much influenced by both Weber and Meyerbeer, but as he matured he began to reject the "light" approach of the former and the chaotic-virtuoso approach of the latter. By the time he was thirty, Wagner had fully formed his aesthetic, which was to present philo-sophically interesting plots in lush, powerful, yet experimental or-chestral-vocal settings. Interestingly, however, this aesthetic slowly deteriorated over time, while Verdi's grew in depth and power. With each success, Wagner fed his ego to such an extent that he began to believe in himself as a demigod of music and poetry; his "music-dra-mas" became more bombastic and pretentious, eventually culminat-ing in a work (*Parsifal*) that presented his ideal of a Christ-like figure with no Jewish background. By this time, of course, his anti-Semi-tism had become almost as legendary as his music, but even the music waned in both interest and complexity, eventually culminating in rambling passages of elongated notes that conveyed nothing.

Nevertheless, he was a great composer, and as such has maintained a hold on the standard repertoire in which his works stand virtually alone.

Wagner, like Verdi, also "created" some new types of voices; but where Verdi drove them up and over the top in his ingenious-conservative style, Wagner pushed them out from the middle, following the radical-revolutionary style of Gluck and Berlioz. As a result, where Verdi's "spinto" sopranos and tenors reached for the skies, Wagner's dramatic sopranos and tenors (also known as *Heldentenors*, from the German word for "hero") had a touch of the contralto and baritone, respectively, about their voices. Without question, the most famous Wagner soprano and Heldentenor in the past 100 years were Kirsten Flagstad (1895–1962) and Lauritz Melchior (1890–1973), who sang together at Covent Garden, the Berlin Opera, and the Metropolitan Opera. Indeed, Flagstad's all-Wagner recital on RCA Victor 7915-2/4-RG (CD/cassette) includes a duet with Melchior in addition to famous arias from *Tristan und Isolde*, *Lohengrin*, *Die Walküre*, and *Götterdämmerung*, while Angel CDH-69789 gives us earlier recordings by Melchior, before he teamed with Flagstad, from *Rienzi*, *Tannhäuser*, *Lohengrin*, *Die Walküre*, *Siegfried*, *Götterdämmerung*, *Tristan und Isolde*, and *Die Meistersinger*.

Because Wagner's music only *ventured* high, as opposed to *staying* in the upper registers like Verdi's, it didn't really affect the standard contralto voice, but it did affect the two lower male voices. As the *Heldentenor* must have a touch of baritone in him, the *Heldenbaritone* must have a touch of the bass; not surprisingly, most Heldenbaritones start out as strong lyric basses who can reach unusually high notes. Though some Heldenbaritones also sing Verdi roles, those who specialize in Wagner usually have a darker, more penetrating low range, more like a lyric bass. One of the best and most famous was Friedrich Schorr (1888–1953); Pearl GEMM-CD-9379 features his performances of excerpts from *Tannhäuser* and *Die Meistersinger* in addition to the related music of Beethoven and Weber. The *dramatic bass*, on the other hand, was simply an extension of the Mozartian deep bass, or "basso profundo," but like Wagnerian dramatic sopranos they, too, had to project a huge middle range. An excellent example was Alexander Kipnis (1891–1978), who sings excerpts from *Tristan und Isolde*, *Die Walküre*, and *Die Meistersinger*, in addition to related music by Mozart and Meyerbeer, on Pearl GEMM-CD-9451.

It should also be noted that Wagner put the forces into motion that led directly to both the "age of the conductor" and the "age of the director." Although he personally loved the Italian school of singing—even for his own operas!—Wagner was very upset with the Italians' slipshod method of stage productions and the lackadaisical rehearsal schedules for orchestra. Because so many of his operatic "effects" were achieved through the orchestra and staging, more so than even the voice, he eventually had an opera house, Bayreuth, built especially for him. It was the first and last time that an opera house was built for the exclusive use of one composer. Wagner raised the standard for conducting and staging that was eventually to influence other opera houses worldwide. In addition, Wagner wrote most of his operas in a continuous, interlocking style, where set "arias" were generally combined with the music before and after them, which discouraged superfluous applause during an act.

Der Fliegende Höllander (The Flying Dutchman)
1843   Richard Wagner

Matti Salminen, bs (Daland); Lisbeth Balslev, s (Senta, his daughter); Robert Schunk, t (Erik); Anny Schlemm, c (Mary); Graham Clark, t (Steersman); Simon Estes, br (The Dutchman). Bayreuth Festival Chorus and Orch., cond. by Woldemar Nelsson. Philips home video 070506-3. *CD alternate*: Philips 416 300-2 (two CDs).

Following near-misses in his light, Weber-styled comedy *Die Feen* (*The Fairies*, 1833–34) and the sprawling, Meyerbeer-influenced *Rienzi* (1842), Wagner captured the imagination of an international public with this excursion into the legend of the Flying Dutchman. It is often considered, rightly so, his first major step on the road from conventional opera to music-drama; but, more than that, it is his tightest and most exciting stage work. Unlike his later operas, there is no waste music in *Höllander*; all is taut, cogent, logical, and inevitable. Even the two "wayside" arias of Daland and Erik have an urgency unlike the rambling, inconsequential passages later written for such characters as Fricka, Lohengrin, and Parsifal.

The character of Senta, the chaste maiden who has devoted her life to the single thought (or *idée fixe*) of being the Dutchman's salvation, can be interpreted from several different angles. Wagner saw her as the pure spirit who redeems the damned, but in the light of modern psychology she can also be seen, as she is in this production, as a slightly mad woman living in a world of her own. This interpretation is underscored by her often excitable state of mind, as well as by the fact that the Dutchman himself is unconvinced of her fidelity to him. The story begins when Daland, Senta's father, returns from his merchant voyage a bit shaken by a terrible storm. The Dutchman's ship also pulls into port; he disembarks, singing a long aria describing his torturous voyage and his condemnation to sail the seas forever until a pure maiden gives herself to him unconditionally. Meanwhile, Senta, spinning yarn with her old nurse Mary, is singing the "Ballad of the Flying Dutchman." Erik, a huntsman smitten with love for Senta, announces the arrival of her father's ship and a ghastly looking stranger. Senta, immediately sensing this to be the Dutchman, greets him when he arrives with Daland. In a long duet, Senta offers herself to the damned sailor; Daland, who thinks the stranger just another wealthy merchant, gives his blessing to their betrothal.

Erik, discovering this, pleads with Senta to remember his love for her. The Dutchman overhears them, thinks himself abandoned, and bids Senta farewell over her protestations of love and fidelity. She tries to follow him to his ship, but is held back by Erik and his friends. As the Dutchman puts to sea, Senta, freeing herself, rushes to a cliff overhanging the ocean, cries out "Here I stand faithful, even to death," and throws herself onto the rocks. The Dutchman's curse is lifted as the curtain falls.

Keynotes

The opera begins with a restless, exciting overture that contains many themes heard later in the work, principal among them Senta's ballad. Though the opera was originally presented in three short acts, totaling a little over two hours, Wagner always wanted it presented in one unbroken act, as it is here. The effect of this condensation is overwhelming: the music surges and dips, but pushes inevitably on from scene to scene. Practically any excerpt will prove the excellence and economy of this score, but particular attention should be paid to the Senta-Dutchman duet, the Senta-Erik duet, and especially the final scene that comes to a stunning conclusion with three crashing chords from the orchestra. Daland's aria adds a light touch that comes as a relief amidst such dramatic events, and Erik's aria, though stretching the limits of the average Wagnerian tenor, contributes a weird tension to the proceedings.

The Recording

Bass-baritone Simon Estes has an unusual voice that takes about five minutes of continual singing to warm up, but once that is achieved his slow wobble turns into a burnished glow that is startling in its power and organ-like resonance. Matti Salminen sings well as Daland, and the little-known Lisbeth Balslev and Robert Schunk are superb as Senta and Erik, especially from a dramatic point of view. Yet the star of this performance is undoubtedly Woldemar Nelsson, the conductor, who pulls the variegated threads of music together into a cogent whole that subsides from the overture only to rise in a long, slow crescendo to the tumultuous finale.

Tristan und Isolde
1865   Richard Wagner

Horst Laubenthal, t (Sailor); Birgit Nilsson, s (Isolde); Ruth Hesse, c (Brangäne); Jon Vickers, t (Tristan); Bengt Rundgren, bs (King Marke); Walter Berry, br (Kurwenal). Philharmonia Chorus; Orch. National de l'ORTF, cond. by Karl Böhm. Lyric Distribution videotape 1868. *CD alternate*: Flagstad, Blanche Thebom, Ludwig Suthaus, and Dietrich Fischer-Dieskau, cond. by Wilhelm Furtwängler. Angel CDCD-47321 (four CDs).

Following the success of *Der Fliegende Höllander*, Wagner plunged himself into Teutonic and Scandinavian legends for more or less the remainder of his operatic career. This resulted in one extraordinary opera, *Tannhäuser* (1845, 1861), and one semi-excellent music drama, *Lohengrin* (1850); but in 1865, at which time he was already involved in the legends that would eventually formulate *The Ring of the Nibelungs*, he was sidetracked into the realm of Irish legend. The result was *Tristan und Isolde*, the work often considered his masterpiece.

Typical of all his work from *Der Fliegende Höllander* on, Wagner completely "remodeled" the Tristan legend before setting it to music. He cast aside all side incidents, working the main episodes into a concise, fast-paced, cogent drama. He also turned the love potion from a mere chemical substance into one that releases a flood of pent-up emotions that cannot be reversed by any process known to man. In the events that transpire before the opera begins, Tristan, an orphan, was raised by his uncle, King Marke of Cornwall. He has killed Morold, an Irish knight engaged to Isolde, in combat; having been dangerously wounded, he was ironically saved by Isolde, and the two fell in love with each other without knowing the other even cared. Soon after Tristan's return to Cornwall, he is returned to Ireland by Marke in order to bring Isolde back—to marry the King!

Thinking Tristan doesn't love her, Isolde decides to drink a death potion. Tristan, feeling that life without Isolde wouldn't be worth living anyway, determines to join her. But Brangäne, Isolde's companion, recognizes the true situation and so substitutes a love potion for the death-draught. Shortly after reaching Cornwall, the lovers are caught embracing by the King and his retinue; Tristan is mortally wounded by Melot, one of Marke's knights. Kurwenal, Tristan's faithful servant, takes him to Kareol where he lived before he was orphaned. Isolde is not far behind, and arrives just as Tristan is breathing his agonized last. Drinking at last her death-potion, Isolde sinks upon his corpse and dies.

Upon this humble plot Wagner hung a rich tapestry of music, ranging from the violence of Isolde's curse in Act I to the penultimate "Love-Death," or *Liebestod*, that she sings before dying. In between are scenes that, though long, have a strange logic and fascination to them; although the music occasionally rambles, it never lapses into self-pity or artificial mysticism as in the case of Wagner's later works. An excellent example of this is the *Liebestod*. Though it expresses the Oriental philosophy of two spirits, pure in their love for each other, being absorbed by nature, there is nothing maudlin about it. On the contrary, the music rises in a slow spiral from low, soft passages to ecstatic, long-held notes at full volume.

Keynotes

The opening bars of *Tristan*, moving immediately into a strange-sounding chord that seems to belong to no particular key, plunge us into a world of mystery as no other opera before it. Nor is this opening a freak aberration; throughout the score, Wagner combines lush tonal fantasies with chords and extra notes known as "passing tones" that take us out of the comfortable world of "regular" key-changes and into a miasma of uncertain tonalities. In this way, the door was opened for future composers to experiment with keys that were not part of the recognized harmonic structure, and to combine two unrelated chords, one on top of the other, to create tension. Undoubtedly the most famous passage in the opera is the long love duet in Act II, which starts in a frenzy of excitement, settles into a lush, warm environment where the two protagonists indulge in a little musical foreplay, and then almost rises to a peak of climax when the proceedings are broken up by the arrival of Marke and his knights. If ever there was such a thing as *coitus interruptus* in music, this is it.

The Recording

Wagner always stressed the importance of the Italian bel canto vocal style in the performances of his music-dramas, but contemporary and more recent German singers either didn't believe him or didn't care. As a result, most singers in these roles tend to belt and bark their way through them. Two glorious exceptions to this rule were Kirsten Flagstad and Lauritz Melchior, but their live performances together are marred by poor subsidiary casting. Fortunately their heirs apparent, Birgit Nilsson and Jon Vickers, managed to make this interesting videotaped performance in 1972. The production features, sadly, one of those typically bleak "minimalist" sets that add little or nothing visually, though the acting of Vickers and Walter Berry is superb. If you want the best possible *audio* performance, however, the CD version with Flagstad and company on Angel, listed above, is a sublime alternative.

THE RING OF THE NIBELUNGS

The four-opera "trilogy" that comprises *The Ring of the Nibelungs*, or *Der Ring des Nibelungen* to give it its German title, is often considered the greatest project conceived by the mind of a single man. Wagner spent many years transforming several combined Teutonic and Norse legends into the "poetry" of the *Nibelung* dramas, and published these in book form in 1863. Six years later the first completed opera, a two-hour-ten-minute "prologue" (as Wagner saw it) called *Das Rheingold*, premiered at the Court Theatre in Munich. A year later *Die Walküre* popped up, but he withheld the last two works—*Siegfried* and *Götterdämmerung*—until the famed Bayreuth Theatre was built and the whole cycle could be presented intact in August 1876.

While Wagner's achievement remains in some respects monumental, audiences today should look upon certain aspects of this work with a grain (or maybe a barrel) of salt. For one thing, though this is not the time or place to discuss it in detail, Wagner altered several portions of the old legends to suit his own purposes. In a few instances, he mistranslated certain words, which led him to draw erroneous conclusions about the original myths. And, last but not least, his written "poetry" from which the librettos are taken is turgid, clumsy, racist, and more than a little ridiculous. Many would-be philosophers have waxed eloquent over the "relationships" among Wagner's characters and the moral dilemmas they find themselves in, but today they seem alternately heavy-handed or pointless. In addition, the overblown lyrics practically forced Wagner to compose music that was in itself overblown. As one wit of a critic remarked, the *Ring* has splendid moments and long half-hours.

The most consistently remarkable detail of the *Ring* cycle is its rich orchestration: not even in *Lohengrin* or *Tristan* did Wagner present audiences with such a feast of sound, and the orchestral score of the *Ring* laid the groundwork for practically everything accomplished symphonically by Gustav Mahler and Richard Strauss. He also developed, to a high degree, the use of short "themes" that represented various characters or motives (e.g., greed, hate, the ring), which he called *leitmotifs*. The recurrence of these *leitmotifs* cues discerning listeners so that they can recognize what is about to happen. The problem is that Wagner's drama is so transparent, even heavy-handed, that most of the action is pretty predictable even without them. Readers who are music-literate can explore the various *leitmotifs* if they wish; I will simply touch on a few of the most obvious in the present discussion. Because the plot is so convoluted, we will discuss it opera by opera.

Most critics are unanimous in their praise for the complete integral *Ring* recorded between 1959 and 1966 by Sir Georg Solti, but I have always found much of his conducting in this cycle to be stiff and lacking momentum. His tempos are generally good, and most of the singers are solid, but inevitably there is little life to the proceedings: It sounds like a *Ring* bred in a hothouse. The 1950 La Scala *Ring* is superbly conducted by Wilhelm Furtwängler, but some of the principal singers are inferior, and the first Siegfried (Set Svanholm) literally runs out of voice long before the end of his long love duet. As a result, I have selected what I feel are the best performances from three complete *Rings*: La Scala 1950, Bayreuth 1954, and Bayreuth 1966.

Das Rheingold
1869 Richard Wagner

Dorothea Siebert, s (Woglinde); Helga Dernesch, s (Wellgunde); Ruth Hesse, c (Flosshilde); Gustav Neidlinger, br (Alberich); Erwin Wohlfahrt, t (Mime); Theo Adam, bs-br (Wotan); Annalies Burmeister, ms (Fricka); Anja Silja, s (Freia); Kurt Böhme, bs (Fafner); Martti Talvela, bs (Fasolt); Wolfgang Windgassen, t (Loge); Gerd Nienstedt, bs-br (Donner); Vera Soukupova, c (Erda). Bayreuth Festival Orch., cond. by Karl Böhm. Philips 412 475-2 PH2 (two CDs).

Das Rheingold opens in the river Rhine, where three water nymphs known as the Rhinemaidens guard a magic lump of gold. Legend has it that any being who renounces love forever can forge the gold into a magic helmet and ring that will give him power over all living creatures. Alberich, prince of the subterranean Nibelung dwarfs, flirts with the Rhinemaidens, but when it becomes apparent that they are merely teasing him, he steals the gold. Meanwhile Wotan, king of the gods, is having a grand palace called Valhalla built by two giants, Fasolt and Fafner. The price they have agreed on as payment for the job is the hand of Freia, Wotan's sister-in-law. When Valhalla is finished, however, Wotan refuses to give her up. Loge, another god, suggests that the giants accept the gold hoard of the Nibelungs in exchange; they agree. Thus emboldened, Wotan slips down to Nibelung-land and tricks Alberich into giving him the magic ring and helmet. Enraged, Alberich puts a curse on the ring. Wotan, paying no heed, collects the remainder of the Nibelung gold and returns to Valhalla.

Wotan piles the gold, minus the helmet and ring, in front of the giants, but it is not quite as high and wide as Freia. Wotan adds the magic helmet, or Tarnhelm, but the giants also clamor for the ring. Erda, the earth goddess, rises from the ground and warns Wotan that he will be sorry if he does not turn over the ring as well. Reluctantly, he adds the ring to the pile. The giants argue over the division of the treasure, and Fafner kills Fasolt in the argument. Donner, the god of thunder, strikes his hammer on a huge rock. A rainbow bridge appears, and the gods use it to cross over into their new home, Valhalla.

Keynotes

There is little conventional melody in *Rheingold*; even the solo spots are more like dramatic *recitative* than arias, and much of the vocal music "skips around" in an angular fashion rather than following a "smooth" melodic line. Yet the Rhinemaidens' "theme song," a lilting 6/8 melody, is one of the most recognizable of all the *leitmotifs*, as are Alberich's curse and the heavy thud of the giants' tread. Only in the final moments of this "prologue" do we get a recognizable tune, Wotan's *Abendlich strahlt*, in which he eloquently greets his new home. Yet the orchestral writing, especially in the "Descent into Nibelheim" and the buildup to Donner's striking the rock, is consistently stunning, and the music demands the utmost of vocal power and richness from the singers despite the angularity of its structure.

The Recording

Vera Soukupova and Theo Adam are not the steadiest of Erdas and Wotans, but Annalies Burmeister is superb as Fricka, the three Rhinemaidens are excellent, Gustav Neidlinger and Kurt Böhme practically held a patent on the roles of Alberich and Fafner, and both Wolfgang Windgassen and Martti Talvela are surprises in the roles of Loge and Fasolt. More to the point, Karl Böhm's conducting moves this work with a smoothness and control that Georg Solti can only hint at.

Die Walküre
1870   Richard Wagner

Günther Treptow, t (Siegmund); Hilde Konetzni, s (Sieglinde); Ludwig Weber, bs (Hunding); Ferdinand Frantz, bs-br (Wotan); Kirsten Flagstad, s (Brünnhilde); Elisabeth Höngen, c (Fricka); Ilona Steingruber, s (Helmwige); Walburga Wegener, s (Gerhilde). La Scala Orch., cond. by Wilhelm Furtwängler. Fonit-Cetra CDC-15 (four CDs).

Undoubtedly the most popular and best-written of the four Nibelung operas, *Walküre* can and has stood alone in an opera season. Unlike its predecessor or successors, it contains the largest amount of consistently lyric music, and, despite the somewhat banal melody of the "Ride of the Valkyries," it remains theatrically effective. Of course, some of this attractive, lyric music was purposely contrived in order for Wagner to make the thought of incest palatable to prudish 19th-century audiences.

Siegmund and Sieglinde are fraternal twins and illegitimate children of Wotan, whom they know under the name of Wälse. Separated as children, Sieglinde has since been married to Hunding, a hunter. Siegmund, now an adult, staggers accidentally into their home during a heavy storm. He is tended to by Sieglinde, who initially thinks it is her husband. After Hunding returns, he demands to hear the stranger's name and story; Sieglinde recognizes it as the partner to her own. When Hunding is asleep, Siegmund recognizes his father's magic sword stuck into a tree that grows through the house. He pulls it out, sings a love duet with Sieglinde, and the two rush into the night.

Wotan and Brünnhilde, one of his nine daughters who are also Valkyrie warriors, are confronted by Wotan's wife, Fricka, who demands that they pursue Siegmund and Sieglinde to preserve the sanctity of marriage. As a result, Wotan orders Brünnhilde to side with Hunding in the coming battle, but she disobeys his orders and helps the Wälsung couple. Wotan, angry, arrives in time to break Siegmund's sword with his spear; Siegmund is slain by Hunding, Sieglinde rushes off to give birth to Siegmund's and her child, and

Brünnhilde is put to sleep on a rock, around which Wotan places magic fire that can only be penetrated by a hero pure-of-heart.

Keynotes

The first-act love duet contains some of Wagner's best-known melodies, including Siegmund's song to the magic sword (*Wälse! Wälse!*), the beautiful *Winterstürme*, and Sieglinde's *Du bist der Lenz* and *Der manne sippe*. The second act introduces the *Ho-yo-to-ho* as a solo aria, which later becomes the famous ensemble "Ride of the Valkyries." In addition, there is a long and dramatic scene in which Siegmund pleads with Brünnhilde to change her mind despite Wotan's orders, a gorgeous arioso for Brünnhilde in which she pleads with Wotan for forgiveness, and the long finale known as the "Magic Fire Music" in which Wotan sings a reluctant farewell to his favorite Valkyrie daughter.

The Recording

This particular portion of the 1950 Furtwängler *Ring* is absolutely splendid in every respect: Günther Treptow is an ardent Siegmund, Hilde Konetzni a luscious-voiced Sieglinde, Ferdinand Frantz an imposing Wotan, Elisabeth Höngen an exciting Fricka, and the legendary Kirsten Flagstad the most rapturous and lyrical of Brünnhildes. In addition, Wilhelm Furtwängler sets an almost frantic pace at the outset that, despite the inclusion of slower tempos, never flags in tension from beginning to end. The sonics are, admittedly, a little flat, yet there is no other *Walküre* ever recorded—not even Furtwängler's fairly good Radio Italiana remake of 1953—that can equal this one in its combination of clarity and drive.

Siegfried
1876   Richard Wagner

Erwin Wohlfahrt, t (Mime); Wolfgang Windgassen, t (Sieg-fried); Theo Adam, bs-br (The Wanderer [Wotan]); Gustav Neidlinger, br (Alberich); Kurt Böhme, bs (Fafner, now a dragon); Erika Köth, s (Forest Bird); Vera Soukupova, c (Erda); Birgit Nilsson, s (Brünnhilde). Bayreuth Festival Orch., cond. by Karl Böhm. Philips 412 483-2 PH4 (four CDs).

Siegfried, though an even longer opera than *Walküre*, has an even skimpier plot, and is practically a pastoral interlude between the swift, furious drama of its predecessor and the heavy-handed muscle of *Götterdämmerung*. Siegfried is the son of the doomed Siegmund and Sieglinde; he has been raised by Alberich's dwarf-brother, Mime, who plans to take advantage of the boy's naïveté to kill the giant Fafner, who has since used the Tarnhelm to turn himself into a dragon, and thus claim the magic ring. To protect and avenge himself, Siegfried forges the broken parts of his father's sword together.

There are two long and rather superfluous scenes between Wotan, disguised as a Wanderer, and each of the two Nibelung brothers (Mime and Alberich), leading to Siegfried slaying Fafner. After he licks a drop of the dragon's blood from his finger, he understands the singing of the bird who tells him about the secret of the helmet and ring. Siegfried dons the ring, which allows him to understand the treachery behind Mime's supposedly kind words. He kills Mime, then discovers Brünnhilde asleep on the rock. Mistaking her for a man, he is able by magic powers to penetrate the fire; as he wakes her, he realizes that she is not a man, but (having never seen a woman before) he doesn't know what she is. He quickly finds out, however, and the two sing a long and rapturous love duet, after which they repair to a nearby cave for lovemaking while the curtain falls.

Keynotes

The best-known sections of *Siegfried* are the "Forging Song," the passage known as the "Forest Murmurs," the song of the forest bird, and the penultimate love duet which, though not quite as erotic as the one Wagner wrote for Tristan, is nevertheless effective.

The Recording

Wolfgang Windgassen was famous for being able to sing the long, exhausting role of Siegfried without running out of voice; this 1966 "live" performance shows how. In addition, Birgit Nilsson was the greatest Brünnhilde of the sixties, Theo Adam is in spectacular voice as the Wanderer, Kurt Böhme and Gustav Neidlinger are back as Fafner and Alberich, and Karl Böhm's conducting has a sweep and lilt that only Wilhelm Furtwängler ever equaled.

Götterdämmerung
1876   Richard Wagner

Maria von Ilosvay, c; Ira Malaniuk, ms; Regina Resnik, s (Three Norns); Astrid Varnay, s (Brünnhilde); Wolfgang Windgassen, t (Siegfried); Hermann Uhde, br (Gunther); Josef Griendl, bs (Hagen); Natalie Hinsch-Gröndahl, s (Gutrune); Gustav Neidlinger, br (Alberich). Bayreuth Festival Chorus and Orch., cond. by Clemens Krauss. Laudis LAU-4005 (four CDs).

Götterdämmerung, or "Twilight of the Gods," begins with a long, rather boring scene in which the three Norns (or Fates), who weave the tapestry of life, recount the entire tale over again from the beginning. There was no reason for Wagner to write this scene at all, except that he was so much in love with his own "poetry" he couldn't bear cutting a word. After that we hear the "Dawn Music," in the midst of which Siegfried and Brünnhilde emerge from their cave where they have presumably been making love since the end of *Siegfried*. At the end of their duet they part company so that Siegfried can go in search of more heroic deeds.

We are then transported to the hall of the Gibichungs: the brave knight Gunther, his fair sister Gutrune, and their half-brother, a sinister plotter named Hagen who has long had designs on the magic ring. He knows that Siegfried has killed the dragon that guarded it and given it to Brünnhilde as a symbol of his love. Hagen knows all this because he is the son of Alberich, the Nibelung dwarf who started this entire chain of events. When Siegfried arrives, he naïvely shows the Gibichungs the equally magic Tarnhelm; Hagen slips him a love potion that makes him forget Brünnhilde and instead fall in love with Gutrune. Under its spell, Hagen talks Siegfried into traveling with Gunther to capture Brünnhilde, whom he no longer knows.

Brünnhilde is visited on the Valkyrie rock by her sister Waltraute, who begs her to toss the magic gold ring back into the Rhine, but she refuses. Siegfried, disguised as Gunther by the Tarnhelm, approaches her and demands it; she tries to defend herself, but finds herself strangely powerless. Alberich urges Hagen to murder Siegfried and regain the ring, while Brünnhilde and the real Gunther (who has now claimed her for his own) arrive at Gibichung Hall for a double wedding ceremony with Siegfried and Gutrune. Brünnhilde, naturally, recognizes Siegfried and demands his loyalty and love, but Siegfried, under the spell of the love potion, is still enamored of Gutrune. Brünnhilde takes an oath of vengeance against Siegfried on Hagen's spear; Hagen calls for Siegfried's death, but Gunther, his new friend, is sworn to protect him. The next day, during a hunt, Hagen slips Siegfried another potion that restores his memory of Brünnhilde and how he found her. Siegfried tells this story to Gunther, who is aghast at the revelation. When Siegfried turns his back to observe two ravens who fly overhead, Hagen stabs him in the back with his spear. This is followed by "Siegfried's Funeral March."

Back in Gibichung Hall, Hagen informs Gutrune that Siegfried is dead; wild with grief, she hurls violent accusations at Gunther, who simply points to Hagen. Hagen draws his sword and kills Gunther. He tries to get the ring off Siegfried's finger, when the corpse suddenly raises its hand in a grisly warning. All, including Hagen, fall back in fear. Meanwhile Brünnhilde has learned from the Rhinemaidens the plot that deceived both her and Siegfried; stricken with grief, she has a funeral pyre built. In the long but exquisite "Immolation Scene," Brünnhilde and her horse Grane ascend the pyre and she starts the flames. The massive fire burns down Valhalla, which in turns causes the Rhine to flood its banks. Borne on the flood, the Rhinemaidens swim to the pyre and reclaim their ring; Hagen, who witnesses all this, plunges in after them. Two of the maidens firmly hold his arms and drown him while the third holds the ring up in triumph.

Keynotes

Once past the dismal Norn scene, there's much to admire in *Götterdämmerung*, not least of which is the exciting Siegfried-Brünnhilde duet, *Zu neuen Taten*. The music of the Gibichung hall is interesting, combining elements of gaiety and doom, and the passage known as "Hagen's Watch" is fascinating in its continual use and transformation of a single chord. The trio that leads up to "Brünnhilde's Curse" is exciting, as is the latter half of the "Immolation Scene"; and the orchestral "bridges," "Siegfried's Rhine Journey" and "Siegfried's Funeral March," are among the greatest instrumental passages Wagner ever composed.

The Recording

Clemens Krauss is not a name that excites any but aficionados, but during the 1930s and forties he was considered one of the greatest of all opera conductors, especially of Wagner's dramas. This 1954 *Ring* cycle was his last and greatest testament; unfortunately, his versions of the first three operas are not up to the quality of the competing versions already chosen. In *Götterdämmerung*, however, he combined a near-perfect cast with excellent conducting to produce what is undoubtedly the most consistently dramatic and well-sung performance ever recorded.

Follow-up Listening

The excellent 1845 opera *Tannhäuser* is best represented (in its 1861 Paris revision) by an early-seventies recording with Helga Dernesch, Christa Ludwig, René Kollo, Victor Braun, and Sir Georg Solti conducting on London 414 581-2 LH3 (three CDs), and there are also moments of excellence in *Lohengrin* (1850), particularly the performance by Elisabeth Grümmer, Christa Ludwig, Jess Thomas, and Rudolf Kempe on Angel CDCC-49017 (three CDs).

Kidding the Ring

Perhaps because of its exhaustive length and convoluted plot, no opera or group of operas has been so exhaustively parodied as Wagner's *Ring des Nibelungen*. Aside from the numerous comediennes who need only don a winged helmet and metal breastplates to make an audience guffaw, there have been several clever and vicious digs at old Richard's four-opera "trilogy."

The most famous and clever of these is undoubtedly the "plot synopsis" given by singer-comedienne Anna Russell, who for thirty-five years has been delighting listeners with her version of the Ring dramas (available on CD and cassette, Sony Classical MDK-47252/MGT-44677). Perhaps her funniest line comes halfway through, when she tells an incredulous audience, "I'm not making this up, you know!" Another variation came in the halcyon days of NBC's "Saturday Night Live", when Dan Aykroyd as "Leonard Pinth Garnell" presented a "Bad Opera" entitled *Der Goldene Klang*, or *The Golden Note*. In this version, soprano-comedienne Madeline Kahn (dressed in Brünnhilde getup) sings part of the "Magic Fire Music" from *Die Walküre* while John Belushi, the lightning-god, descends from heaven on wires and sticks her in the neck with a piece of cardboard lightning. At this point, as Aykroyd put it, "She sings a note of such a pitch and duration that the singer develops larynx-lock, and is stuck on the note—FOREVER!!" As a result, poor Madeline is forced to emit a continuous high A-flat while paramedics rush to her aid with oxygen tanks as the curtain falls.

For me, however, the very funniest *Ring* spoof of all came in a 1956 comedy revue called *Carousel* by a little-known comedienne named Frances Osborne. The record is long out-of-print (and I unfortunately forget the label), but the lyrics she sang to *Ho-yo-to-ho* are etched on my memory forever:

Each night willy-nilly, perched up on this filly, I feel rather silly but isn't it odd: I whoop like a demon, the audience beamin', the louder I'm screamin' the more they applaud! *Ho-yo-to-ho! Ho-yo-to-ho! Ho-yo-to-ho-o-o-o-o-o!!*

I'd rather be standing secure on a landing, like Juliet handing a rose to Romeo. These nightly Valhallas, they fill me with malice, I'm getting a callous on my Ho-yo-TOE! *Ho-yo-to-ho! Ho-yo-to-ho! Ho-yo-to-ho-o-o-o-o-o!!*

Since I was just a young 'un, I've hated Nibelungen; I hate to sing in German—I'd rather be Ethel Merman! But most of all . . . of course . . . I hate this GODDAMNED HORSE! I hate his humps and hollows, I hate the way he swallows, I wish they'd put a net up, *I HATE THE WHOLE DAMN SETUP! Ho-yo-to-ho! Ho-yo-to-ho-o-o-o!! WHOA!!!*

SEVEN

The Romantic Era

Verdi and Wagner were not the only composers writing operas in the latter half of the 19th century. Some very great works were coming out of France and Russia as well, though the majority of these composers were heavily influenced by one or the other of the "big two." Some composers combined Verdi's use of realistic literary subjects and Wagner's advanced harmonies with interesting results; but by and large, the most extraordinary creations of the time were pretty much *sui generis*, in a class of their own. Indeed, though music historians credit the Italian composers of the 1890s with creating the "verismo" or "realism" school, it was in fact started many years before, and the composer who first got it under way was a Russian maverick named Modest Mussorgsky (1839–1881).

These composers generally used the same types of voices that had been developed by Verdi and Wagner: dark basses, dramatic baritones, spinto tenors, and dramatic mezzos. They did, however, emphasize different aspects of the voice, basically combining the dramatic aspects of Wagner with the higher range of Verdi. Two singers in this style, at opposite ends dramatically, are Feodor Chaliapin (1873–1938) and Kiri te Kanawa (b. 1942). Chaliapin, in range and voice color a lyric bass (or *basso cantate*), gave a greater emphasis to the words than the music; as a result, his performances had a dramatic urgency not even found in singers of the Wagner school. His recital on Angel CDH-61009 features arias from *A Life for the Czar*, *Russlan und Ludmilla*, *Rusalka*, *Prince Igor*, *Sadko*, *The Demon*, *Aleko*, and his starring role, *Boris Godunov*. Te Kanawa, a much more lyric singer, represents the new sort of "creamy" soprano favored by the French school. Her recital on Angel CDC/4DS-49863 (CD/cassette) includes excerpts from *Louise*, *L'Enfant Prodigue*, *Damnation de Faust*, *Hérodiade*, *Tales of Hoffmann*, *Manon*, *Les Pêcheurs de Perles*, *Le Cid*, and Verdi's French-influenced *Don Carlos*. These two singers, then, adequately display the disparate qualities of the Russian and French styles.

Boris Godunov
1874   Modest Mussorgsky

Andrei Sokolov, t (Mitiukha/Shuisky); Evgeny Nesterenko, bs (Boris Godunov); Valery Yaroslavtsev, bs (Pimen); Vladislav Piavko, t (Grigori [The False Dmitri]); Arthur Eisen, bs (Varlaam); Vitaly Vlassov, t (Missail); Glafira Koroleva, ms (Feodor); Irina Arkhipova, ms (Marina); Alexei Maslennikov, t (Idiot). Bolshoi Opera Chorus and Orch., cond. by Boris Khaikin. Kultur videotape 1138 (two tapes).

When *Boris Godunov* premiered at the Maryinsky Theatre on January 27, 1874, it created shock waves throughout the musical world. Here was a sprawling canvas of life in 16th-century Russia, written by a self-taught composer with no previous operatic credits, that almost completely bypassed conventional melody in its presentation of a violent and curious episode in Russian history. Various versions of the different scenes, and one different version of the complete opera, had already been rejected by the committee of the Imperial Theatre. Considering the inflammatory subject matter, which did not show the royal ruling class in a particularly good light, it is surprising that any version was approved at all. With all of the principal characters (excepting, perhaps, old Pimen the monk) being somewhat shady, one could with justice claim that this was the first "anti-hero" opera ever written. But that would not be entirely true. The true heroes of *Boris Godunov* are the Russian people, long-suffering but stubborn in their loyalty to the Motherland, and in fact it is in the choruses of the opera that one finds the most uplifting and cheerful music. This facet was not lost on the Communist regime that ruled the Soviet Union with an iron fist between 1918 and 1989, and *Boris* became, in latter years especially, as much a propaganda tool as a work of art.

In the prologue, Boris, the brother-in-law and chief minister of Czar Feodor, is being "pressed" to accept the reigns of power. In actuality, we later learn, this had been Boris's master plan all along: to that end he has had Dmitri, the young half-brother of the Czar and next in line for power, killed. Only Boris and a few others know that it was a murder. Boris is crowned czar amidst much rejoicing and ringing of church bells.

Five years later, Act I begins. Pimen, an old monk, who is writing a history of Russia, tells how the years of Boris's rule have brought only famine and plague to the land. Grigori, a young monk who shares Pimen's cell, suddenly awakens from a recurring dream in which he sees himself standing on a high tower with all Moscow lying at his feet. Grigori laments that his entire life has been spent inside the monastery; after he learns that the murdered Dmitri would have been about his age, he decides to leave the cloister and pretend he is the "missing" heir in order to seize power for himself. To this end he heads for the Lithuanian border. At an inn, he runs into Varlaam and Missail, two beggars with a taste for adventure. He learns from the inn's hostess that police are out looking for him, and she tells him how to cross the border safely. The police arrive; they question Grigori, but think him harmless and turn their attentions to Varlaam. While they are questioning him, Grigori jumps out of the window and escapes.

At the Czar's apartments in the Kremlin, his son Feodor and daughter Xenia are being entertained by their old Nurse. Alone with his son, Boris confides in him that his iron rule of Russia has caused him great distress. Prince Shuisky, a sly, power-hungry Boyar, informs Boris that disaffected nobles have been contacting Poles at Krakow, including himself, to rise up against Boris. He also tells him that a pretender to the Russian throne, claiming to be Dmitri, has arisen in Poland, and has the support of the Pope and the Polish King. At the mention of Dmitri's name, Boris sends Feodor away and makes Shuisky swear that the Czarevich is indeed dead. As soon as Shuisky leaves, a clock chiming in the shadows triggers fear and remorse in the Czar's overloaded mind; he becomes hysterical and sinks sobbing to the floor while he prays to God for forgiveness.

Meanwhile, in Poland, the Polish princess Marina receives the Jesuit priest Rangoni. He learns that she plans to marry "Dmitri", who has come to their country seeking aid to overthrow the Czar; Rangoni reminds her of her duty to the Roman Catholic Church if she becomes czarina to promote the Christian religion over the Russian Orthodox Church, which is led by Boris. In the second scene, Dmitri meets with Marina and declares his passionate love for her. As his social superior, she stings him unmercifully. However, when he angrily offers to leave her in Poland, she butters him up with love talk while Rangoni watches gleefully from behind.

The rest of the opera becomes somewhat confused, depending on which version is performed. The final act is divided into two scenes; one depicts the triumph of "Dmitri" and the other the death of Boris; the order of these two scenes varies from production to production. Mussorgsky wrote two similar versions of Dmitri's triumph, one set in front of St. Basil's Cathedral and the other in the Kromy Forest. In both versions, Dmitri's apparent victory over Boris is darkened by an idiot savant's prediction that misery and bloodshed will come to "poor Russia." This scene is supposed to be the end of the opera, but for dramatic purposes it is sometimes placed before the death of Boris. The second scene opens with Pimen's arrival at the Kremlin. He tells Boris that a blind shepherd has had his sight miraculously restored after praying at Dmitri's tomb. Boris is horrified by the mention of Dmitri, and falls unconscious in the arms of the Boyars. He realizes he is dying, and sends for his young son to whom he passes the throne, warning him to be wary of the plotting nobles.

Keynotes

The music of this opera is more brutal than melodic, but that isn't to say there are no tender moments. Pimen's first scene is rather lyrical, if foreboding; Varlaam's famous aria *In the town of Kazan* is swashbuckling; the love duet in the Polish act is as beautiful as anything written by Wagner at his best; and Boris's two principal monologues, *I have attained the highest power* and the "Prayer and Death of Boris," are as moving as any of Verdi's dramatic scenes.

The Recording

The Bolshoi Opera's production of *Boris* has been cast in stone for roughly thirty years: as late as 1987 they were still using the same sets and costumes as in the 1960s, and only a very few singers alternated in the principal roles. As a result, this video presents a performance that is so well rehearsed by an ensemble company that every move in every scene becomes almost as natural as life itself, and the sets and costumes are gorgeous. On the negative side, the first half of the Polish scene (Act III) is deleted; *both* the St. Basil and Kromy Forest scenes are included (back to back, no less), ending with the death of Boris. This offbeat rearrangement, however, is offset by the magnificent performances of Evgeny Nesterenko and Irina Arkhipova the greatest Russian bass and contralto of the modern era; Artur Eisen's Varlaam is also a classic interpretation.

Carmen
1875   Georges Bizet

Faith Esham, s (Micaëla); Placido Domingo, t (Don José); John Paul Bogart, bs (Zuniga); Julia Migenes-Johnson, ms (Carmen); Lilian Watson, s (Frasquita); Susan Daniel, s (Mercédès); Ruggero Raimondi, bs (Escamillo); Julien Guiomar, br (Lillas Pastia). Radio France Chorus; Orch. National de France, cond. by Lorin Maazel. RCA/Columbia videotape (no number). *CD alternative*: Erato/Musifrance 45207-2 ZB (three CDs).

Georges Bizet (1838–1875) was a competent composer whose previous operas (including *Les Pêcheurs des Perles* [1863], *La Jolie Fille de Perth* [1867], and *Djamileh* [1872]) contained some excellent moments but were, overall, nothing to get excited about. Yet his last work has become one of the most popular and critically acclaimed operas ever written. No composer other than Verdi was able to combine dramatically cogent scenes with such strikingly memorable melodies. Though he only used fragments of authentic Spanish tunes, the entire work has, somehow, an authentically Spanish flavor about it; and *Carmen*, more so than *Boris Godunov*, became the opera that most greatly influenced the "verismo" school that flourished in the 1880s and nineties.

The plot, based on the excellent novelette by Prosper Merimée, is one of those simple yet fascinating love triangles that always seem to have a universal appeal. Instead of concerning itself with countesses, dukes, and kings, however, its principal characters are a corporal, a toreador, and a gypsy woman who, in the original story, was not even particularly pretty. The historical Carmen seldom bathed and had but one eye, yet she also possessed an earthy sex appeal that transcended physical beauty. The baseness of the subject matter horrified contemporary critics, but the public responded enthusiastically; contrary to popular myths, Bizet lived just long enough to see his brainchild take off in popularity, although it did not earn a constant spot in the opera repertoire until some four years later.

Don José is a corporal in the army stationed in Seville. He is visited by Micaëla, a character concocted by Bizet's librettists, who is his sweetheart from home; she brings him news of his mother. Carmen, who works in a nearby cigarette factory, is involved in a knife fight with one of the other girls and arrested for disturbing the peace. Don José, charged with putting her in jail, is seduced by her; she promises to meet him in Lillas Pastia's somewhat seedy inn on the edge of town. José frees her bonds so she can escape; as she does, she mockingly throws a rose at him. Naturally, José is arrested for dereliction of duty, but upon his release he goes to meet Carmen, who greets him with enthusiasm yet taunts him when the call of retreat summons him back to the base. Meanwhile Escamillo, a handsome but vain toreador, has also come to the inn; he flirts with Carmen, but for the time being she is loyal to José. When Captain Zuniga comes to bring José back to camp, José pulls his sword on him, a distinct act of insubordination. Rather than face another prison charge José flees into the mountains where Lillas Pastia, Carmen, and their cronies have set up a smuggling ring. He is now a fugitive.

Despite the fact that they now see each other on a daily basis, Carmen is becoming bored with her soldier boy. She does not seem to realize that he has forfeited everything dear to him—his home, girl, and career—just so he can be with her, nor does she care. Carmen reads a deck of cards to tell her own fortune, and sees violent death in her immediate future. José, now a guard for the smugglers, fires a warning shot when a stranger appears: It is Escamillo, come to see Carmen, apparently at her invitation! Enraged, José and Escamillo duel; Escamillo's knife is broken, but he is saved when the rest of Pastia's gang arrives. Sneering, Escamillo invites the entire company to see his next bullfight in Seville. After he leaves, Micaëla comes to beg Don José to return home. Carmen taunts him and tells him to leave, but he resists until he discovers that his mother is dying.

The last act is short and to the point. The bullfight is going on in the arena; Escamillo, dressed in his finery, dedicates his fight to Carmen's love. A gypsy girl tells Carmen that José is outside, and warns her to stay away from him, but Carmen claims that neither fear nor any man will rule her life. When she goes outside, José begs her to start over again with him, but her only reply is "It's all over." Swearing that if he cannot have her neither will anyone else, he stabs her to death.

Keynotes

Like *Trovatore*, *Carmen* is a veritable "greatest hits" opera in which constantly memorable melodies are woven into a dramatic fabric. Among the many highlights are the choruses of the soldiers and cigarette girls; Don José's *Flower Song*; Carmen's three solos (*Habañera*, *Gypsy Song*, and *Card Song*); the four major duets (*Seguidilla*, the duet after the Flower Song, *Je suis Escamillo*, and the concluding scene); and, of course, the famous Quintet and Escamillo's *Toreador Song*.

The Recording

There are many decent recordings of *Carmen* available, but none so strongly cast, well conducted, and well acted as this one. When the film version first appeared in 1984, critics were practically unanimous in proclaiming it one of the finest visual representations of an opera ever made, and the consequent release of the soundtrack on CD has verified that the musical performance was equally fine. Ironically, this was the performance that both made Julia Migenes-Johnson's name and ruined her career. Originally a high coloratura soubrette, she worked for months to bring her voice down low enough to sing Carmen, a role she planned on performing only for this film and recording. Unfortunately, the film was such a success that she found herself in demand all over the world—but only as Carmen. Because she had since reset her voice in the upper stratosphere, this was patently impossible. Unfair? Certainly, but at least this filmed performance will attest to the fact that she was one of our finest singing-actresses.

Samson et Dalila
1877   Camille Saint-Saëns

Anton Diakov, bs (Abimélech); Jacques Potier, t (First Philistine); Jean-Pierre Hurteau, bs (Second Philistine); Rita Gorr, ms (Dalila); Jon Vickers, t (Samson); Ernest Blanc, br (High Priest). René Duclos Chorus; Paris Opéra Orch., cond. by Georges Prêtre. Angel CDCB-47895/4AV-34052 (two CDs/cassettes).

Unlike Bizet, who wrote several operas, Camille Saint-Saëns (1835–1921) was known primarily as a composer of sonatas and symphonies. He was a well-grounded musician, a man more impressed by the musical innovations of Beethoven, Berlioz, and Wagner than by the emotional appeal of his fellow countrymen Aubér, Gounod, and Offenbach; as a result, when he came to write what would become his operatic masterpiece, he approached it more in the manner of *Fidelio* than *Faust*, which is to say more as a musically cogent whole than as a string of sweet little tunes that audiences could hum on their way out. Not so curiously, then, *Samson et Dalila* has suffered much the same fate as *Fidelio*: It is often looked upon as a musically brilliant but theatrically static opera, one more admired than loved by the populace. And yet it has endured, simply because the music really is excellent.

The opera closely follows the biblical tale of Samson's attack on the Philistines. Samson kills Abimélech, the Philistine leader of Gaza. In retaliation, they send their chief seductress, Dalila, to worm her way into Samson's heart. Once that is accomplished, she cuts off his hair, which is the source of his super strength; now the Philistines easily overcome him, blind him, and chain him to a mill. The Philistines defeat the Samson-less Hebrews; during their victory feast, Samson realizes that his hair has grown back. He places himself between the pillars of the Philistine temple, gives them a mighty push, and brings the marble crashing down on them.

Keynotes

Because very little actually happens on stage, Saint-Saëns had to make things happen in the music, and this he accomplished to brilliant effect. There are several gorgeous arias: Samson's *Arrêtez, ô mes frères, Israel! romps du chaines*, and *Vois ma misère, hélas*; Dalila's *Amour, viens aider* and *Mon coeur s'ouvre à ta voix*; and the brilliant trio *Je viens célèbrer*. More interesting than any particular melody, however, is the clever way in which Saint-Saëns weaves them into the tapestry of the surrounding music. Scenes blend seamlessly into one another, in a way unknown in France since Berlioz and Gluck, to create a cumulative effect of almost overpowering intensity. Particularly interesting in this regard is Act II, which combines familiar and unfamiliar musical material in a cohesive whole with an almost unbelievable effect. The music envelops rather than overwhelms the listener, and the result is a listening experience in which the music becomes the drama.

The Recording

Because *Samson* is not a particularly popular opera, complete recordings have been scarce—there are only four in the current catalog—but this 1962 version is such a classic that there is practically no need for another. Rita Gorr ended her career at the height of her powers which, as one can hear in this recording, were considerable: She was undoubtedly the greatest French contralto of her time, and the finest we have had in the quarter-century since she retired. Jon Vickers made Samson something of a signature role, along with his Otello and Peter Grimes, and his voice seldom sounded fresher or more alive with dramatic feeling. Ernest Blanc was not the most voluptuous-sounding French baritone of the LP era (that honor goes to the almost unknown Jean Borthayre), but he was a consummate musician with a pleasant and somewhat distinctive voice. Georges Prêtre leads the Paris Opéra Orchestra and Chorus in what can only be termed a monumental interpretation; and, amazingly, the spacious sonics and close miking combine to produce a remarkably lifelike soundstage. All in all, a perfect recording.

The Tales of Hoffmann
1881   Jacques Offenbach

Huguette Tourangeau, ms (Muse/Niklausse); Gabriel Bacquier, bs (Lindorf/Coppelius/Dapertutto/Dr. Miracle); Paul
Guigue, br (Hermann); Placido Domingo, t (Hoffmann);
Hughues Cuénod, t (Andrès/Cochenille/Pitichinaccio/
Frantz); Joan Sutherland, s (Olympia/Giulietta/An-
tonia/Stella); André Neury, bs (Schlemil). Chorus and Orch.
de la Suisse Romande, cond. by Richard Bonynge. London
417 363-2 LH2 (two CDs).

Jacques Offenbach (1819–1880) was almost alone among serious
opera composers in that he came from the world of "light music":
ballets, cancans, and operettas such as *La Belle Hélène* (1865), *La
Perichole* (1868, 1874), and *Orpheus in the Underworld* (1858, 1874)
that were the French equivalent of Johann Strauss or Gilbert and
Sullivan. Late in his life, however, he became attracted to the tales of
Ernst Theodor Amadeus Hoffmann, a famous critic and a good
composer (whose own opera, *Undine*, paid homage to both Mozart
and Weber), who was best remembered for his prose fantasies.
Hoffmann's "tales" were unlike any others that came before him.
They were fanciful and/or grotesque nightmares that probed the
depths of the subconscious, and had a profound influence on Edgar
Allen Poe and, much later, H. P. Lovecraft. Because Hoffmann was
widely known as an alcoholic, Offenbach's librettists, Barbier and
Carré, set the opera's prologue in a tavern and strongly hinted that
the three "tales" they chose were alcoholic delusions. This may not
been fair to Hoffmann, but it did provide a framework for what was
the first "anthology" opera in history, one which contained more
than one separate plot.

The Tales of Hoffmann received solicitous reviews when it premiered in February 1881, largely because the composer had died
during rehearsals, but within a quarter-century it began to fall out of
favor as "sugary" and "too fantastic." Since the mid-sixties, however,
due largely to revivals by Nicolai Gedda, Joan Sutherland, and
Beverly Sills, the opera has seen not merely a renaissance of interest
but in fact greater interest than before. One may now place it firmly

next to Bizet's *Carmen* as one of the most popular French operas ever written.

The Prologue, as already mentioned, opens at Luther's Tavern, next door to an opera house where a performance of *Don Giovanni* (Hoffmann's favorite opera) is taking place. Councillor Lindorf, a sinister figure, enters with Andrès, the servant of the prima donna Stella, who is singing in *Don Giovanni*; Lindorf urges him to hand over a letter that Stella has written to Hoffmann, arranging for a tête-à-tête and enclosing the key to her room. A crowd of students enter and sing rousingly in appreciation of the beer that Luther is bringing them. Hoffmann enters, straight from the performance, with his friend Niklausse; the writer is prevailed upon to sing a song to the students, and launches into "The Legend of Kleinzach." But he is in a haunted, meditative mood, and soon begins to reminisce about the features of his lady love. Hoffmann notices Lindorf, whom he claims has been shadowing his steps and bringing him bad luck. Though the curtain is going up on the second act of Mozart's opera, Hoffmann offers to tell the tale of the three great loves in his life; the students stay behind to listen. The first, he announces, was called Olympia.

Here we fully enter the oddball world of Hoffmann's tales. Spalanzani, an inventor, is creating life-sized, lifelike human robots; Hoffmann, arriving, mistakes the doll Olympia for Spalanzani's daughter. Coppelius, who supplied the eyes for Spalanzani's "masterpiece," shows up with an assortment of eyes and spectacles for all occasions, and sells Hoffmann the proverbial "rose-colored glasses." Soon, guests arrive for Olympia's coming-out party; the doll sings a mechanical ditty that enchants them all, but only Hoffmann (on account of the glasses) mistakes her for a real person. He rushes about the room, professing his love for her and attempting to dance with her. Coppelius, learning he is to be cheated out of his "take" in the fraud, returns in an angry mood. As Hoffmann waltzes with Olympia, the automaton goes faster and faster until she breaks down and is put in her room. Suddenly, the noise of smashing machinery is heard; Coppelius emerges from Olympia's room, laughing in triumph and clutching the false eyes as Hoffmann suddenly realizes that his "ideal love" was nothing more than a doll.

Act II is set in Venice and opens with the famous "Barcarolle." Giulietta, a courtesan and agent of the evil magician Dapertutto, is hosting a gambling party that Hoffmann, Niklausse, and other society swells are attending. Hoffmann is attracted to Giulietta, but Niklausse warns him that she is an untrustworthy woman who will abandon him at the first opportunity. Dapertutto uses a magic mirror to steal people's souls. He has bought Giulietta's assistance by bribing her with a great diamond, and so she has agreed to assist him in his sinister schemes. When Hoffmann becomes discouraged after losing money gambling, the pretty Giulietta persuades him to stay, and they sing an impassioned duet. Suddenly, the poet Schlemil enters. He was Giulietta's lover in the past when he lost his soul to Dapertutto, and is seeking revenge; Hoffmann fights him and, using the magician's sword, kills him. He removes a chain from Schlemil's neck that carries the key to Giulietta's room, but when he rushes to find her she is already floating away in a gondola in the arms of another.

Act III takes place in Munich at Crespel's house. His daughter, Antonia, has inherited a beautiful singing voice from her mother. But Antonia, like her mother, has signs of consumption (tuberculosis), and each time she sings—despite the fact that it brings great pleasure to her father—she dies a little bit. Crespel blames the girl's excitable condition on Hoffmann, with whom she is in love. Hoffmann, looking at a song that is lying open on the harpsichord, begins to sing it when she enters; they perform a duet, much to Crespel's displeasure. Suddenly the third of Hoffmann's villains, Dr. Miracle, shows up. He purports to treat Antonia for her illness, but Hoffmann senses that he is evil, as does Crespel, who believes the doctor poisoned her mother with his treatments but feels powerless to get rid of him. Hoffmann tries to persuade Antonia to give up her singing for the sake of her health; she agrees, but as soon as Hoffmann leaves, Dr. Miracle re-enters. Miracle seizes a violin from the walls and plays wildly on it; Antonia, against her better judgment, breaks into an impassioned song. Dr. Miracle magically brings the oil painting of her dead mother to life and it encourages her to continue singing, higher and higher. She does so until she falls, dead, on the ground. Miracle leaves; Crespel enters to hear his daughter's dying words. He again blames Hoffmann, who wants to call a doctor—but you-know-who is the only doctor who answers his summons.

The epilogue brings us back to Luther's tavern. Hoffmann's stories are finished; so too is the performance of *Don Giovanni*. Niklausse suggests that Stella is the personification of the three loves of his life, but Hoffmann (urged on in his drinking by Lindorf) is too hopelessly drunk to care. The Muse of Poetry appears by his side, claiming him for her own. As Lindorf leads Stella from the room, she turns and throws a flower from her bouquet at Hoffmann—who looks blankly at her and collapses, dead drunk.

The original premiere had the Antonia act second and Giulietta third, as Offenbach intended, but after the composer's death others rearranged it as they saw fit. First, Giulietta disappeared entirely, the Antonia act being set in Venice so as to keep the "Barcarolle"; then, Giulietta returned, this time in her more familiar second spot, with Antonia completing the triumvirate. Dramatically, the Giulietta act makes more sense coming last, but the inspired trio Offenbach wrote for the climax of the Antonia scene was far and away his greatest piece of music, and so modern directors often succumb to the now- "traditional" setting with Antonia last.

Keynotes

There are many fine melodies in *Hoffmann*, the best of which are Hoffmann's two arias ("The Legend of Kleinzach" and *O Dieu, de quelle ivresse* in the Giulietta scene), Olympia's "Doll Song," Dapertutto's *Scintille, diamant* (*Sparkle, diamond*), the "Barcarolle," and the arias of Niklausse, Frantz, and Antonia. Yet by far it is the trio for Dr. Miracle, Antonia, and her mother that grips you the most, not only in performance but on record with its unearthly power that builds to a frenetic conclusion. A really good staging that complements the musical treatment can easily make this one of the most overwhelming and unforgettable moments in all of opera.

The Recording

One of the reasons why *Hoffmann* is so difficult to perform, despite its popularity, is that the composer wished the same singers to perform all of the villains (including Lindorf) and all of the female leads (including Stella); more often than not, the former is complied with but not the latter. Generally, three different sopranos are used for Olympia, Giulietta, and Antonia, which may help the performers cope with the different musical portrayals but weakens the drama. In this recording, Offenbach's wishes are complied with, and although Joan Sutherland may not make the most seductive-sounding of Giuliettas, her Olympia is brilliant and her Antonia limpid in its creamy tone. Placido Domingo is a bit gruff and bluff of voice for Hoffmann, not as poetic-sounding as others (notably Robert

Rounseville, Nicolai Gedda, and Stuart Burrows), but Gabriel Bacquier's villains are so superb that he almost gives a 3-D effect even on record; and, with such a strong supporting cast and excellent conducting, this is by far the best *Hoffmann* available. It is interesting to note that, when this album first came out on LP, the last two acts were in their proper (original) order, but in its CD reissue they have been returned to the "popular" sequence.

Pique Dame (The Queen of Spades)
1890   Peter Tchaikovsky

Andrei Sokolov, t (Tchekalinsky); Vladimir Valaitis, br (Count Tomsky); Vladimir Atlantov, t (Herman); Andrei Fedoseyev, br (Prince Yeletsky); Tamara Milashkina, s (Liza); Valentina Levko, ms (Countess); Galina Borisova, c (Pauline); Nelya Lebedeva, s (Masha); Vitaly Vlasov, t (Tchaplitsky). Bolshoi Theater Chorus & Orch., cond. by Mark Ermler. Philips 420 375-2/4 (three CDs/cassettes). *Video alternate*: Milashkina, Atlantov, Yuri Mazurok, Elena Obratsouva. Kultur videotape 1164.

Peter Ilyich Tchaikovsky (1840–1893) was one of the most popular composers who ever lived, but—like Saint-Saëns—he is much better known for his orchestral works, especially his symphonies and ballets, than for his operas. (It is interesting to note that his popular ballet, *The Nutcracker*, was also based on a story of Hoffmann.) Unlike the fairy-tale world of his ballets, Tchaikovsky wanted more realism in his operas; he was much taken not only by Mussorgsky's *Boris*, but also by Bizet's *Carmen*, and wanted to produce an opera along those lines. His first operatic success, *Eugen Onegin* (1879), is for some reason a very popular work, despite its long, rambling, and uneven quality; but in 1890 he (by his own admission) really "hit the nail on the head" with *Pique Dame*, which, though *not* derived from Hoffmann, certainly has a nightmarish, Hoffmannesque "twist ending" that is fantastically dramatic even today.

The opera opens in the Summer Garden of St. Petersburg where children are playing. Two officers of the guard enter and dicuss the gambling habits of their fellow officer, Herman. Even as they speak, Herman enters with his friend Tomsky, who asks him about the sorrow that seems to hang over his life. Herman explains that he has fallen in love, but doesn't even know his beloved's name. Prince Yeletsky enters, rejoicing because of his recent engagement; he points out his beloved Lisa to them, and to his horror Herman recognizes her as the woman he loves. Lisa and her grandmother, the Countess, notice Herman's ardent looks though they do not know his name; Tomsky greets the Countess, who asks about the stranger, and is told who he is as Yeletsky goes to Lisa.

After the two women leave, the others speculate about the rumors surrounding the Countess, who was supposedly a great cardsharp at one time. One of her most ardent admirers was the Count St.-Germain; when she lost everything at the gambling tables, the Count offered to teach her the secret of the "three cards" if she would grant him one rendezvous. The next morning she was back at the tables, where nothing could stop her winning streak. It was whispered that she passed the secret on to her husband, and years later to a young man who had taken her fancy, but in a dream she had been warned that she would die if anyone else sought to learn it from her.

Lisa and her companion Pauline are singing a duet for friends; after Lisa sees her friends to the door, she wonders whether her promised marriage to Yeletsky is the answer to her dreams. Herman appears at the window, declares his love, and sweeps Lisa away as she falls into his arms.

At a masked ball, Tchekalinsky and Sourin plan to play a trick on Herman, who is obsessed with cards. Yeletsky accompanies Lisa to the ball; as they leave together, Herman enters with a note from her proposing to meet him in her room afterward. He immediately wishes to know the secret of the "three cards," so that he can become wealthy and offer Lisa his hand. Tchekalinsky and Sourin whisper in his ear that he should gain the secret for himself; Herman wonders if it is the voice of a ghost. After an interlude in which the story of Daphnis and Chloë is given as entertainment, Herman waits for Lisa. She gives him a key and tells him to go through her grandmother's room to open the secret door behind the Countess's portrait that leads to her own bedchamber. Herman enters the Countess's room, hears voices, and hides; the Countess enters with her servants, begins undressing and reminiscing about earlier, more gallant times, then sends the servants away. Herman appears, begs her not to be frightened, and asks for the secret of the cards. Frozen with fear, she cannot speak; in desperation Herman draws his pistol, and the Countess dies of shock. When Lisa discovers what has gone on, she assumes that it was for love of gambling, not of her, that Herman wanted access to the room, and makes him leave.

Later, Herman sits in his quarters in the barracks, reading a letter from Lisa in which she apparently has forgiven him, understanding that he did not intend to kill her grandmother, and asks him to meet her at midnight by the canal. He is overcome by conscience, however, and obsessed by memories of the Countess's funeral. Suddenly the door opens, the candle is blown out, and the Countess's ghost is seen in the doorway. She tells him that he must marry Lisa, and that the secret of the three cards shall be his: "Three! Seven! Ace!" He mutters the formula as the curtain falls. In the second scene, Lisa waits by the canal for Herman; he appears, and sings of their future together. All seems well until Herman announces his intention to leave her to go gambling. Lisa thinks him mad; he admits his obsession, pushes her aside, and goes his way. Lisa rushes to the parapet and throws herself over the edge.

Tomsky and Yeletsky are already at the gaming house when Herman arrives. Only Tchekalinsky will take him up on his offer to play cards; Herman plays huge stakes and wins twice, on the three and the seven. Tchekalinsky backs out, but Prince Yeletsky offers to take him up. Herman reluctantly agrees and turns up a card, proclaiming it an ace without even looking at it. But the Prince says, "No, it is the Queen of Spades." With a wild cry, Herman sees the Countess's ghost; everyone moves away from him as he gibbers with rage and fear. He stabs himself, asks the Prince's forgiveness for taking Lisa away from him, and dies.

Keynotes

The musical palette Tchaikovsky used to paint his drama is a rich one, building from the lighthearted, skittish chorus of the playing children to the stark, dramatic finale. There are two "pastiches," or borrowed tunes, in the opera, the duet of Lisa and Pauline and the Countess's aria, which is from André-Ernest-Modeste Gretry's *Richard the Lion-Hearted*, yet the originality and dramatic sense with which Tchaikovsky uses them is uncanny. Herman's two arias and duets with Lisa show, quite admirably, the change in mood from the first act to the third: the first is ardent but conventional, like the Micaëla-Don José duet from *Carmen*, while the second is more impetuous and a little crazy, like *Carmen*'s finale. Lisa's aria at the canal is one of the greatest pieces of dramatic music ever composed; after Herman's death, Tchaikovsky has one more surprise in store, a heartrending Russian hymn for the repose of his soul. Indeed, anywhere you turn in *Pique Dame* the music is taut, well constructed, and—above all—creative.

The Recording

Because it is not quite as popular as *Eugen Onegin*, *Pique Dame* has not been granted many complete recordings. This one holds the edge over the performance on Sony Classical (S3K-45720, three CDs) because of the superiority of the male singers, particularly Vladimir Atlantov and Andrei Fedoseyev as Herman and Yeletsky. Tamara Milashkina's voice is wiry and acidic, like so many Russian sopranos of recent vintage, but her phrasing is musical and her dramatic sense unerring, and Mark Ermler has just an extra edge in his conducting over Sony's Emil Tchakarov. The video alternate is not quite as well conducted, and Milashkina is ten years older (and more wiry), but Atlantov, Yuri Mazurok, and Elena Obratsouva are superb—the first two vocally, the third histrionically.

Follow-up Listening

There are some other fine operas from this period that, although they are not as superb and/or as popular as these, may nevertheless interest you. Among these are Bizet's *Les Pêcheurs de Perles* (*The Pearl Fishers*, 1863), especially the performance by Barbara Hendricks, John Aler, Gino Quilico, and Michel Plasson on Angel CDCB-49837 (two CDs); Offenbach's semi-serious operetta *La Belle Hélène* (1865), in the recording with Jessye Norman, John Aler, Gabriel Bacquier, and Michel Plasson on CDCB-47156 (two CDs); Massenet's *Manon* (1864) with Ileana Cortubas, Alfredo Kraus, and Gino Quilico on Angel CDCB-49610 (two CDs), and *Werther* (1892) with Ninon Vallin, Germaine Feraldy, and Georges Thill on Angel CDHB-63195 (two CDs); and Tchaikovsky's *Eugen Onegin*, most especially the legendary 1961 recording with Galina Vishnevskaya, Sergei Lemeshev, Ivan Petrov, and Boris Khaikin on Legato Classics LCD-163-2 (no libretto—check your local library).

Enklish in Five Queasy Lessins

In latter years, having given up the tradition of performing opera in the vernacular of each country, European opera houses have taken not only to doing works in their original languages but trying to entice opera-loving American tourists by giving English translations of the plots in their programs. Most of these, to be sure, are competently done; but one famous example heads my list of translation faux pas. This is the way the plot of Bizet's *Carmen* was described in a program from Genoa, Italy—and this is EXACTLY the way it appears:

Act 1. Carmen is a cigar-makeress from a tabago factory who loves with Don Jose of the mounting guard. Carmen takes a flower from her corsets and lances it to Don Jose (Duet: "Talk me of my mother"). There is a noise inside the tabago factory and the revolting cigar-makeresses burst into the stage. Carmen is arrested and Don Jose is ordered to mounting guard her but Carmen subduces him and he lets her escape.

Act 2. The Tavern. Carmen, Frasquito, Mercedes, Zuniga, Morales. Carmen's aria ("The Sistrums Are Tinkling"). Enter Escamillio, a balls-fighter. Enter two smuglers (Duet: "We Have in Mind a Business"), but Carmen refuses to penetrate because Don Jose has liberate from prison. He just now arrives (Aria: "Slop, here who comes!"), but hear are the bugles singing his retreat. Don Jose will leave and draws his sword. Called by Carmen shrikes the two smuglers interfere with her, but Don Jose is bound to dessert, he will follow into them (final chorus: "Opening Sky, Wandering Life").

Act 3. A roky landscape, the smuglers shelter. Carmen sees her death in cards and Don Jose makes a date with Carmen for the next balls fight.

Act 4. A place in Seville. Procession of balls-fighters, the roaring of the balls is heard in the arena. Escamillio enters (Aria and chorus: "Toreador, Toreador, All Hail the Balls of a Toreador"). Enter Don Jose (Aria: "I Do Not Threaten, I besooch you"). But Carmen repels him wants to join with Escamillio now chaired by the crowd. Don Jose stabbs her (Aria: "Oh Rupture, Rupture, You May Arrest Me, I Did Kill Her") he sings, "Oh my beautiful Carmen, my subductive Carmen."

EIGHT

Verismo Opera and Puccini

As the 19th century drew to a close, there appeared on the scene a number of Italian composers who rejected both the technical vocal writing of Verdi and the dramatic complexities of Wagner. These were the "verismo" composers, who took the name of their style from the Italian word for "truth."

In actuality, the verismo style was no more truthful or realistic than the works of Mussorgsky, Bizet, and Tchaikovsky that had preceded it, and in some respects these works were far less complex and musically interesting. But they were strongly melodic, and soon overtook the more graceful and gracious repertoire of Verdi, Donizetti, and Rossini in Italian opera houses. In addition, these operas and their composers closed the door forever on the lyric grace that had prevailed, despite changing tastes and fashions, since the early 18th century. Their music emphasized, even more so than Verdi's and Wagner's, the purely dramatic aspects of the voice. Elegance was passé; from here on out, drama was everything.

Nevertheless, the early verismo singers managed to retain some lyric grace even in the most pressing and passionate of scenes. Primary among these was Enrico Caruso (1873–1921), the most famous Italian tenor of all time, who was unique in that his chest voice (the voice as pushed up from the chest muscles) was as beautiful as his head voice (the voice placed in the sinus cavities), and he

117

often mixed them with stunning results. His organ-like resonance was pretty well captured by the recording technology of his time, and the 1902–1904 recordings on Angel CDH-61046 find him at the very outset of his international career, in arias from *Germania*, *Mefistofele*, *Tosca*, *Iris*, *Fedora*, *La Gioconda*, *Pagliacci*, *Cavalleria Rusticana*, *Adriana Lecouvreur*, and other, non-verismo operas such as *Aida* and Massenet's *Manon*. Caruso's baritone counterpart was Titta Ruffo (1877–1953), who pressurized the voice even more, as can be heard on Nimbus NI-7810-2. Sopranos of the verismo era either produced a metallic sound like Ruffo, or tried to combine a chesty low range with a creamy upper register. One of the best of the latter type was Claudia Muzio (1889–1936), who managed to overcome short breath control to produce performances that were unsurpassed in their combination of musicality and depth of interpretation. In her recital on Angel CDH-69790, we can hear how effective she was, not only in such verismo fare as *Mefistofele*, *Cavalleria Rusticana*, *La Bohème*, *Tosca*, *Andrea Chénier*, *L'Arlesiana*, and *Adriana Lecouvreur*, but even in such earlier music as *La Sonnambula*, *Il Trovatore*, *La Traviata*, and *La Forza del Destino*.

Cavalleria Rusticana
1890 Pietro Mascagni

Jussi Björling, t (Turiddu); Zinka Milanov, s (Santuzza); Margaret Roggero, ms (Mamma Lucia); Robert Merrill, br (Alfio); Carol Smith, c (Lola). Robert Shaw Chorale; RCA Victor Orch., cond. by Renato Cellini. RCA Victor 6510-2-RG.

When *Cavalleria Rusticana* burst on an unsuspecting world in 1890, Italian audiences were still becoming acclimated to the dramatic power of Verdi's *Otello*. But Pietro Mascagni (1863–1945), a struggling composer just twenty-seven years old, had written his masterpiece. Despite later operas, some of which have had a vogue in recent years, he is largely remembered as the composer of *Cavalleria*.

A one-act opera, *Cavalleria*'s plot is fairly simple and straightforward. Turiddu has made love to Santuzza, a village girl, who as a result of this out-of-wedlock liaison has been excommunicated. But Turiddu has no thoughts of remaining faithful to her; even as the opera opens, he sings passionately of Lola, the young and sexy wife of the teamster Alfio. Santuzza sings an aria to Turiddu's mother, Mamma Lucia, telling her how her son has abused her. Turiddu enters; the two sing an impassioned duet in which Santuzza chastises him for pretending to go away. She is interrupted by Lola who mocks Santuzza, claiming Turiddu as her own. Turiddu throws Santuzza aside, and she curses him. When Alfio arrives on the scene, Santuzza informs him of the affair between Turiddu and Lola.

After an intermezzo, Turiddu sings a drinking song. Alfio joins him; Turiddu offers him wine, but Alfio rejects it. In a brief scene, Alfio challenges Turiddu to a duel with knives. Turiddu calls for his mother: He is going away, he tells her, and if he should not return she should be a mother to Santuzza. A peasant woman comes out screaming that Turiddu has been murdered; Santuzza faints, and Mamma Lucia grieves for her lost son.

Keynotes

Cavalleria takes a while to build up steam—first there is a long orchestral prelude, interrupted by Turiddu's aria (called the "Siciliana"), and an extended chorus sung by villagers as they go to church on Easter Sunday. Alfio's brusque aria, *Il cavallo scalpita*, characterizes his personality; Santuzza's *Voi lo sapete* is one of the most passionate Italian arias ever composed; and the long Santuzza-Turiddu duet is one continuous musical inspiration. After this, the drinking song and finale almost seem an anticlimax, yet they too can be highly entertaining.

The Recording

Zinka Milanov's soprano voice is perhaps a little less metallic and "chesty" than those of her Italian sisters, yet her attention to text makes her interpretation memorable. Jussi Björling and Robert Merrill have rich, attractive voices, well used in context, and Renato Cellini's conducting is brisk even if the orchestral sound is a little thin.

Pagliacci
1892   Ruggero Leoncavallo

Leonard Warren, br (Tonio); Jussi Björling, t (Canio); Paul Franke, t (Beppe); Victoria de los Angeles, s (Nedda); Robert Merrill, br (Silvio). Columbus Boy Choir and Robert Shaw Chorale; RCA Victor Orch., cond. by Renato Cellini. Angel CDC-4503-2.

Ruggero Leoncavallo (1857–1919) was one of the least known of operatic composers, but like Mascagni he managed to enter the standard repertoire with this verismo hit. Oddly enough, though it debuted only two years after *Cavalleria Rusticana*, it did not occur to impresarios to pair these two short operas on a regular basis until well after 1910. Before then, they were often coupled with such oddities as Gounod's *Philemon et Baucis*, which bore no musical or stylistic resemblance to them. Though *Pagliacci* is ostensibly in two acts, they are short and the opera's overall length is just about equal to *Cavalleria*. Since the 1920s they have been known as the "operatic twins," referred to as simply "Cav and Pag." It is hard to imagine, nowadays, the one being performed without the other.

The plot concerns an aging clown, Canio, and his young wife, Nedda. Canio is a jovial fellow, kindly toward all but insanely jealous of Nedda. Tonio, a hunchbacked jester in his company, makes advances to her behind Canio's back but is spurned by her; in revenge, he spies on her and discovers that she is seeing a young villager named Silvio. Tonio tortures her with this knowledge, hoping for emotional blackmail, but Nedda is too stupid and naïve to take him seriously. She'd much rather sing songs to the birds, and go on seeing Silvio on the sly. Finally, Tonio makes good his threats to tell Canio, who rushes in just in time to hear Nedda saying goodbye to her lover. Nedda blocks his way while Silvio escapes, and Canio is kept ignorant of his identity. As he puts on his makeup for the evening's performance, Canio sings his famous aria *Vesti la giubba* (*On with the play*).

The second act revolves around the performance itself. Villagers arrive to see Canio's troupe; Nedda tries to warn Silvio to stay away. The clowns portray the story of Columbine (played by Nedda) and Pagliacci (played by Canio), a tale of a wife betraying her husband so that she can have a rendezvous with her lover, Harlequin. By the time Canio enters, he is mad with rage and jealousy; breaking out of character, he demands to know the name of Nedda's lover. She refuses. Canio, driven beyond the breaking point, pulls out a knife and stabs Nedda; Silvio, rushing forward to protect her, is also stabbed. Canio stands in shock while the knife falls from his hand. "The comedy is ended!"

Keynotes

Though much of Act I is actually less dramatic than *Cavalleria*, *Pagliacci* is actually a more musical opera. Tonio's famous prologue before the curtain was an afterthought by Leoncavallo, to please the famous baritone Victor Maurel, but it was an ingenious afterthought. Canio's song to the villagers, entreating them to come to his performance, is lovely and engaging; so are Nedda's birdsong, or "Ballatella," and the Nedda-Silvio duet.

With *Vesti la giubba*, however, we enter another world, one of dark emotions and shattered feelings. Even as the Harlequin sings his serenade to Columbine, at the beginning of the "play-within-a-play," we sense that this darkness pervades the atmosphere and will soon take over. There is a delicious tension between Nedda's idiotic little waltz-song, in the character of Columbine, and Canio's delicate mental state, which breaks out in *No, Pagliacci non son* (*No, Pagliacci no more!*), and a touch of irony as the "audience" on stage blindly applauds Canio for his great "acting." In fact, the final moments are among the most emotionally compelling of all operatic finales. Small wonder that Leoncavallo was never able to top this.

The Recording

Oddly enough, for an opera as popular as this one, there are actually very few available recordings (seven, as of the Summer 1991 *Schwann Opus* catalog), and excepting the "live" performances (one of which is in German) only two really capture the "stage flavor" that is such a necessary ingredient. One of these is the 1934 Iva Pacetti–Beniamino Gigli–Mario Basiola–Franco Ghione recording (Angel CDH-63309), the other is this 1953 gem. Jussi Björling and Robert Merrill are in fabulous voice, in fact even a shade better than in *Cavalleria*; Leonard Warren, though rough and woolly in places, is superbly dramatic; and even Victoria de los Angeles, one of the most reserved of sopranos, gets caught up in the drama of the last act.

Andrea Chénier
1896   Umberto Giordano

Gino Bechi, br (Carlo Gérard); Maria Caniglia, s (Maddalena); Giulietta Simionato, ms (Countess); Maria Huder, ms (Bersi); Giuseppe Taddei, br (Fléville/Fouquier-Tinville); Beniamino Gigli, t (Chénier); Italo Tajo, bs (Roucher); Vittoria Palombini, ms (Madelon). La Scala Chorus and Orch., cond. by Oliviero de Fabritiis. Angel CHS-69996-2 (two CDs).

Unlike Leoncavallo, Umberto Giordano (1867–1948) was one of the more conscientious and musical of composers, and yet, he too is largely remembered as a "one-opera" composer nowadays. Despite the hot-and-cold interest in his 1898 *Fedora*, it is the 1896 *Andrea Chénier* that has managed to maintain a hold on the public's affections.

The fact that it was based on a true story (as was *Pagliacci*) may have something to do with it, but the fact remains that *Chénier's* music and drama is among the very best that the operatic stage has had to offer, in and out of the verismo period.

One stroke of genius that Giordano and his librettist, Luigi Illica, hit upon was to contrast Chénier's circumstances before and after the French Revolution. In Act I, Carlo Gérard is a servant who mocks the aristocratic life, but is deeply in love with the noble Madeleine de Coigny (Maddalena). Chénier, a famous poet, is a dinner guest of the de Coigny family; but when Madeleine's mother, the Countess, asks him to recite a poem, Chénier contrasts the beauty of nature with the misery man has made around him—priests, politicians, aristocrats, all of whom inhibit freedom and individuality of expression. The wealthy guests are horrified, but Gérard and the other servants find in Chénier's poem part of the inspiration for their revolution.

After the first phase of the Revolution (Act II), Chénier sits at a café table; at another is Bersi, Madeleine's mulatto maid, and the Incredibile, a spy. Roucher, Chénier's friend, stops at his table and gives him a passport; he urges him to flee, hinting that Chénier has powerful enemies, but Chénier declines. He has been receiving anonymous letters from a woman, whom he has built up in his mind as the most beautiful creature who ever existed; it turns out to be

Madeleine. When she meets Chénier, she tells him her secret; the Incredibile, overhearing them, realizes that she is a woman wanted by the revolutionary leaders—one of whom is Carlo Gérard. Gérard happens by, followed by the spy and Roucher. Chénier urges Roucher to take Madeleine into his charge, and fights Gérard without recognizing who he is. Gérard falls wounded, recognizes his opponent, and changes from anger to concern, warning Chénier to be on his guard because the poet is on the revolutionary leadership's list as a "counter-revolutionary." When the Incredibile returns with the police, Gérard says that he did not recognize his attacker.

Act III is the Revolutionary Tribunal. Mathieu, a former waiter, tries unsuccessfully to get the assembled crowd to contribute money and valuables to the common fund. Gérard enters and makes an impassioned speech urging their participation. Then he asks the Incredibile about Chénier and Madeleine: the woman was arrested, and Chénier is expected to arrive soon looking for her. Gérard is torn between conscience and feelings; he wants to denounce Chénier as an enemy of his country in order to have Madeleine for himself, but cannot forget that this was one of the men who inspired his revolutionary fervor in the first place. Madeleine is brought in, and offers her love to Gérard in exchange for Chénier's freedom. She tells him how her mother, the Countess, died in flames as her house was burned by a mob, and vows that she will die as well unless Chénier is set free. When Chénier is brought before the Tribunal, he is at first refused permission to answer the charges against him, but Gérard fights for his rights. Chénier says he has fought for his country as both a poet and a soldier; Gérard defends him, claiming that the indictment was false, but the death sentence is duly given.

In the courtyard of the prison of St. Lazare, Chénier waits for the wheeled cart to take him to his execution. Roucher is with him, and asks him to read the poem he has just written. Gérard appears at the outer gate with Madeleine; the jailer lets them in, and agrees to let her take the place of a condemned female prisoner so that she may die with Chénier. Their final duet is so resplendent, so impassioned, that it acts as a fitting climax to the entire drama.

Though Chénier is the principal character, and an interesting and likeable one, many of the opera's best moments (dramatically and musically) revolve around Carlo Gérard. In the first act his music is light, brusque, and cynical, as befits an underling waiting for the coming revolution; but in the second and third, we see (and hear) the character deepening before our eyes and ears. The conflict between his emotions and his sense of loyalty is actually the dramatic crux of the opera; he at first tries to make Madeleine give in, threatening her with Chénier's life, but when he realizes that she would rather kill herself than be unfaithful to Chénier, he decides to do all he can to save the poet. Gérard even puts himself in a difficult position at the Tribunal, working to reverse the charges against Chénier after he himself had signed the indictment. Though the lovers die together, singing grandly up to their respective high Cs, it is the redemption of Gérard's character that touches us most. He is, in a sense, an operatic villain, but a villain with misgivings and a sense of justice that supersedes even his "duty" to the Revolution.

Keynotes

Chénier's first-act *Improvviso*, third-act *Si, fui soldato*, and fourth-act *Come un bel di di Maggio* are all superb solos, growing out of the dramatic situation rather than just being inserted set pieces for the tenor to sing. The same goes for Madeleine's *La mamma morta*, and the scene in which Gérard tries to make her love him. The latter's famous aria, *Nemico della patria?*, is more of a standard piece of dramatic declamation, but even here Giordano has kept true to his ideals, and instead of a sugary tune he composed a well-constructed piece. As for the final duet, *Vicino a te*, it is one of the most magnificent musical-dramatic structures ever assembled, ending with a burst of flame rather than an anticlimax.

The Recording

Only two versions of this opera have really stood out over the years, the early-sixties recording by Antonietta Stella, Franco Corelli, Mario Sereni, and Gabriele Santini (Angel CDCB-49060) and this one; the singing of Maria Caniglia and Gino Bechi is far better than that of Stella and Sereni, despite the superior sound quality of that recording, and the subsidiary casting here is much stronger.

Follow-up Listening

For those who wish to hear other operas by these composers, I can recommend Giordano's *Fedora* in the performance with Renata Tebaldi, Giuseppe di Stefano, Mario Sereni, and Arturo Basile on Legato Classics LCD-158-2, and Mascagni's *L'Amico Fritz* (1891) in the recording by Mirella Freni, Luciano Pavarotti, Vicente Sardinero, and Gianandrea Gavazzeni on Angel CDCB-47905 (two CDs).

PUCCINI

By rights, there was no reason why Giacomo Puccini (1858–1924) should emerge as the "King of Verismo"; he was neither a well-schooled composer such as Giordano, nor a great conductor such as Mascagni. In addition, many of the melodies used in his arias had a distinctly "light-classical" feel to them, being closer to café music than Amilcare Ponchielli or Giuseppe Verdi. Yet he was a theatrically effective composer. Puccini knew how to cut to the heart of the plot, dramatically, and write music that moved things along. He also knew that, by remaining within the sugar-coated style of operetta, he would reach the masses in a way that a more complex style would not. In short, he knew what it took to be popular, and he exploited the high ranges of his singers in a way that made even Verdi wince.

Manon Lescaut
1893   Giacomo Puccini

Magda Olivero, s (Manon); Vicente Sardinero, br (Lescaut); Richard Tucker, t (Des Grieux); Eugene Green, bs (Geronte); José Mantanegro, bs (Captain); Bernard Fitch, t (Edmondo/Music Master); Alfredo Izyulerdo, t (Lamplighter); Aurora Cipriani, ms (Musician). Caracas Opera Chorus and Orch., cond. by Michaelangelo Veltri. Legato Classics LCD-113-2 (two CDs).

Manon Lescaut was not Puccini's first opera, and in fact when it premiered in 1893, Jules Massenet's opera *Manon* (1884), based on the same story and less than ten years old, was already established as a popular favorite. Yet, it managed to become a world-wide favorite in about five years, and since the early 20th century, it has more or less usurped the Massenet opus. The reasons aren't difficult to fathom: Where Massenet, in true French style, concentrated more on the love affair between Manon and Des Grieux, Puccini cut some of the story and zeroed in on the dramatic aspects. Puccini's opera, then, was much shorter and easier to assimilate (not to mention sit through). As a result, where the Massenet work stresses a lyric, erotic feeling, Puccini emphasizes Tragedy with a capital T.

Act I opens at an inn where Des Grieux is being teased by his friends because he looks unhappy; when it is suggested that he has had an unsuccessful love affair, he rebuffs them. Lescaut, a sergeant in the King's guards, arrives with his sister Manon. He is accompanying her to a convent so she can complete her education, but the wealthy satyr Geronte plots with the innkeeper to abduct her and make her his wife. Des Grieux spots her and asks what her name is. Falling in love at first sight, Des Grieux saves her from the clutches of Geronte; they elope, using the carriage Geronte has ordered. But because Des Grieux is not wealthy and Manon likes jewels and furs, by Act II she is living with Geronte anyway.

She soon tires of luxury for its own sake and complains to her brother, who tells Des Grieux where he can find Manon. Des Grieux rushes to her; Geronte sees them together, and calls for the police; the fickle Manon, by now back in love with luxury, insists on gathering up her jewels to take with her before they can leave. The delay proves disastrous. The police arrive and arrest her on Geronte's charge that she is an "abandoned woman."

In Act III, we learn that her sentence is banishment, with other "women of loose virtue," to the then-French possession of Louisiana. Des Grieux and Lescaut plan to rescue her before she embarks from Havre, but are foiled. A lamplighter enters, and sings a little aria. There is a great fuss when the roll is called of the women who are to be transported; when it is Manon's turn, Des Grieux stays by her side. He begs the ship's captain to let him come along, even if he is forced to serve on board. The captain relents and agrees to take them both to the New World.

In the last act, set in a vast plain on the border of New Orleans, the two lovers have been forced to leave the overcrowded city settlement. Manon is physically and emotionally exhausted, and begs Des Grieux to leave her to die alone. He goes off to seek help, but when he returns she is already dying. Des Grieux collapses by her side.

Keynotes

The score of *Manon Lescaut* is undoubtedly Puccini's finest. Among the best moments are Des Grieux's arias, *Tra voi belle*, *Donna non vidi mai, Ah Manon mi tradisce*, and especially the impassioned, dramatic *Guardate, pazzo son!* in which he begs the sea captain for help. Manon also has three fine solo moments, *In quella trine morbide, L'ora o Tirsi*, and her farewell to life, *Sola, perduta, abbandonata.* Yet it is in the duets that we appreciate the unhackneyed approach that Puccini brings to this score; these are fully explored dramatic entities in which the composer has understood the difference between the merely beautiful and the beautifully effective. There are lighter moments that are harbingers of Puccini's later works, but these are limited to short set pieces such as the lamplighter's aria and are unrelated to the dramatic thrust of the plot. Despite the great success of his later works, Puccini was never able to top *Manon Lescaut*.

The Recording

Very few sopranos, then or now, have been able to serve both the lyric and dramatic demands of this score with equal success, but Magda Olivero was definitely one of them. Though her voice tended to sound brittle and thin, her complete mastery of both singing and acting made her a supremely effective singing actress. She is partnered by a superb cast, including Richard Tucker as a somewhat blustery, old-sounding, yet ardent Des Grieux, and the vastly underrated Vicente Sardinero as Lescaut. (This recording does not come with a libretto, so you must hie yourself to your local library to get one, but it's worth it!)

La Bohème

1896   Giacomo Puccini

Rolando Panerai, br (Marcello); Luciano Pavarotti, t (Rodolfo); Nicolai Ghiaurov, bs (Colline); Gianni Maffeo, br (Schaunard); Michel Sénéchal, br (Benoit/Alcindoro); Mirella Freni, s (Mimi); Elizabeth Harwood, s (Musetta). Deutsch Opera Chorus; Berlin Philharmonic Orch., cond. by Herbert von Karajan. London 421 049-2 LH2 (two CDs).

Only three years after *Manon Lescaut*, Puccini gave the world *La Bohème*—without question the most famous, popular, and widely imitated opera of the last 100 years. Despite its derision by many critics and musicians, there is a certain quality to its melodies and the way Puccini ties things together that makes it his second-best score. Indeed, the Earl of Harewood, revisor and editor of *Kobbe's Complete Opera Book* (New York: G. P. Putnam's Sons, 1976), makes very few editorial comments regarding the operas his predecessor had already written about, but in his discussion of *Bohème* he writes: "Puccini's melodic invention and its turn to expressive use is at fullest flood and most apt, and he combines it moreover with an epigrammatic, conversational conciseness that is unique in his output" (p. 1158). It was a favorite opera of both Arturo Toscanini, who conducted the world premiere, and Sir Thomas Beecham—two very hard-nosed conductors not generally swayed by this composer's sentimentality, and who in fact disliked him personally.

The plot is fairly simple. Four Bohemians—Rodolfo the poet, Marcello the painter, Schaunard the musician, and Colline the philosopher—share a cold, drafty loft in the Latin Quarter of Paris. At the opera's outset, it is Christmas Eve. Colline enters with books that he burns in place of firewood, Schaunard with food and money. Benoit the landlord interrupts their horseplay to collect the rent, but the quartet make him forget his errand by encouraging him to boast about his female conquests; they pretend to be scandalized and throw him out. They divide the rent money and plan to go to Café Momus, but Rodolfo wants to stay and finish his poem. After he is alone, Mimi, a seamstress, knocks at the door; her candle has gone out. As she turns to leave, she collapses in a fit of coughing; both candles go out, and she drops her key. Rodolfo finds it but doesn't tell her; they introduce themselves to each other with arias, fall in love, and then leave together for the café when Rodolfo's friends call him.

The second act, set in the outdoor café, is largely memorable for its extended choral writing, the entrance of Parpignol the toy seller, and the arrival of Musetta. She is a shameless flirt who is being supported by her current "sugar daddy," old Alcindoro, but has a crush on Marcello. As a result, she pretends that her shoe hurts and sends Alcindoro to the cobbler's to have it fixed while she embraces Marcello. Later, she forsakes her rich lover and moves in with Marcello.

Act III takes place at a gate to the city of Paris. Musetta, Rodolfo, and Marcello are sharing a drink at a nearby tavern; Mimi sends in a note, asking Marcello to meet her outside. She is racked with a cough, and tells Marcello that Rodolfo is so insanely jealous that she fears they must part. When Rodolfo comes to look for Marcello, Mimi hides behind a tree; Rodolfo tells Marcello that Mimi is seriously ill, which she overhears. She comes out, pretends she heard nothing, and agrees to part from Rodolfo without bitterness. Marcello, meanwhile, has found Musetta flirting with a stranger, and they quarrel and decide to end their relationship.

In Act IV we are back in the attic loft. Rodolfo longs for Mimi and Marcello for Musetta. Schaunard and Colline enter, and the four engage in horseplay. Suddenly, Musetta enters; she tells them Mimi is dying and, as a last request, has asked to be brought back to Rodolfo's chambers. Colline goes to sell his coat so he can buy medicine. When Mimi enters, Rodolfo tries to console her, and they remember their former happiness, but it is too late. Mimi appears to go to sleep, but Marcello discovers she is dead. When Rodolfo learns the news, he staggers across the room and lies sobbing on her lifeless form.

Keynotes

Like *Il Trovatore*, *La Bohème* is chockful of famous melodies that even non-opera lovers recognize, among them the tenor aria *Che gelida manina*, the soprano aria *Si, mi chiamano Mimi*, the famous "Musetta's waltz" (turned into a pop hit in the early 1950s), the closing quartet of Act III (*Addio, dolce svegliare*), and the opening duet of Act IV (*O Mimi, tu piu non torni*). Other notable moments include the love duet, *O soave fanciulla*; the famous children's chorus at the

Café Momus; Rodolfo's Act III narrative, *Mimi e tanto malata*; and Colline's "coat song," *Vecchio zimarra*.

The Recording

Unlike many previous operas, where subtlety of expression is necessary to convey the drama properly, all *La Bohème* really needs are the types of voices that the verismo era created: a creamy lyric soprano, a pungent lyric baritone and lyric bass, two character singers, and a tenor who can produce both a good legato and a youthful, ardent sound. As a result, there are probably more good recordings of *Bohème* than any other famous opera—including no less than six with Mirella Freni and three with Luciano Pavarotti! Nevertheless, this recording has the advantage of great sonics, an excellent supporting cast, and the sensuous conducting of Herbert von Karajan, which makes for a truly winning combination.

Madame Butterfly
1904   Giacomo Puccini

Cesare Valletti, t (Pinkerton); Mario Carlin, t (Goro); Rosalind Elias, ms (Suzuki); Renato Cesari, br (Sharpless); Anna Moffo, s (Cio-Cio-San [Butterfly]); Fernando Corena, bs (Bonze); Nestore Catalani, br (Prince Yamadori). Rome Opera Chorus and Orch., cond. by Erich Leinsdorf. RCA Victor 4145-2-RG/AGK2-4145 (two CDs/two cassettes).

With the success of *La Bohème*, one would think that Puccini could do no wrong as far as general audiences were concerned; and, indeed, over the decades *Madame Butterfly* (1904) established itself as a perennial favorite. Yet in the beginning, it was scarcely a success: It ran on too long, and the first Butterfly, soprano Rosina Storchio, was having an affair with Arturo Toscanini. As a result, when Butterfly came out in Act II with her child, "little Trouble," the La Scala audience shouted hoots and catcalls—"Il piccolo Toscanini!" ("The little Toscanini!"). Puccini spent two months revising it; when it resurfaced at Brescia, this time with Toscanini conducting but without Rosina Storchio, it was a smash success, and has remained so ever since. *Butterfly* is a sweet little opera, perhaps saccharine in spots yet with a great appeal to audiences.

The plot is, in some respects, even simpler than *Bohème*. Navy Lieutenant B. F. Pinkerton enters into a "Japanese marriage," basically a way of legalizing his relationship with his mistress, Cio-Cio-San, a fourteen-year-old girl. She, however, takes the marriage seriously, and renounces her religion so she may marry the Westerner; her uncle, a Bonze (or Japanese priest), calls curses down on her head. But Butterfly stands by her man, engages in a rapturous love duet, and goes with him to the "bridal chamber" as the curtain falls.

Three years later, Pinkerton is long gone but Butterfly still believes in his promise to return. When he does, he arrives with an American wife, Kate, who is to join him in Nagasaki. Sharpless, the American consul to Japan, tries to convince Butterfly of Pinkerton's faithlessness, but she produces her son (little "Trouble") and insists that Pinkerton will return to her once he sees their fine child. Butterfly and her servant, Suzuki, spread a carpet of flower petals for Pinkerton's arrival. When he arrives, he realizes how much he has meant to the girl and how deeply he must now wound her; he sings a tearful farewell to the little Japanese house, leaving Sharpless to break the news to her. When Butterfly meets Kate Pinkerton, she realizes the awful truth. Once Kate and Sharpless leave, Butterfly commits hari-kari.

Keynotes

Though it was much praised in the early years of this century, Puccini's pseudo-oriental music (especially the Butterly-Suzuki "Flower Duet") is now seen as the opera's least original and likeable feature. On the other hand, he did work a snatch of "The Star-Spangled Banner" very cleverly into the first Pinkerton-Sharpless duet (*Dovunque al mondo*), he blended chorus and soloist exquisitely in the famous "Entrance of Butterfly," and in the principal moments— Butterfly's aria *Un bel di vedremo* (*One fine day he will return*), Pinkerton's farewell aria *Addio, fiorito asil*, and the famous love duet (one of the longest and best constructed of Puccini's entire career)— there is scarcely a hint of orientalisms.

The Recording

Like *La Bohème*, *Madame Butterfly* is fairly easy to cast: just insert great singers and let the music take over from there. As a result, there are several good versions to choose from, though one must decide whether to select a "heavy" cast (as in the Leontyne

Price-Richard Tucker-Erich Leinsdorf version on RCA 6160-2-RC or Maria Callas-Nicolai Gedda-Herbert von Karajan on Angel CDCB-47959, both two-CD sets) or a "light" one (as with Renata Scotto-Carlo Bergonzi-John Barbirolli on Angel CDMB-69564 [two CDs], or the present recording). In my opinion, the lighter voices work better, bringing a subtle "chamber-opera" effect to the music that suits it admirably. As a result, despite some dropped notes in the orchestral prelude, I recommend this performance for home listening: it draws you inward, rather than knocking you over the head, and there is wonderful attention given to the lyrics and the subtle mood changes of Butterfly and Pinkerton by Anna Moffo and Cesare Valletti.

Follow-up Listening

Those who find themselves drawn to Puccini may also want to investigate his somewhat noisy, unsubtle, yet popular opera *Tosca* (1900), especially in the version with Maria Callas, Giuseppe di Stefano, Tito Gobbi, and Victor de Sabata on Angel AV-34047/CDCB-47174 (two cassettes/CDs); the somewhat strange and modern-sounding "spaghetti Western," *La Fanciulla del West* (1910), in the performance with Renata Tebaldi, Mario del Monaco, Cornell MacNeil, and Franco Capuana on London 421 595-2 (two CDs); and the composer's most dramatic opera, *Turandot* (1926), especially the recording with Birgit Nilsson, Renata Scotto, Franco Corelli, and Francesco Molinari-Pradelli on Angel CDMB-69327 (two CDs).

"Gallipacci's" Comin' to Town

The problem with too many opera spoofs nowadays is that the spoofers are ignorant of opera, either generally or specifically. Because they don't know what they're spoofing, the end result may amuse a similarly ignorant audience but leave an informed listener both embarrassed and angry.

This, however, was not a problem in the days of Sid Caesar's legendary comedy programs, *Your Show of Shows* and *Caesar's Hour*. Sid, Carl Reiner, Imogene Coca, and later Nanette Fabray all had a working knowledge of good music, and knew how to make it funny for both general audiences and those in the know. Their finest moment came in a 1956 spoof of Leoncavallo's *Pagliacci*, retitled *Gallipacci*, with popular and folk songs rewritten in reasonable operatic facsimile for laugh after laugh. The opening chorus, "Gallipacci's Comin' to

Town," was a rewrite of "Santa Claus is Comin' to Town"; Nedda's aria telling how much she loved Silvio came from "My Man"; the soprano-baritone duet was a version of "Begin the Beguine" set to a galloping, *William Tell* overture-type of rhythm; and the final chorus was a variation on "The Yellow Rose of Texas."

The various performers also added their own subtleties. Howard Morris did a great simulation of the typical "character tenor" with the sprightly gait and wiry, grating voice; Reiner lampooned those baritones who try to steal scenes by holding their high notes longer than the soprano and winking at the audience; and Fabray, who had a beautiful singing voice, added to it with some hysterical mugging. Yet undoubtedly the highlight of this skit was Sid's *Vesti la giubba*, sung to the melody of "Just One of Those Things": making himself up before the mirror, his eyebrow pencil slipped and made a line down his cheek. Without breaking character (or losing a beat of the song), he just kept going—improvising as he went along—and played a game of tic-tac-toe on his cheek while he sang!

NINE

The "Golden Age" of Singing

As we have seen, singers dominated opera from roughly the late 17th century through the late 19th, despite individual efforts by Monteverdi, Lully, Gluck, and Berlioz to emphasize the story lines of their operas. With the coming of Wagner, and the spreading popularity of his music-dramas, critics and audiences alike began re-examining some of their priorities, and they decided that they liked having better conducted and acted performances. Ironically, after decades of complaints about the lack of truly great singing, people began to notice during the 1890s that operatic casts were getting better and better, that in addition to having superb voices in the principal roles there were also some very good singers in subsidiary parts. This was the beginning of what has since become known as the "Golden Age."

Contemporary critics placed the Golden Age as being from circa 1890 to 1915, but many since have extended it to 1920. The Golden Age of Wagnerian singing came a little bit later, during the 1920s and thirties, as the younger generation of singers and their slightly older colleagues matured into great artists. For our purposes here, we will (with two exceptions) limit it to those singers born between 1867 and 1897, a period of roughly thirty years.

Naturally, it is impossible in a book of this limited scope to do full justice to this era. A great many of the best singers only made acoustic recordings, and some of these discs are not technically good enough to appeal to modern ears.* There are also some singers who only made amateur cylinders, which have been worn almost down to the nub and produce as much extraneous noise as they do great vocal sounds. We will, however, examine ten of them in depth, keeping in mind that some of the singers we have already discussed—including Lawrence Tibbett, Kirsten Flagstad, Lauritz Melchior, Friedrich Schorr, Alexander Kipnis, Feodor Chaliapin, Claudia Muzio, Enrico Caruso, and Titta Ruffo—also fall into these years. These ten singers are listed alphabetically rather than chronologically, though the first is also the oldest and the last is the youngest, and their recordings are all quite excellent, even by the standards of their time, so that we can enjoy them to the fullest despite their somewhat dated sound.

Mattia Battistini   1856–1928

Battistini. Arias from *Eugen Onegin, Un Ballo in Maschera, Ernani, Martha, La Favorita, Don Sebastiano, Zampa, Damnation du Faust, Werther, Hamlet, Quo Vadis, La Traviata, Linda di Chamounix, Macbeth, Don Carlos*. Nimbus NI-7831.

Mattia Battistini, called "King of [the] Baritones" and "The Glory of Italy," was one of the greatest singers of any category. He made his debut at the age of twenty-two in Donizetti's *La Favorita*, and continued to sing for the next forty-nine years. Despite singing the role only in Italian, he was Wagner's favorite Wolfram in *Tannhäuser*. He spent most of his best years in Imperial Russia, where he was an honored guest between 1892 and 1910. He sang twice in South America, but became so seasick from his journeys that he refused all offers to sing in the United States. After World War I, he divided his time between England, France, and his native Italy; his only

---

* Prior to 1925, all recordings were made "acoustically"; singers sang into a large horn that collected the vibrations and transferred them to a master disc. In 1925, microphones were introduced to "electrically" transfer sounds to disc. Ironically, however, late acoustic recordings (1918–1925) often captured the contraltos and male voices with a greater richness and fidelity than the earliest electrics (1925–1928), simply because the early carbon microphones had an inherently tinny sound.

disappointment was in not living long enough to celebrate his fiftieth anniversary as an opera singer.

Battistini's voice was smooth and even from the midrange up, with no trace of a wobble and very little vibrato; indeed, his high notes were piercing, vibratoless bells that were the envy of younger and older colleagues alike. After 1911, he increasingly tried to emulate the vehement style of snarling Titta Ruffo, the brassy-voiced baritone who was all the rage in those years; by doing so, Battistini compromised the elegance of his style somewhat, and his low range suffered as a result. Even so, the soundness of his technique and his extraordinary breath control made him a standard by which other baritones were judged; and, except for a rather poor *La Traviata* duet in the present collection, these recordings more than prove the legend. Note especially the samples from *Ernani*, *Ballo in Maschera*, *Favorita*, and *Werther*, which Massenet rewrote for Battistini's voice.

Marcel Journet   1867–1933

Opera Arias & Songs. Arias from *La Damnation du Faust*, *Carmen*, *La Jolie Fille de Perth*, *Louise*, *Faust*, *Thaïs*, *Il Barbiere di Siviglia*, *Lohengrin*, *Tannhäuser*; various songs. Preiser 89021.

Marcel Journet was a great singer who was unappreciated in his time. A superb bass, actually more of a bass-baritone with a range that extended easily up to the high A, Journet sang with distinction at the Brussels and Paris Opéras—but the most famous basso of that time also happened to be French, the great Pol Plançon (1854–1914), whose records are unfortunately tubby and dry and do not do him full justice. In the great opera houses of the world, however, Plançon was the preferred favorite; as a result, Journet often suffered from the comparison, both in France and at New York's Metropolitan Opera, where he was sometimes paired with Plançon in a smaller role. Disgusted by such denigration, he left the Met in 1908 and returned to France. Within a few years, Plançon retired and then died, and Journet finally was able to take his place as the premiere bass of his day. He moved easily between bass and baritone roles for the next twenty-five years. He returned to America often enough to make an impressive array of records for Victor Red Seal, including duts and scenes with such noted artists as Caruso, Edmond Clément, Giovanni Martinelli, and Geraldine Farrar. The titles in this collection are from his period of electrical recording (1925–1933).

Journet's voice had the same plangent resonance and power as the more famous Ezio Pinza, but he was an even more musical artist and (by contemporary accounts) a far superior stage actor. One will notice that, by 1930, some of the focus and much of the power of his voice had faded with age, yet his last recordings are still remarkable specimens for a singer over sixty. Also note the superb tenor voice of the little-known Fernand Ansseau (1890–1972) in the duet from *Faust*. One final bit: When staying in hotel rooms on his journeys to foreign countries, Journet liked to set traps on his windowsill for pigeons, which he would capture, decapitate, and eat. Make of that what you will!

John McCormack   1884–1945

McCormack in Opera. Arias and duets from *Lucia di Lammermoor, L'Elisir d'Amore, La Traviata, La Bohème, Carmen, Lakmé, Faust, Figlia del Reggimento, La Gioconda, Mefistofele, Pescatori di Perle, Manon, Rigoletto, Don Giovanni, Die Meistersinger, Natomah, Semele,* and *Atalanta.* Nimbus NI-7820.

John McCormack is, next to Caruso, the most famous tenor of the acoustic era. Like Caruso, his voice recorded extraordinarily well; some would say even better than Caruso's. Unlike Caruso, however, he was not a singer of inexhaustible power and richness as he was one of finesse and elegance. He had an extensive operatic career in the years before World War I, though few are alive who remember it; after the War, he became the greatest and most highly paid concert artist in the world. When he appeared in New York, for instance, Carnegie Hall was too small for him: He would fill the vast Hippodrome Theater with his fans. He was also one of the very first singers to embark on a true "world tour," including countries in the Middle and Far East in his itinerary. During World War II, the aging tenor gave free concerts for relief aid and earned the title of Count. Though his voice was in decline as a result of asthma after

1936, he died full of honors, a living relic of the more elegant era that disappeared forever in 1919.

McCormack's voice, though light in timbre, had a tremendously tight focus that made it penetrate even the largest halls. The voice could ring out with a clarion quality that bordered on the lyric spinto, as you will hear in the *Natomah* aria, but more often than not his trademark qualities were an unsurpassed legato, phenomenal breath control (listen carefully to the *Don Giovanni* and *Semele* arias), and haunting soft (pianissimo) high notes, which he could float endlessly with apparent ease (as in the excerpts from *Atalanta* and *Figlia del Reggimento*). All of these recordings date from his acoustic period, yet, though the orchestras sound tinny and odd, the voice cuts through the crackle and pops like a hot knife through butter. Also notice the excellent singing of soprano Lucrezia Bori (1887–1960) in the duet from Verdi's *La Traviata*, and baritone Mario Sammarco (1873–1930) in the excerpt from Ponchielli's *La Gioconda*.

Antonina Nezhdanova 1873–1950

Antonina Nezhdanova. Arias and duets from *Harold, Life for the Czar, Russlan und Ludmilla, The Demon, Die Zauberflöte, Winter's Tale, The Czar's Bride, Les Huguenots, La Traviata, Les Pêcheurs de Perles*, and *Lohengrin*; songs by Taubert and Alabiev. Club "99" CL-99-5 (LP/CD).

It's a sad fact that, in the decades after World War II, we've had to settle ofttimes for third-rate singing in Russian operas (and by Russian singers in any repertoire), conventional thinking being that nasality, squalliness, and an overripe vibrato are inherent to Slavic voices. Though this is true to a certain extent, it was certainly not as pronounced in the earlier generation of Russian singers, which included (in addition to Nezhdanova) Chaliapin, Kipnis, Ivan Erschov, Ivan Koslovsky, and Leonid Sobinov (heard here in two duets with Nezhdanova).

Nezhdanova came to opera late, partly as a result of a promise to her father to become a school teacher. When she first began taking formal lessons, in 1899, she was told that she did not have a good enough voice to sing opera; but she traveled to Italy to study and applied herself diligently, and by 1902 was considered good enough to sing at the leading Russian theaters. An avowed patriot, she made few appearances outside her homeland. One of the few was in 1912, when she sang Gilda in *Rigoletto* at the Paris Opéra opposite Caruso and Ruffo, for which she received (as she always did) rave reviews. After the Bolshevik Revolution, she declined to leave the new Soviet Union, but stayed behind to promulgate Russian art; thus, she was denied the international career enjoyed by Chaliapin and Kipnis. Her fame is largely posthumous, and mostly due to her records, rare once, but now considered among the most exquisite ever made.

Nezhdanova had the most unusual Russian soprano voice of all time. She had the timbre of a full lyric soprano, which enabled her to sing Elsa in *Lohengrin*, as well as a high range and coloratura technique that made her more than adequate for roles in *La Traviata*, *Les Huguenots*, *Fra Diavolo*, and *Die Zauberflöte*. In addition, her voice was so headily vibrant, with so many overtones, that it was able to cut through the old recording process with a dramatic impact that is still impressive today.

Eidé Norena 1884–1968

Norena. Arias from *William Tell*, *Le Nozze di Figaro*, *Le Coq d'Or*, *Turandot*, *Die Zauberflöte*, *Otello*, *La Traviata*, *Faust*, *Rigoletto*, *Hamlet*, *Carmen*, *Die Entführung aus dem Serail*, and *Atalanta*; songs by Fauré, Grieg and Gounod. Nimbus NI-7821.

Few great singers have had stranger careers than Eidé Norena. She was born Karolina Hansen in Oslo, Norway, and began her career as a concert singer in 1904. In 1907 she made her stage debut as Amor in Gluck's *Orfeo*; she sang, without any particular distinction, for nearly twenty years, noted as a good stage actress with a tiny but beautiful voice. In 1909 she married stage actor Egel Naess Eidé and changed her name to Kaja Eidé. Then, around 1920, she began restudying in London with Raimund von zur Mühlen, in addition to working with legendary soprano Nellie Melba (1861–1931). These two were instrumental in expanding her vocal size and power; she was engaged to sing at La Scala in 1924, making her debut as Gilda in *Rigoletto* under Arturo Toscanini, the first of many triumphs. She sang at the Chicago, Paris, Covent Garden, Salzburg, and Metropolitan Opera houses until 1939, when she gave up her career and returned to live in Norway.

Norena's voice was, as you will hear, almost as extraordinary as Nezhdanova's. She could sing so lightly and elegantly that you would swear she was just a light-voiced "coloratura" soprano, complete with trills and high notes, but then suddenly expand and enlarge the voice, bringing it (especially in the upper register) into an entirely new dimension. As a result, she was able to encompass an extremely wide range of operas and styles, from Handel to Puccini, and handle them all beautifully.

Rosa Ponselle 1897–1981

Ponselle. Arias and duets from *La Gioconda, Otello, Aida, Ernani, La Vestale, La Forza del Destino, Norma*; songs by de Curtis, di Capua, Arensky, Rimsky-Korsakov, Bond. Nimbus NI-7805.

Rosa Ponzillo's rapid rise to fame, from the world of vaudeville to the stage of the Metropolitan (at only age twenty-one!) was so much the archetypal American success story that singers ever since have been trying to duplicate it. Yet few American-born voices were anywhere near as perfect as hers, and few singers have had the intelligence to "build" a career the way Rosa did after she changed her last name and burst upon the musical scene in 1918 as Leonora in *La Forza del Destino* appearing opposite Enrico Caruso at the Met.

Ponselle was described as "a Caruso in petticoats," but the only similarities she bore to the Neapolitan tenor were similar facial structure and the ability to overwhelm her partners of the evening. Ponselle's voice was pure and creamy, something like Kirsten Flagstad's, but her upper range was more extensive and her style better geared towards the dramatic French and Italian repertoire. She moved slowly through *Aida, Forza,* and *La Juive* until she was able to sing *La Vestale* and *Norma*; yet her trills and coloratura ability suggested better things, as when she dazzled an early-thirties radio audience with the aria *Bel raggio lushingiere* from Bellini's *Semiramide.* Unfortunately, this was an era when impresarios were unwilling to take chances with revivals of unpopular or forgotten operas; as a result, Ponselle was eventually forced into the verismo repertoire where her art and voice simply didn't belong. She retired from opera in 1937 and, though she occasionally sang on the radio, never performed publicly again. Fortunately, we still have her recordings, which are among the most perfect to have been left us by any singer.

Tito Schipa   1890 – 1965

Operatic Arias and Encores. Arias from *Serse, Il Barbiere di Siviglia, L'Elisir d'Amore, La Traviata, Rigoletto, Martha, Lakmé, Mignon, Werther, Pagliacci*; songs by Liszt, Padilla, Arona, Martini, and Barthelmy. Pearl GEMM-CD-9322.

Tito Schipa made his operatic debut at the precociously youthful age of twenty—a feat impossible today in this era of master's degrees over talent. He was not considered to have had the most beautiful voice of his time, as were Caruso and McCormack, yet he has since become the standard by which all light lyric tenors are judged; and his technique was so sound that he was able to continue singing well for forty years, his first period of decline not occurring until the early 1950s.

Schipa was handicapped by a limited high range, a shortcoming that affects most tenors of the classic Italian school. Unlike McCormack, he also drained his voice of the characteristic vibrato, which made it difficult for him to sing coloratura tenor roles. What was left, however, was an Italian tenor voice that appeals greatly to those who normally do not enjoy Italian tenors: pure, well focused, and based on the style of elegance and shading that made him McCormack's natural successor. More interestingly, he was (like contemporary tenor Alfredo Kraus) able to intensify what high range he had to produce performances of great feeling, though never breaking or distorting the vocal line with sobs or glotting. The end result was a tenor who could charm or thrill the listener, depending on the material, and excel in areas thought to be taboo to Italians, such as the works of Handel, Delibes, Thomas, and Massenet. The present collection gives a full range of his effectiveness in a well-chosen program of arias and songs—and note the floated pianissimo high notes!

Ernestine Schumann-Heink 1861–1936

Schumann-Heink. Arias from *Lucrezia Borgia*, *Le Prophéte*, *Das Rheingold*, *Rienzi*, *Rinaldo*, *Götterdämmerung*; songs by Wagner, Reimann, Molloy, Brahms, Böhm, Lieurance, Millöcker. Nimbus NI-7811.

Very few contraltos, then or now, seem to rise above the pack and make an impression; and when they do, it seems as if their success is due to extramusical reasons, such as their looks, personalities, or histrionic ability. Yet Ernestine Schumann-Heink was fat, ugly, and not much of an actress; when she first appeared in an opera, she was told to give it up and become a seamstress! Fortunately she ignored her critics' jibes and won over her audiences through the sheer quality of the voice itself—rich, metallic, dramatically brilliant, and technically perfect—which she made even more expressive through the sensitivity and generally accurate musicality of her performances.

Schumann-Heink had pretty much stopped singing by the early 1920s, but the advent of radio lured her back. Astonishingly, the voice had lost none of its control and focus, and only a little bit of its former power. In 1932 she gave her farewell performance at the Metropolitan Opera, as Erda in a complete *Ring* cycle, and continued to sing popular and light classical songs on the radio until her death. As a result, she remains one of the few singers who was able to continue singing, and well, into their seventies.

The present recital is an excellent cross-section of her abilities, from the bravura coloratura runs of Luigi Arditi's "Bolero" (*Leggiero invisibile*) to the dramatic depths of Erda's *Weiche, Wotan, weiche*, in two versions from 1907 and 1929. Also notice the excellent style in Handel's, Donizetti's, and Meyerbeer's works, in fact in anything she touches.

Conchita Supervia 1895–1936

Opera Arias. Arias and duets from *Il Barbiere di Siviglia, La Cenerentola, L'Italiana in Algeri, Carmen.* Angel CDH-63499.

Conchita Supervia, though very much a 20th-century woman (and one who made electrical recordings, to boot), was an anachronism. The progeny of an ancient Andalusian family, her voice and technique were based on old Spanish traditions rather than modern conservatory training; as a result, her voice had a sound peculiar to Anglo-Saxon ears, with a heavy vibrato, though that vibrato was even and never degenerated into a wobble. Her voice was also well set at a young age: She entered the Barcelona Conservatory at the age of twelve (!) and at fifteen made her stage debut in Buenos Aires. By 1912 she was admired as Carmen, one of her starring roles, and in 1925 she began a mini-revival of bel canto operas at La Scala. These were occasioned as much by her stunningly beautiful face and figure as they were by the character of her voice, yet even on recordings one senses a lively and vivacious personality that carries well beyond the years in which they were made.

Supervia created similar sensations in Turin, Florence, and Rome, and then in Paris and Great Britain; even the usually taciturn critic B. H. Haggin described her as having "an excitingly individual voice and style," rare praise indeed from one to whom singers were merely an appendage to an operatic performance. Yet the career that had started so early in her life ended all too abruptly when she died in childbirth at the age of forty-one. Many mezzo-sopranos have attempted the Rossini roles she sang so well, but few pierced the heart of them, musically or interpretively, as Supervia did almost unconsciously.

Marcel Wittrisch   1901–1955

Marcel Wittrisch. Arias and duets from *Barbiere di Siviglia, Les Huguenots, Ernani, Il Trovatore, La Traviata, Barber of Baghdad, Les Pêcheurs de Perles, Carmen, Tales of Hoffmann, Lakmé, Cavalleria Rusticana, Pagliacci*, and *La Bohème*. Preiser 89024.

Technically, Marcel Wittrisch just misses the period under discussion by a few years; but he is so great a singer, as are some of the other German singers featured on this recital with him (Margarethe Teschemacher, Gerhard Hüsch, and Wilhelm Streinz), that I am more than willing to make an exception. I think, after you have heard him, that you will too.

From a personal angle, sadly, there is little to admire about Wittrisch. A ruthless egotist whose vocal timbre was remarkably similar to that of rival tenor Richard Tauber (1892–1948), he wormed his way into the good graces of the Nazi Party, and was partly responsible for getting Tauber banned in Germany. He also acquiesced to the Nazis' demand to give up the music of such Jewish composers as Offenbach and Meyerbeer, which he sang superbly, and agreed to have the masters of his superb duet from *Les Huguenots* destroyed. He even recorded a song known as the "Hitler Hymn," which has since become an infamous and legendary recording.

Yet, as much as we would like to relegate Wittrisch to the scrap heap of Nazi history, there is no getting around one fact: He was probably the greatest tenor of this century. Indeed, his recordings reveal an almost chameleon-like quality, adapting superbly in both style and sound to such polar opposites as Count Almaviva in *Barbiere di Siviglia* and the lead role in Verdi's *Ernani*; he also sang Rodolfo in *La Bohème*, Don José in *Carmen*, Tamino in Mozart's *Die Zauberflöte*, and Wagner's *Lohengrin*—and he sounded perfectly "right" in each of these roles. He had a perfect command of both his chest and head registers, flawless technique, and a stylistic trick of alternating long phrases with short, declamatory outbursts, which made him consistently interesting and insistently dramatic even in the most lyrical music. After World War II, he paid a heavy price for his Nazi leanings, being virtually banned from performing (except in such distortions of democracy as South Africa). He died of a heart attack at the age of fifty-four.

Sideways Wasn't Her Best Side

As I mentioned earlier, most of the great opera singers were NOT the "homely elephants" so often laughed at in low comedies, but an exception to this rule was Ernestine Schumann-Heink. The great contralto was not only portly but homely, and had some embarrassing trouble with underarm wetness. Once, while rehearsing some lieder with pianist André Benoist on a hot, muggy August afternoon, the pianist—overcome by the heat and humidity—let out a whoosh between numbers. Schumann-Heink, thinking this sound signaled something else, said, "Yes, I know: I alvays get this vay in the heat!"

Once the great tenor Enrico Caruso came into Ernestine's home at dinner-time, and saw her sitting down to an unbelievable meal of roast turkey, stuffing, peas, yams, and cranberry sauce. "Tina!" he yelled in amazement. "Surely you are not going to eat that alone?!?" "Uff course not," she replied. "I am having it mit gravy, und dumplings, und bread!"

Last but not least, at the rehearsal for a concert with orchestra, Ernestine was making her way to the front of the stage from the wings through the musicians' stands. She was knocking everything over—sheet music, stands, and chairs. The conductor looked at her and reproached her. "Tina! Why don't you come in sideways?" She looked at him in disbelief. "Can't you tell?" she said. "I GOT no sideways."

TEN
Modern Opera

Around the turn of the 20th century, opera as an art increasingly began to move away from the vocal-dramatic showcase it had been for nearly 300 years. Much of this change was due to the all-pervasive influence of Wagner, who by the close of the 19th century had become the composer of preference in England and France as well as in Germany and Austria. It might seem strange that such diametrically opposed cultures as England and France should embrace the tenets of the same composer; yet, since the time of Handel, the influence of German composers in Great Britain had been quite strong, and there had been a strong connection between France and Germany since the time of Gluck. Indeed, it is interesting to note that Meyerbeer, originally a German, became the favorite in France; that Berlioz, a Frenchman, was more appreciated in Germany than Italy; that Weber, a German, based his style on French principles; and that Gounod's *Faust*, once the title was changed to *Margarethe*, also became a strong favorite in Germany.

So it was around 1900, when the influence of Wagner was interspersed with a Renaissance of philosophical concepts (by Friedrich Nietzsche, Henrik Ibsen, and Soren Kierkegaard) that European composers and librettists were inspired to elevate their music to a higher plane. Great music, they reasoned, was no longer to be merely "entertaining"; it must have a message, or a philosophical point of view, especially in so complex a form as opera. Singers were no longer permitted to dominate the proceedings, as they had done and continued to do in Italian works, but subjugated themselves, dramatically and vocally, to a new and more disciplined aesthetic. No longer were audiences supposed to applaud high notes and feats of vocal acrobatics (even when they were heard in the context of these new operas), but instead plunge into questions of ethics, motives, and interrelationships. The results of this thinking were interesting, if much less fun, and they continue to influence modern operas to this day.

One of the stylistic hallmarks of the "new opera" was a greater harmonic sophistication. The system of major and minor chords, which had been the underlying basis of all music since the end of the 17th century, was breaking up into a new system of "multitonalism." This meant, in effect, piling one key on top of another to create a dissonant tension, or changing chords subtly and quickly in order to leave the listener unsettled as to what key or keys the music was in. Indeed, the very concept of "keys" was breaking down. The German composer Arnold Schoenberg (1874–1951) invented the "twelve-tone row," a system of composition using every chromatic half-step within an octave (which is to say, every black and white key on the piano between two Cs, for example), with a strict rule to use every half-tone at least once before any of them could be repeated. This form of composition became all the rage in the 1920s and thirties, and it too influenced modern classical music for decades to come.

Naturally, such highly sophisticated and complex musical forms required a greater discipline, not only for singers but for conductors. The "era of the conductor" had been slowly gaining momentum from about 1870, and in the early 20th century it came to dominate all musical proceedings, whether the music performed was Wagner or Verdi, Schoenberg or Puccini. After a few decades of this, singers by necessity became less expressive; they were allowed to do less and less, even to the point that conductors removed their freedom to improvise cadenzas and sing alternate high notes from bel canto operas. At the Glyndebourne Festival in the mid-1930s, impresario Rudolf Bing and conductor Fritz Busch inaugurated the "era of the director," in which the directions of the stage manager became equal in importance to that of the musical content. This principle began to dominate opera productions worldwide after World War II, when a number of great conductors were aging or dying out.

There were, naturally, benefits to be gained from both systems. No longer would you see slapdash productions, and poor or ineffective singing-actors would at least have halfway intelligent stage movements blocked out for them. Singers would no longer be permitted to sing encores of favorite arias, no matter how exquisite their delivery, and musically wayward performers were systematically weeded out. On the down side, freedom of expression was slowly and painfully squashed, damned by conductors, directors, and critics as "old-fashioned," "unnecessary," and "distorted." By the mid-1960s, there were scarcely any singers, who even *could* perform older music with the requisite style, simply because they had not been allowed to for so long that they had lost the way. The dominance of conductor and director "tightened" things up, but there were few if any conductors who were willing or even permitted to lead performances of alternate style. The "new wave" became not merely an interesting alternative, but the law of the land, and so it has continued.

Pelléas et Mélisande
1892–1902 Claude Debussy

José van Dam, br (Golaud); Frederica von Stade, s (Mélisande); Nadine Denize, ms (Geneviève); Ruggero Raimondi, bs (Arkel); Richard Stilwell, br (Pelléas); Christine Barbaux, s (Yniold). Berlin Opera Chorus; Berlin Philharmonic Orch., cond. by Herbert von Karajan. Angel CDC-49350-2 (three CDs).

Like Camille Saint-Saëns, Claude Debussy (1862–1918) was far better known for his instrumental than his vocal music: *Images for Piano*, *Prelude to the Afternoon of a Faun*, and the three *Nocturnes for Orchestra* were all established favorites by the time he debuted his lone opera in 1902. But there had also been such vocal experiments as *La Damoiselle élue* (1888) and *L'enfant prodigue* (1884) that preceded it, so it cannot be said that Debussy was entering the vocal field without any prior experience at all. Interestingly, though he professed to reject the musical aesthetics of Wagner, at least insofar as stage works went, it was Debussy—more than any composer prior to Schoenberg—who stretched the limits of uncertain tonality, which Wagner had initiated, to new heights.

Pelléas et Mélisande introduced a new form of opera to the world. Based on a play by writer-philosopher Maurice Maeterlinck, it gives us an entirely "unreal" world, called *Allemande* ("All the World"), in which characters and motives are not clear-cut, or even clearly explained, but shadowy, without any judgments of values and morals. You are encouraged to make up your own mind about what is going on on stage; Maeterlinck and Debussy do not help you. This opera had no predecessors or followers; it is almost a stylistic dead end, but so interesting and beautiful in a strange, inexplicable way that it has managed to survive as something of a staple. As the Earl of Harewood stated (in the *Kobbé Opera Book*), "its very lack of followers is some indication that what it has to say has been said once and for all" (p. 1259).

In a forest, Golaud is hunting, and comes to a place unknown to him. He sees a girl sitting by a spring; she acts oddly, as if detached from the world. After repeated urging, she tells him her name—Mélisande—and allows him to lead her out of the dark wood. In the second scene, Queen Geneviève (Golaud's mother) is reading aloud a letter to the half-blind King Arkel from his grandson Golaud to Golaud's half-brother, Pelléas. Golaud has been married to the strange Mélisande for six months, but knows no more about her now than the day he met her, and so begs Pelléas to give him a sign that their grandfather would be willing to accept this stranger at the castle. Arkel grants this, and bids Pelléas to convey his best wishes to the couple. When Mélisande arrives at the castle with Golaud, she is even more gloomy and detached than before. The Queen and Pelléas try, without success, to rouse her.

Pelléas and Mélisande go together to a fountain in the park, where her spirits revive somewhat. As Mélisande bends over the fountain and lets her long hair fall into it, Pelléas wonders if she is a water nymph. She plays with a ring that Golaud has sent her, but it slips out of her hand and sinks in the fountain. At that very moment, we learn later, Golaud's horse reared while he was hunting, throwing and injuring him. Later, Mélisande, tending to him, tells Golaud that she does not feel well at the castle. Golaud, trying to comfort her, takes her hands and discovers that the ring is missing; Mélisande lies to him, saying she dropped it in the sea. He drives her out into the night to look for it, and Pelléas offers to help. They go to a grotto by the ocean, so she can at least know the place she claimed to have lost it; they feel the "shadow of death" about them, and see three strange bearded beggars.

At a tower in the castle, Mélisande is standing by the window combing her hair. Pelléas comes by to say farewell; early the next morning he is leaving. He asks her to let him kiss her hand once more, but she can only reach him with her long hair. Pelléas is filled with erotic feelings and admits his love for her, but the mood is broken when Golaud comes by and chides them for their "childishness." The two half-brothers leave together, and go to a chilly vault under the castle. After they exit the vault, Golaud warns Pelléas not to disturb Mélisande because she is about to bear a child. Golaud continues to be disturbed by jealousy, so he asks his little son Yniold (from a previous marriage) to spy on the couple at the window; Yniold does not see any improper behavior, but Golaud nevertheless senses that something odd is going on.

Arkel, who has taken Mélisande to heart, is sorry that she appears unhappy. When Golaud enters, his inner rage is fueled by his wife's calm innocence; in a mad rage, he knocks her down and drags her across the room by her hair. The tension continues to build. Mélisande meets Pelléas, at his request, for one last time at the fountain where the ring was lost; they sense impending doom, and say their farewells in the tone of doomed lovers, almost rejoicing in death together. Golaud comes on them and kills Pelléas with his sword, and Mélisande flees into the night. Golaud catches her and brings her back to the castle, but her will to live has left her. Golaud blames himself for her illness, but when Mélisande regains consciousness he presses her to admit that she has been unfaithful to him with Pelléas. She denies it; Golaud keeps insisting; and, suddenly, all earthly tensions fall away from her soul as if she were already free. Arkel brings her child to her. Mélisande says her farewells, and dies.

Keynotes

Pelléas is such a strange opera, almost completely devoid of standard arias and duets and certainly devoid of the conventional Italo-Franco melody we've come to expect, that approaching it for the first time (or the hundredth) leaves you feeling that there is something here that you've not grasped. This was Debussy's genius. Even the most acerbic critics have had lifelong love-hate relationships with *Pelléas*, but they keep coming back to it because it is so unconventionally brilliant. Opaque orchestral preludes introduce each scene, and equally opaque orchestral interludes connect them; and it is in these orchestral passages that the true drama takes place. The vocal line is so shadowy, so "insignificant" by contrast, that it almost seems a running commentary rather than an imposition of operatic characterization. Nevertheless, the brief arietta for Mélisande at the beginning of Act III, *Mes longs cheveux*, is a more-or-less "conventional" melody that listeners can remember, and the ensuing love duet is a masterstroke by Debussy, who creates here an erotic mood easily the equal of Wagner's *Tristan und Isolde*.

The Recording

Despite its not being as popular as the works of Puccini, *Pelléas* has fared pretty well on records, from the legendary 1941 recording conducted by Roger Désormière (EMI CHS-7610382, three CDs) to the now out-of-print 1950s mono recording with Suzanne Danco, Heinz Rehfuss, and Ernest Ansermet. The von Karajan recording, however, has unusually spacious sonics, which help capture the ambience of both the orchestral and vocal texture; Frederica von Stade never gave a finer performance in her life; and the singing of Richard Stilwell, Nadine Denize, José van Dam, and Ruggero Raimondi is sheer perfection, not only for their beauty of tone but also for their legato style and subtlety of expression.

Salome
1904–1905   Richard Strauss

Wieslaw Ochman, t (Narraboth); Bernd Weikl, br (Jokanaan); Teresa Stratas, s (Salome); Hanna Schwarz, ms (Page); Hans Beirer, t (Herod); Astrid Varnay, c (Herodias); Nikolaus Hillebrand, bs (A Cappadocian). Vienna Philharmonic Orch., cond. by Karl Böhm. DG 072209-1 NTSC (video laserdisc).

The emergence of Richard Strauss (1864–1949) in the late 19th century as the "Renaissance man" of German music was (by his own admission) somewhat overblown. Strauss was certainly a fine composer, and also (coincidentally) a superb conductor; but he knew his limits, and was honest enough to admit them. "I am well aware," he once wrote, "of the tremendous gulf which separates my tone-poems from the great symphonies of Beethoven, and of that which separates my operas from the masterpieces of Wagner." Nevertheless his third opera, *Salome*, remains his masterpiece, a near-perfect fusion of interesting text with inventive, creative music.

The plot is based on the Oscar Wilde play, which in turn was based on the biblical story of Jokanaan (John the Baptist) and his incarceration in a well by King Herod and his wife, Herodias. The Princess Salome, Herodias's daughter by a previous marriage, is a strange, somewhat wild creature; her beauty ensnares men, but when she tires of them she has them put to death. She is fascinated, however, with the strange prophet held prisoner in the cistern, but when she tries to seduce him he rebukes her with biblical epithets. She has him taken out of his prison, and desires to touch his "white body" and kiss his "red lips." Jokanaan, appalled by her sensuality, tells her to seek out the "Man of Galilee," who can be her only redemption; realizing that his words are falling on deaf ears, he retreats into his cistern.

Herod and Herodias come out to have a feast; Herod lusts after his stepdaughter, and asks her to do the "Dance of the Seven Veils," a prehistoric striptease. Salome refuses until Herod promises to give her anything she wants; after the dance is over, she demands the head of the Prophet be brought to her on a silver platter. Herod, who is somewhat afraid of his captive, at first refuses and tries to offer her other prizes, but Salome holds him to his promise. When the head is brought to her, Salome sings a long, mad, erotic monologue, that ends with her kissing the dead red lips. Even Herod is revolted, and orders her killed; the guards crush her under their shields.

Keynotes

Like *Pelléas*, there is little conventional melody in *Salome*, but the music swirls and eddies and creates an undeniable atmosphere of its own. The scene between Salome and Jokanaan is masterful; the Dance of the Seven Veils has become a concert staple, divorced from the opera; and Salome's final scene, despite its length, captivates one with its strangely shifting moods and rising ecstasy.

The Recording

When I first saw this performance broadcast on public television in the 1970s, I was so captivated that I taped the soundtrack (this was in pre-VCR days). This video laserdisc version is even sharper and clearer than the original telecast, and remains the most moving and powerful performance I have ever seen or heard. Teresa Stratas, who gives the performance of her life here, is so charismatic from start to finish that it is difficult to think of anyone who could better her; Hans Beirer is a loathsome, lecherous Herod; and Astrid Varnay outdoes herself as the equally repulsive Herodias. For those who do not own a laserdisc player, I can recommend the recording with Birgit Nilsson, Gerhard Stolze, Waldemar Kmentt, and Eberhard Wächter, with Sir Georg Solti conducting, on London 414 414-2 LH2 (two CDs), but only as a second-best version.

Wozzeck
1914–1921   Alban Berg

Gerhard Stolze, t (Hauptmann); Dietrich Fischer-Dieskau, br (Wozzeck); Helmut Melchert, t (Tambour-Major); Fritz Wunderlich, t (Andres); Karl Christian Kohn, bs (Doktor); Evelyn Lear, s (Marie); Alice Oelke, c (Margret); Kurt Böhme, bs (1st Apprentice). Berlin Opera Chorus and Orch., cond. by Karl Böhm. DG 435 705-2 GH3 (three CDs, also includes Berg's *Lulu* cond. by Böhm).

Alban Berg (1885–1935) was a follower of Arnold Schoenberg, which means that he composed within the twelve-tone system. Unlike Debussy, who wrote only one opera, Berg wrote two; and, in recent years, the popularity of his second opera *Lulu* (1928–1934), has been something of a cause célèbre *Lulu's* plot is, to some, even more perverse and unpalatable than that of *Salome*, while even Berg's severest critics admit that *Wozzeck* is one of his masterpieces.

Wozzeck is based on an incomplete drama written by an obscure writer named Büchner; it depicts the unbalanced mental state of a soldier who, in addition to the pressures of his profession, also has to cope with a flighty, unfaithful lover and a series of "medical experiments" to which he subjects himself in order to supplement his meager army pay. This story was easily 100 years ahead of its time, and may be considered the first "existentialist" drama.

The opera opens with Wozzeck shaving the Captain, then moves to Wozzeck and Andres (another soldier) cutting sticks in a field. In both locales, Wozzeck feels haunted, somehow unreal. Later, his girlfriend, Marie, is flirting with a Drum Major in her room; Wozzeck comes to her window, and though it is too late for him to enter, she is disturbed by his confused talk. We learn that the Doctor has been using Wozzeck for dietary experiments; his scientific talk further confuses Wozzeck. Meanwhile, Marie continues to flirt with the Drum Major, who finally makes his advances on her.

In the second act, Marie is admiring herself and her new earrings (that the Drum Major gave her) in a piece of broken mirror. She tries to put her child to sleep, but goes back to admiring herself; Wozzeck enters, and she tells him that she found the earrings to avoid mentioning her liaison with the Drum Major. Wozzeck says that he has never had luck finding things like that in pairs, then reflects that life is nothing but work. He gives Marie the money he has earned from the Captain and Doctor, and leaves. The Doctor and Captain run into each other on the street. The Doctor doesn't think that the Captain looks too healthy, and warns him of apoplectic fits; the Captain reflects on the thought of his own death, but cheers himself by reflecting on what nice things people will say of him when he is dead.

The remaining scenes reflect Wozzeck's descending mental state, the most important of these being in a beer garden where Wozzeck sees Marie dancing with the Drum Major, and in the barracks where the drunken Drum Major taunts Wozzeck with his conquest. Wozzeck and Marie meet at a pond in the woods; in a frenzy, he pulls his knife and cuts her throat. He flees to an inn, where he dances with Marie's neighbor, Margret. Wozzeck tries to make love to her, but she stops when she spots blood on his hand. He rushes back to the pond, trying to find the knife; when he does he throws it into the water and watches it sink. Then the entire pond seems to him to be filled with blood; he sees spots on his hands and clothes, and walks into the water to wash them off. He keeps on walking until he disappears and drowns.

Marie's child is playing with others in the street; different children enter, and one of them says that Marie has been found dead. Her child does not understand what has happened, and goes on playing with his hobbyhorse as the curtain falls.

Keynotes

The opera's fifteen scenes (five apiece for three acts) are tightly interwoven and, like the play, jump around in depicting various incidents and emotions in Wozzeck's life. Utilizing atonal and twelve-tone techniques, and Schoenberg's device of *sprechstimme*, or "speech-song," Berg presents Wozzeck in the beginning of the opera as a man struggling to keep a grip on reality. He composed Wozzeck's songs in a bland, emotionless monotone, while the voices of those around him appear to sound mad, distorted, and surreal. In this way Berg was able to give us the "insider's view," as it were, of a man going insane. Not all of the opera, by the way, is twelve-tone music, though many neophytes automatically assume it to be so.

The Recording

Though *Wozzeck* does not demand conventionally expressive voices, they must at least be well focused. Also, because of this opera's complexity, it demands great discipline from both cast and conductor in order to perform it properly. This 1962 recording meets both of these tests; it is the only accurately sung and conducted *Wozzeck* available today. Evelyn Lear sings Marie with rare beauty of tone and elegance; Dietrich Fischer-Dieskau brings to the title role both warmth of timbre and depth of expression; and Karl Böhm's conducting, though lacking the excitement of some others (notably Dmitri Mitropoulos and Claudio Abbado), has a wonderfully transparent 3-D effect. This performance is also notable for the excellence of the subsidiary casting, and the new CD repackaging includes Böhm's recording of the unfinished version of *Lulu*.

Peter Grimes
1945   Benjamin Britten

Norman Bailey, br (Balstrode); Jon Vickers, t (Grimes); Heather Harper, s (Ellen); John Tomlinson, bs (Hobson); Forbes Robinson, bs (Swallow); Elizabeth Bainbridge, c (Auntie); Philip Gelling, br (Ned Keene). Covent Garden Chorus and Orch., cond. by Sir Colin Davis. Thorn-EMI videotape HTVE-3562.

Despite several bids by British composers to enter the standard operatic repertoire, only Lord Benjamin Britten (1913–1976) was really able to compete on an international basis. This was undoubtedly due, in part, because he pursued neither the old-fashioned post-Romantic style, typified by Ralph Vaughan Williams and Edward Elgar, nor the completely atonal (or twelve-tone) style of Berg. Britten certainly liked, and used, many modern harmonies—there are several passages in his operas that are tonally ambiguous—but he never went so far out on a limb, tonally, that he lost the listener entirely.

That being said, his operas have been as much out of the standard repertoire as in it, especially in the years since his death, due to a critical backlash claiming that they aren't modern enough, and because his works are so difficult to perform that new singers tend to shy away from them. Singers don't like to sing music that isn't really popular, especially if they must commit themselves to the arduous task of both singing and acting, which Britten demands, at an extremely high level.

Peter Grimes, based on a poem by George Crabbe entitled "The Borough," concerns a fisherman whose young apprentices die mysteriously one after the other. Britten and his librettist, Montagu Slater, softened Grimes somewhat from the plain sadist depicted by Crabbe to a strong-willed misfit who does not understand what is happening to him yet refuses to accept help. The opera opens with an inquest, led by Swallow, into the death of Grimes's latest apprentice. Grimes claims that he and his apprentice were beset by a storm at sea and, after three days without food or water, the boy died. The other characters are called up to corroborate the evidence, and the apprentice's death is ruled accidental. Ellen Orford, a widow and schoolmistress, tries to console Grimes; afterwards, as the fishermen and their women go about their business, Grimes calls for help with his boat, but only the retired Captain Balstrode and apothecary Ned Keene are willing to come to his aid. Keene tells Grimes that he has found another apprentice for him whom he can claim from the workhouse. But Hobson, the carter, refuses to help Grimes fetch the boy until Ellen offers to take care of him.

Balstrode remarks that Grimes seems determined to isolate himself, and suggests that he'd be better off working as a merchant seaman rather than piloting his own boat. But Grimes wants to be his own man in his own town. He tells the Captain of the horrors he suffered being alone at sea with the dead boy's corpse. Grimes then goes to The Boar, the local pub, where Auntie (the inn's "Madame") holds court; Mrs. Sedley, a rentier widow, faints as Grimes sings a monologue on the mystery of human destiny. Keene picks up everyone's spirits by singing an old round, "Old Joe has gone fishing." A storm is approaching, and Hobson finally arrives with Ellen and the new young apprentice.

In the second act, Ellen tries talking to the boy about school and the workhouse, but discovers that his coat is torn and there is a bruise on his neck. As Grimes comes to get him, she pleads with him to show a little mercy for the boy's youth, but Grimes drives the boy off. Ellen goes to the inn to tell the villagers what's going on. The assembled crowd begin to suspect worse than a mere cuff on the neck, and are soon whipped up into a cry of "Murder!" Grimes, in his hut (an overturned boat) with the boy, reflects on the bleak reality of his situation in contrast to his plans for himself and Ellen. The vigilantes arrive, angering Grimes; he rushes the boy out of the hut and down the cliff, and hears the scream as the boy falls to his death. Grimes quickly hurries out and runs down the cliff himself.

Act III opens with a wild dance at The Boar, where Auntie's "nieces" are being chased lustily by Swallow and Ned Keene. As the dance breaks up and the neighbors say goodnight to each other, Mrs. Sedley hides outside in the darkness. She sees Ellen and Balstrode walk up from the beach, and hears the Captain explaining that Grimes's boat is in but Peter cannot be found, while Ellen tells how she has found the boy's jersey that she made for him. Mrs. Sedley goes back to The Boar and calls for Swallow; another posse is quickly formed to search for Grimes. As the search-party calls Grimes's name, Peter emerges from the shadows: He has gone mad, and alternately babbles about going home, how his apprentices died in "accidental circumstances," and sings a snippet of "Old Joe has gone fishing." Ellen arrives with Balstrode, and tells Peter she has come to take him home, but he does not recognize her. Balstrode suggests that Grimes take his boat out to sea, and sink it there. By the next morning, the posse has grown tired of its search; Swallow confirms that he has seen a boat sink out at sea, but nobody is interested.

Keynotes

Despite the unsettled tonality of the opera, there are some moving passages in *Peter Grimes*, among them Ellen's arioso *Let her among you without fault*, her duet with Grimes, and Peter's three arias. The last of these, *Steady! There you are! Nearly home!* is the heart of the mad scene, and it is one of the most effective since *Boris Godunov*'s "Clock Scene." Also of interest are the orchestral passages, known as the "sea interludes," which are often performed separately as concert pieces.

The Recording

In our time, two tenors were indelibly identified with the role of Grimes: Sir Peter Pears, who debuted the part, and Jon Vickers. But Pears's recording of the opera (London 414 577-2 LH3) has the inferior soprano Claire Watson performing the part of Ellen instead of Heather Harper, who was Britten's first choice. Harper sings Ellen beautifully in the present "live" performance, and Vickers is an intense, fascinating Grimes.

The Tender Land
1954–1955 Aaron Copland

Elisabeth Comeaux, s (Laurie); Janis Hardy, c (Ma Moss); LeRoy Lehr, bs (Grandpa Moss); Dan Dressen, t (Martin); James Bohn, br (Top); Vern Sutton, t (Mr. Splinters); Agnes Smuda, ms (Mrs. Splinters); Merle Fristad, br (Mr. Jenks); Sue Herber, s (Mrs. Jenks). Plymouth Music Series Chorus and Orch., cond. by Philip Brunelle. Virgin Classics VCD-91113-2/4 (two CDs/cassettes).

I have decided to end this operatic survey with an American opera. American and immigrant composers have been trying, with some interest, to compose American operas for decades; these range from embarrassing stereotypes such as Louis Gruenberg's *The Emperor Jones*, through interesting but small-scaled chamber works like Virgil Thomson's and Gertrude Stein's *Four Saints in Three Acts*, to such pretentious drivel as Victor Herbert's *Natomah*, Carlisle Floyd's *Susannah*, and Samuel Barber's *Vanessa*. Part of the problem, it seems to me, is that we Americans as a whole are fairly simple, uncomplicated people. Despite the fact that many of us suffer stress, as a nation we have had it relatively easy; emotional and/or politically complex situations do not come easily or naturally to us, as witness the "make-believe" worlds we create in nighttime TV soap operas like "Dallas" and "Twin Peaks," whose very artificiality make them escapist entertainment.

But that is exactly why *The Tender Land* works so well. Aaron Copland (1900–1990), certainly one of the finest and most popular of American composers, didn't try to paint his musical canvas with big, splashy, inappropriate colors, just as librettist Erik Johns didn't try to write *The Great Gatsby*. Instead, they chose to set their opera in rural America during the Depression, which even by 1954 seemed like another time and place. Their story, which was wholly original, is based on a young girl's coming of age and the dilemma she faces between remaining at home or trying her luck in the outside world. And Copland's score, rather than trying to be something it wasn't, filled in these elemental conflicts with simple, uncomplicated, yet subtle and interesting music.

Laurie Moss is an eighteen-year-old girl who lives on a Midwestern farm with her mother, grandfather, and little sister Beth. She is about to graduate from high school, and her family wants her to stay at home and help with the spring harvest. Into the picture come Martin and Top, two vagrant workers typical of the Depression; they offer to help Grandpa Moss with his chores in return for food and shelter, to which he reluctantly agrees. Ma Moss has heard of two men molesting young girls in the neighborhood, but Martin and Top are allowed to sleep in the shed anyway.

Laurie falls in love with Martin, as much because he represents freedom and places she's never been as for any physical attraction. Top warns Martin against dallying with the old man's granddaughter; Grandpa Moss catches Laurie and Martin kissing, and tells the drifters that they'd better be gone by sunrise. Laurie makes plans to leave with them, but the two men leave early because Top convinces Martin that a roaming life would not be good for a sweet girl like Laurie. Despite the fact that she has been jilted, Laurie decides to leave home anyway, breaking the family cycle on the farm that has existed for generations.

The Tender Land is as much symbolic of the changes that took place in America after World War II as it is a portrayal of the Depression era. Grandpa Moss's mistrust of strangers, for instance, is both indicative of the typical rural farmer's attitude toward outsiders and a subtle condemnation of Senator Joe McCarthy's communist "witch-hunts": It is no accident that Martin and Top, suspected by the townsfolk of being the molesters, turn out to be completely innocent. The nice thing about the opera, though, is that it is not pretentious or "preachy," and we can enjoy it as much today, simply for its excellent music and idyllic, pastoral setting, as the original audiences did in 1954.

Keynotes

Copland, who began his career composing in the twelve-tone idiom, had by the late 1930s created a "modern-tonal" style that made his music much more popular while still garnering critical acclaim, and it is this style in which *The Tender Land* is written. As a result, one may enjoy the lovely, ethereal aria for Laurie, *Once I thought I'd never grow*; the jaunty Martin-Top duet, *We've been north*; the excellent quintet *The promise of living*; Laurie and Martin's love duet; and Ma

Moss's concluding aria, *All thinking's done*, which is both the finale and dramatic crux of the opera.

The Recording

Because of subtle political pressure against Johns and Copland during the 1950s, *The Tender Land* never received the exposure it so richly deserved, and no complete recording was available before this one (though Copland had made an excellent disc of about sixty-five minutes of the work in the early 1960s for Columbia). Fortunately, this performance is fully worthy of the music. Elisabeth Comeaux's sweet lyric voice is perfect as Laurie, Dan Dressen is a good Martin, and James Bohn a superb Top; LeRoy Lehr and Janis Hardy are a bit dry and brittle of voice, but good enough for Grandpa and Ma Moss, and Maria Jette is excellent in the thankless role of the young girl, Beth.

Follow-up Listening

If you're more interested in modern opera, you'll also enjoy Strauss's *Ariadne auf Naxos* (1916), in the performance with Elisabeth Schwarzkopf, Rita Streich, Rudolf Schock, Hermann Prey, and Herbert von Karajan on Angel CDMB-69296 (two CDs), and his somewhat gushingly Romantic *Der Rosenkavalier* (1910) in the version with Schwarzkopf, Teresa Stich-Randall, Otto Edelmann, and von Karajan on Angel CDCC-49354 (three CDs). Béla Bartók's symbolic opera *Duke Bluebeard's Castle* (1911) is given a fine reading by Eva Marton, Samuel Ramey, and Adam Fischer on CBS MK/MT-44523 (CD/cassette), and Berg's *Lulu*, its third act reconstructed and orchestrated after the composer's death, has a definitive reading by Teresa Stratas, Hanna Schwarz, Kenneth Riegel, and Pierre Boulez on DG 415 489-2 GH3 (three CDs). In addition, there are the Benjamin Britten operas *The Rape of Lucretia* (1946), with Janet Baker, Heather Harper, Sir Peter Pears, John Shirley-Quirk, and the composer conducting (London 425 666-2 LH2, two CDs), and *A Midsummer Night's Dream* (1960) with Pears, Elisabeth Harwood, Josephine Veasey, Helen Watts, and the composer conducting on London 425 663-2 LH2 (two CDs).

So Who Can Tell?

One of the jokes constantly made about atonal or multitonal music is that no one would know the difference if some notes were sung or played wrong, because it all sounds "wrong" anyway. Of course, to those who can read scores and own a pitch pipe, this is not the case, yet it still amazes critics when good musicians just blaze away through a mistake and don't catch it or know the difference.

The atonal opera most often performed, and as such the one most open to these problems, is Alban Berg's *Wozzeck*. In a famous 1951 performance (once available on Columbia and Odyssey LPs—that's right, they even reissued it!), soprano Eileen Farrell was bound and determined that she would sing the part of Marie better than it had ever been sung before. She was in glorious voice; it just sailed over the orchestra and chorus; and in her aria, it sailed so high that she went way past the written high B-flat all the way to D above high C—a full third higher!

But we shouldn't pick on Eileen alone. In the Columbia recording from the late 1960s, every singer makes either pitch or rhythmic mistakes throughout their performances. Yet conductor Pierre Boulez is so widely regarded as a musical genius, that to this day some critics select this as the "finest performance" on record, and complain about the accurate DG recording (conducted by Karl Böhm)—because it doesn't sound the same!

Unfortunately, some singers claim that performing atonal opera ruins their voices—even when they do it well. Evelyn Lear, the Marie in my recommended recording, complained that singing this role "completely ruined" her voice for Mozart. But I guess we should wonder about those singers who go the other way, such as Hildegard Behrens, who was once a superb dramatic soprano but who later picked up a "wobble" so bad that you couldn't tell what pitch she was singing. It was at THAT point in her career (you guessed it!) that she decided to sing Marie in *Wozzeck*.

ELEVEN

The Great Opera Houses/Singers of Today

Now that you've had a taste of opera history, it might be a good idea to become acquainted with the world's largest and most famous opera houses and today's star performers. This will give you some idea of the grand platforms that the world has provided for the presentation of these musical spectacles, plus the leading lights who have graced these stages. Bear in mind that, like much of the material in this book, this listing reflects my personal views as accumulated over the past thirty years, though I have consulted with other authorities in the operatic world before making my selections.

RUSSIA

The Bolshoi Opera, Russia's largest and most famous opera house, was founded in 1780 in Moscow, and has been housed in its present location since 1825. Its repertoire is mostly nationalistic, with the addition of a few of the most famous foreign operas. In years past, foreign operas were usually translated into Russian for the benefit of local audiences, but in the last decade or so more of them are being performed in their original languages. The Bolshoi, like all arts organizations in Russia, has seen its budget shrink since the decline and fall of the Soviet Union; only time will tell if the company, like the country itself, will be able to retain its former glory.

AUSTRIA

Despite the fact that Vienna has been the home of great opera for over 200 years, it was not until 1869 that the Vienna State Opera (or *Staatsoper*) was founded. The architects who won the competition to design the house, Eduard van der Nüll and August Siccard von Siccardsburg, chose for their design what they called a modification of "the principles of the French Renaissance," which turned out to be pure 19th-century Viennese. The design evoked derision and laughter when it was made public, though today it is ironically considered a masterpiece of its time. The State Opera's most famous music director was the composer-conductor Gustav Mahler (1860–1911), who battled against a tradition of lax musical practices. He omitted the practice of singers taking extra encores, insisting on a dramatic presentation of each opera.

The other famous Austrian house, the Salzburg Opera, is located on the Salzach River seventy-one miles southeast of Munich. It is located in the birthplace of Mozart but, ironically, was not a major opera house during that composer's lifetime, only achieving its fame in our century. Its success may be traced to the great soprano Lilli Lehmann (1848–1929), one of the few singers of the past who also directed an opera house. Her conception, to make Salzburg a shrine to Mozart as Bayreuth is for Wagner, took shape from 1901 until the outbreak of World War I in 1914. After the War, it took a number of years for Salzburg to regain its status as a major house, but in the past half-century its stock has gradually and consistently risen.

GERMANY

Though it might be surprising to Americans, Germany is second only to Italy in the number and quality of great opera theaters; indeed, some might claim (with justification) that Germany has maintained even higher standards over the years. The most famous house is, of course, the Berlin State Opera (*Staatsoper*), a project initiated by Frederick the Great when he took the throne in 1740; it opened in an incomplete state (amidst scaffolding and sheets!) two years later. Oddly enough, it was for decades a showplace for Italian operas rather than German ones, probably because there were few great German operas before Mozart. Not so oddly, it was first available only to the aristocracy, not opening to the general public until 1806, at which point the body of the house—which had contained only standing room and boxes—was remodeled into an auditorium with seats and tiers. Its most famous music director was the conductor Otto Klemperer, who in the 1920s made Berlin the scene of many avant-garde productions, including Alban Berg's *Wozzeck*.

The Dresden Staatsoper is another outstanding house. Dresden has been home to a succession of music palaces. The first was founded in 1548, long before opera itself began, as a "Musikalische Kapelle" where orchestral performances were given; in 1627, it was the site of a production of Heinrich Schütz's opera *Dafne*. The first house dedicated solely to opera was built in 1667, the second in 1719. During the mid-18th century, two rival opera houses opened up in order to allow the general public to attend. The most famous of early Dresden opera houses opened in 1841; designer Gottfried Semper aimed at serving the art of drama-in-music rather than creating a rococo showcase. After two replacements, caused by fire and war respectively, the present- day house was rebuilt in the 1960s.

The third great German opera house is the Munich Nationaltheater (no translation necessary, I hope). Like Dresden, Munich went through a few previous houses, the first one having been opened in 1657. During the 19th century, before Bayreuth was built, Munich was the site of most of Richard Wagner's great operatic premieres. Like Dresden, the Munich house was damaged in World War II, though it was rebuilt several years before Dresden's.

And then, of course, there is the Bayreuth Festspielhaus. Built in 1876 in a modest Franconian town, on a mound known affectionately as "the green hill," it was considered at the time a marvel of opera-theater architecture. Not the least amazing quality of Bayreuth is its "sunken" orchestra pit, completely hiding the conductor and musicians so that nothing can detract from the stage drama. Another interesting aspect is its wide-open backstage, whereby props and sets can be wheeled on and off the stage in record time. Some connoisseurs argue that the sound seems too distant and instruments cannot "bloom," but the "Bayreuth acoustic" has a quality all its own, instantly recognizable even in recordings and broadcasts. The secret? The middle frequencies, e.g., those around the cello-to-French horn range (and including the bulk of vocal frequencies as well), reverberate for 1.6 seconds, probably longer than in any other major opera house.

FRANCE

The famed Paris Opéra has been around for more than three centuries (it was founded in 1669); the present building opened in 1875, two years after the death of Napoleon III, to whom its architecture had been dedicated. Like many older European houses, it is smaller than one expects, though the acoustics are splendid—indeed, one of the best of any opera house in the world—and when it opened it was the largest opera house in the world. Its instantly recognizable main façade (re-created in Lon Chaney's 1925 horror classic, *The Phantom of the Opera*) is colonnaded, with just enough "roundness" in its design to give it a soft, pleasing look. Unlike the Austrian and German houses, Paris is associated more with great and famous singers than with any particular music director.

The other great French house is Le Capitole, Toulouse. It is almost Italian in its outlook: not because it presents a great many Italian operas, but because its audiences cheer and jeer the singers (as Italians do) with the enthusiasm of a sporting event. Here, singers insist on encores of famous arias if their high notes do not come out right; singers apologize to the public when their singing is out of form; when a singer is roundly booed, the public demands that the singer apologize; and foreign singers, no matter how famous, generally "beg the indulgence of the public" if their French diction is not up to snuff. In short, Toulouse is no Munich, Salzburg, or Bayreuth; but its vocal standards are among the highest in the world.

ITALY

La Scala, Milan, is probably the single most famous opera house in the world, though few know that it was built to replace the Ducale, which was the older and more famous house. Despite a virtually complete reconstruction after 1945, La Scala (which translates as "The Ladder") has changed very little since it opened in 1778. Whereas the Paris Opéra's façade is its most recognizable feature, La Scala's is the horseshoe-shaped auditorium, with the ceiling coming right down to the sixth (and top) row of seats. La Scala's most famous music director was conductor Arturo Toscanini (1867–1957) who, like Mahler, refused to allow his singers to perform encores and insisted that the operas were presented virtually complete. Toscanini left La Scala, and Italy, in 1930 when the Fascists began to wield their political muscle, though he survived to return and conduct its reopening in 1946.

The Teatro la Fenice in Venice opened in 1792, was rebuilt in 1836 and 1854 and remodeled in 1936, and stands today as one of the loveliest and most intimate of theaters. It was the site of many great premieres of the operas of Giuseppe Verdi, as Dresden was for Wagner, and its audiences are noted for their warmth and generosity—which, I assure you, is often a rarity in Italy, where opera singing ranks as a sport not too dissimilar from bullfighting in Spain or boxing in America.

The Teatro San Carlo, Naples, was originally opened in 1737, redecorated in 1768, and (like so many European theaters) "fixed up" after World War II. It holds a place of affection for many American and British soldiers who patronized it during the War. The façade is solid yet unspectacular, its lower half consisting of brick arches, with a colonnade capped by statues of angels to top it off. Like Toulouse, it has long been associated with only the best in singing, and in fact was the principal home of Naples's native son, tenor Fernando de Lucia (1860–1925). Unfortunately, de Lucia's fame was so great that another native-born tenor—Enrico Caruso—managed to obtain only one engagement there in 1901. He was booed by the de Lucia claque, and never sang there again.

Other noted European-Asian theatres are the Kirov Theatre, St. Petersburg; the Warsaw Opera; the National Theatre, Prague; the Royal Opera of Stockholm; the Hamburg Staatsoper; the Monte

Carlo Opera; Il Teatro Regio, Parma; the huge Verona amphitheater; the Rome Opera; and Le Grand Théâtre, Bordeaux.

ENGLAND

Next to La Scala, the most famous foreign opera house (as far as Americans are concerned) is the Royal Opera House, Covent Garden, usually referred to simply as "Covent Garden." The first theater was built in Covent Garden in 1732, though it wasn't until the King's Theatre in the Haymarket burned down in 1789 that opera performances were increased and more full-scale operas were presented there. In 1808 Covent Garden itself burned down and was rebuilt, though performance time was still shared with plays. Covent Garden was substantially expanded after the façade burned down in 1856; it reopened in 1858 and is substantially the same Covent Garden we see today. A period of relative eclipse occurred, but a revitalized Covent Garden opened in 1888 under the directorship of Augustus Harris—a little-known and much-underrated theatrical genius—to present a bevy of great singing talent such as baritone Jean Lassalle, sopranos Zélie de Lussan and Lillian Nordica, and the famous de Reszke brothers (tenor Jean and bass Edouard). Nellie Melba joined the company in the following year, and soon became a Covent Garden favorite (and legend).

The other famous British opera house, Glyndebourne, is the brainchild of one farsighted eccentric, wealthy opera-lover John Christie. Glyndebourne was welded onto a manor house in the Sussex downs in 1934. Christie built the theater to promote the career of his wife, soprano Audrey Mildmay (who was competent but hardly a major star). He proposed that servants wait on each of the 300 spectators (shades of the old aristocratic system!). Glyndebourne could easily have folded as a mad dream, but Christie was lucky: He had taste as well as money, and he managed to attract two refugees from Hitler's New Order, conductor Fritz Busch and director Rudolf Bing. They were both fanatic perfectionists who saw in Glyndebourne the chance to perfect the concept of "ensemble opera" that has become pivotal in our lifetimes. As a result, Glyndebourne not only did well in and of itself, but for decades its recordings of Mozart's operas were considered benchmarks.

AUSTRALIA

Sitting on a peninsula close to the famous Sydney Harbour Bridge is the Sydney Opera House that, if it is not the most famous or most prestigious cultural citadel in the world, is certainly the most recognizable. This is because Danish architect Jorn Utzorn chose to astonish as well as attract, with the result that its exterior consists of ten or twelve eggshell-like roofs, broken in half and jutting their corner peaks high into the sky. Actually, the Sydney house is a multitheater edifice, containing the opera house, a dramatic theater, a cinema, and a concert hall. Despite its imposing and unforgettable image, it could very well have sunk financially as a very expensive albatross; but conductor Richard Bonynge and soprano Joan Sutherland, the latter a native Sydneyan, have managed to build it into a major opera forum.

AMERICA

No other name, in our century, can conjure up an immediate image of Opera with a capital "O" as New York's famed Metropolitan Opera. Enrico Caruso in *Pagliacci*—Rosa Ponselle in *Norma*—the dynamic Wagnerian duo, Kirsten Flagstad and Lauritz Melchior—Ezio Pinza as Don Giovanni—Maria Callas and Tito Gobbi—the immortal tenor Jussi Björling—Leontyne Price as Aida—that modern-day dynamic duo, Joan Sutherland and Luciano Pavarotti—all appeared here, some as near-permanent fixtures, some as fleeting meteors, some as occasional guests. But they were all here, and they all became identified with opera in New York.

The first Met opened in 1883, and was as much famed for its huge seating capacity and larger-than-life stage as it was for its cramped backstage quarters and what was probably the ugliest façade in opera-house history (it was often referred to as "The Yellow Brick Brewery," because that's what it looked like). In 1892 it was gutted by fire and rebuilt; in 1966 an entirely new, more modern, and airier theater opened in Lincoln Center, where the Met has been ever since. (I was taken backstage to interview Francis Robinson in 1975, and can attest to the fact that it is, if anything, even huger and more confusing "around the back" than it is in front.) Nevertheless, despite a recent decline in artistic quality, the Met is still the Met, which is to say the greatest opera house in the New World.

The Civic Opera House, Chicago, is second only to the Metropolitan in terms of importance; indeed, some would go so far as to say that it has surpassed the Met in recent decades at least in terms of quality. Its austere appearance is no thing of beauty, but what transpires on the stage is often of greater importance (and attraction).

The first Chicago Opera Company was formed at the end of 1909, part of a "package deal" that included all rights to the repertory of Oscar Hammerstein's New York company (which had been a serious rival, and thorn in the side, of the Metropolitan). In 1915, it went bankrupt and was reformed as the Chicago Opera Association; its most famous director was Scottish soprano Mary Garden (1874–1967), who imported some astounding singers not invited to perform at the Met (e.g., soprano Rosa Raisa and baritone Riccardo Stracciari) and made them a force on the American opera scene. The company collapsed in 1932, rose phoenix-like from its own ashes in 1933, and ground to a halt again in 1946. The company as we know it today was founded in 1954 by a remarkable one-woman operatic tornado, Carol Fox, who brought to the city some of the finest singers and conductors in the world: Maria Callas, Renata Tebaldi, Anita Cerquetti, Giuseppe di Stefano, Jussi Björling, Ettore Bastianini, Cesare Siepi, Sir Georg Solti, and Nicola Rescigno, among others.

The San Francisco Opera began in 1932, and like Chicago it was better known for its imported talents than for the brilliance of its visual presentation. The two men who raised it to its present preeminence were conductor-director Gaetano Merola and his successor, Kurt Adler. Adler was responsible for the American debuts of such luminaries as sopranos Leonie Rysanek and Birgit Nilsson, mezzo-soprano Oralia Dominguez, and bass Boris Christoff. Like Otto Klemperer, he became associated with the avant garde through his productions of Walton, Poulenc, and Berg operas. In recent years the company has become increasingly noted for the luxuriance of its visual presentation, the revival of unusual Romantic and post-Romantic works by Boito and Meyerbeer, and the formation of its own "ensemble company," a group of studio singers that has produced (among others) the ear-ravishing soprano Ruth Ann Swenson.

In a competitive market that includes just about every opera theater west of New York, east of San Francisco, and south of Chicago, the Houston Opera has become a major American theater. Founded in 1955, it struggled for seventeen years to compete with Dallas–Fort Worth for major imported singers. Then, in 1972, artistic director David Gockley took over, and during the next decade he turned heads and stunned audiences by making Houston the nation's number-one "avant-garde" house, as Otto Klemperer did in Berlin of the 1920s. Over the years, Houston has made it a point to premiere at least one new opera each year, including such controversial productions as *Nixon in China* and Philip Glass's *Einstein on the Beach*, as well as presenting such standard repertoire as *Madame Butterfly* in the controversial productions of Ken Russell and Hal Prince.

After occupying two former homes, Houston Opera moved into the Wortham Theatre Center in 1987. The lobby has an art-deco feel; the auditorium is a deep maroon, with the Star of Texas on the founder's boxes and above the proscenium. Thanks to Gockley's ceaseless efforts, Houston has also become one of our nation's few "full-season" opera houses, offering performances between October and July.

Other noted opera houses in North and South America are the New York City Opera, Boston Opera, Miami Opera, Pittsburgh Opera, Cincinnati Opera, Phoenix Opera, Dallas–Fort Worth Opera, San Diego Opera, Vancouver Opera, Mexico City Opera, and the Teatro Colon in Buenos Aires.

SINGERS OF TODAY

Now that you know where to go, you might want to know who to listen for. As you may have noticed throughout this text, my concentration has been on singers of the recent or distant past rather than the present. The reason for this is that, despite the fact that conservatories churn out hundreds of students each year, the operatic talent pool has thinned considerably in the past two or three decades. If you don't believe me, just ask yourself one question: Why has there not been any successor to Luciano Pavarotti or Placido Domingo since they both established themselves in the early 1970s?

Nevertheless, there are some good, famous singers of today—Pavarotti and Domingo included—who are worth seeking out. Let's critique a few.

Sopranos

Kathleen Battle is the premiere light lyric soprano of our time, and has been since she first burst on the international scene in the late 1970s. Her voice has a shimmering, "mother-of-pearl" quality that is difficult to describe in words; the best I can muster are "liquid" and "fluorescent." She is also an exquisitely musical singer, whose phrasing is always elegant and enchanting, though her vocal acting sometimes suffers in comparison with the sheer high quality of her voice production. She is often featured on public television broadcasts (see Appendix B).

Jessye Norman is the greatest dramatic soprano of our time, a statement I make based on the fact that, over the twenty years I've been listening to her, her voice has not lost one iota of power, resonance, beauty, or technical control. As with many dramatic sopranos, Norman can alternate mezzo-soprano roles (see, for instance, her assumption of the role of Cassandre in *Les Troyens* in Chapter 5). Like Battle, Norman occasionally misses the mark dramatically, but more so in the recording studio than in person. She is an artist with a tremendous stage presence and dramatic imagination, who responds to live audiences in such a way as to positively rivet them with the overwhelming power of her portrayals.

Kiri te Kanawa, recently made a Dame of the British Empire, is as noted for her great beauty (according to reports, the result of extensive plastic surgery) as for the lovely timbre of her voice. She is not a great interpreter, either in the studio or the opera house, but in a limited repertoire (Mozart and the French lyric roles of the 19th century) she is a fine singer, with a caressing legato and silvery quality. In her earlier years (1968–1974) she was able to sing a little wider range of material, such as Desdemona in Verdi's *Otello*, but since the late 1970s her carrying power has waned.

Another outstanding singer is **Carol Vaness,** whose voice is slightly smaller than Norman's as well as brighter or more "metallic." Vaness tends to specialize in dramatic Mozart roles (Elektra in *Idomeneo*, Donna Anna in *Don Giovanni*), the heavier bel canto parts (*Lucia di Lammermoor*, Elvira in *I Puritani*), and Verdi's dramatic-coloratura roles (Donna Elvira in *Ernani,* Leonora in *Trovatore*). Like Norman, she can also sound detached on commercial recordings, but responds in live performance with a superb dramatic flair.

Mezzo-Sopranos

There are only two modern mezzos of note; both have been around awhile, and both sing more or less the same repertoire. **Frederica von Stade** specializes in Mozart, Rossini, and French-lyric parts; her voice is light and has an odd "flicker-vibrato" that sometimes can obtrude on her legato singing, but in recent years she has overcome vocal problems to reassume her high place. **Agnes Baltsa,** who is a little younger, sings the same repertoire, but adds to it dramatic coloratura parts like Donna Elvira in *Don Giovanni* and verismo roles like Santuzza in *Cavalleria Rusticana.* Because her voice is a little larger, fuller, and more metallic than von Stade's, she can encompass this repertoire without too much strain.

Tenors

Once one has discussed **Luciano Pavarotti** and **Placido Domingo,** there doesn't seem to be anywhere else to go. Their voices, faces, and personalities are as familiar to opera goers and viewers of public television as they are to denizens of "The Tonight Show" and "Entertainment Tonight." Both have had long, distinguished careers, and both have high-powered press agents who constantly place them before the public eye. They also happen to be pretty fine singers, though both have had down moments, seasons, or (in Domingo's case) decades (the 1970s). Pavarotti is the more popular of the two, primarily because of his exuberant personality that he invokes in his stage roles, but those who have never heard him in person should be told that the voice is medium-small in size, and not the large-sounding force it appears to be on recordings. Domingo's voice is rather larger, though not as graceful, and he does not distinguish very much between his operatic characters. In 1989 he suffered a hernia while searching through the rubble of the Mexico City earthquake for his relatives and other victims, and since then has canceled several performances. He is currently in the process of redirecting his career from singing to conducting, which he also does quite competently.

Another tenor of note, though not as famous, is **Richard Leech,** who is being groomed as Domingo's successor. He has a beautiful, good-sized voice, but normally sings poorly in studio situations. If you catch him on a good night in an opera house, however, you will be delighted by his singing. And, before we leave tenors altogether, we should mention the up-and-coming Rossini-Mozart tenor **Stanford Olsen,** whose recent work at the Metropolitan Opera suggests great things. Though Olsen's voice is small (about the size of Pavarotti's), it is even more technically fluent, more practiced in runs and trills, and capable of greater tone-coloring.

Baritones

The two finest baritones of today are unquestionably **Gino Quilico,** the son of French-Canadian baritone Louis Quilico, and **Giorgio Zancanaro.** Quilico has a light, bright voice, what the French used to call a "bariton-matin"; his specialties are the French and light Italian roles, which he performs to perfection—musically, vocally, and histrionically. Zancanaro, on the other hand, is a good, old-fashioned Italian "spinto" baritone, a successor to such illustrious names as Lawrence Tibbett, Gino Bechi, and Mario Sereni. He has a lovely timbre, good technical finish, and a fine dramatic sense, and has successfully filled a void that has existed in Italy since Sereni's retirement.

Basses

Though **Samuel Ramey** has become, perhaps, the most famous of modern basses, he tends to overact and push the voice out of shape with his gruff, blustery over-accenting. Nevertheless, he is a potent stage presence, despite a propensity for performing every role with his shirt off. This leaves us, at present, with only two other outstanding basses, the veteran German singer **Kurt Rydl,** who specializes in Mozart and other lyric German works, and Italian **Ruggero Raimondi,** whose voice has deepened in resonance over the years while actually improving in interpretation.

EPILOGUE

I've tried to convey as much as I can of opera's rich history and many facets without getting bogged down in too many technicalities. I have also recommended what I feel are the best available performances, regardless of age or label, though in all but three cases I stayed within the bounds of post–World War II recordings. Naturally, you are free to make your own choices regarding the performances you like best, but as a starting point I don't honestly feel you can do better than my recommended recordings. Some readers might feel that some of the less well-known recordings are difficult to obtain, but in the past decade I've found that, if anything, service and availability have actually gotten better; and besides, there is no guarantee that even some of the big "commercial" labels can be easily obtained in record stores. When it comes to ordering classical fare, I've found that the telephone is your best friend, and until some of these recordings are rendered completely unavailable I shall stick to my recommendations.

I also tried to strike a balance between all phases of opera, though naturally concentrating on works written between 1814 and 1924 that constitute the bulk of the "standard repertoire." And yet, even here I know from experience that you cannot predict a reader's taste; I know several new opera lovers who are much more attracted to pre-1800 opera than to the Romantic works, and even some who are only pleased by more modern idioms. Because a book of this scope can of necessity only scratch the surface, independent investigation is of course heartily encouraged. All I really wanted to do was spark a lively interest in opera, point you in what I felt were the right directions, and let you go on from there.

As for whether opera will continue to be a viable artform in the 21st century, that is anyone's guess. My own feeling is that, in our fast-paced society, opera has become an anachronism replaced by rock-music videos; but it is an enticing, richly rewarding anachronism, and the great works chronicled in this volume have little chance of dying out.

GLOSSARY

Aria A set piece or "song" within an opera, usually lasting three to seven minutes (though some of Wagner's lasted almost a half-hour) for a solo singer.

Arietta A shorter, simpler aria lacking the aria's characteristic middle section.

Bass-Baritone The rarest category of voice, implying a low male singer who can reach both the low notes of a bass and the high notes (at least up to an A-flat) of a baritone.

Bel Canto Italian for "beautiful singing," often applied to the elegant style of the early-to-mid-19th century. Singers in this style have come to possess an even tone production, smooth *legato*, and the ability to move from high to low notes and from soft to loud singing effortlessly. Trills and *coloratura* are also often a requirement.

Cabaletta The faster "tag ending" to arias, generally those in 19th-century Italian operas. These can last anywhere from two to four minutes, are often sung loudly at full voice, and sometimes are accompanied by a chorus.

Cadenza Vocal flourishes added toward the end of an aria.

Castrati The general term used for castrated male sopranos and altos who were featured in 17th- and 18th-century operas. These singers also contributed to the development of "normal" sopranos, tenors, and baritones in the bel canto era (early-to-mid-19th century) through teaching.

Cavatina Slow legato arias, generally those meant to be interpreted as love songs. The two most famous examples are Count Almaviva's aria *Se il mio nome* from *Il Barbiere di Siviglia*, and Faust's *Salut, demeure* from *Faust*.

Coloratura Vocal "tricks" such as rapid scale passages, *staccato*, and trills, which enhance a melody, especially in Italian and French operas of the early-to-mid-19th century (though some lyric German works, such as *Martha*, *The Merry Wives of Windsor*, and Mozart's operas, also call for them). Nowadays this term is most often, and wrongly, attributed only to light, high sopranos who can produce such tricks (see *Soubrette*). In the old days, every singer in all vocal ranges was expected to have some coloratura ability.

Contralto The lowest female voice-range, going from a C below middle C to, say, no higher than an F or G above.

Countertenor An artificial male soprano or alto voice created by developing the falsetto range—the same part of the voice used for yodeling—with increased strength and resonance (the vibration of the voice in the nasal and forehead cavities of your face). These singers serve, today, as pseudo-castrati, though even the best of them often lack the focus and carrying power of the real thing.

Dotted Notes Short, fast notes, usually of the same pitch, sung rapidly. This is also more formally known as "spotted-flute" technique, because the singer simulates that instrument, and more informally (usually wrongly) called "the Baroque trill."

Dramatic Soprano The biggest, loudest, heaviest of soprano voices, usually suitable for only a few different kinds of roles (in the operas of Wagner, Gluck, and the title part of Puccini's *Turandot*). Nowadays most of these singers don't have much flexibility (the ability to sing trills and *coloratura*).

Dramatic Tenor The biggest, loudest, heaviest of tenor voices, like the *dramatic soprano*, suitable for only a few different kinds of roles (in the operas of Wagner, Gluck, and the title part of Verdi's *Otello*). Sometimes referred to as a *Heldentenor*.

Forte The Italian term for "loud."

Heldenbaritone A large, loud, heavy baritone voice, developed specifically by Wagner for his music-dramas. Most of the best Heldenbaritones are usually bass-baritones, though being a bass-baritone does not always ensure that a singer will have the proper volume to be a Heldenbaritone.

Heldentenor Similar to the dramatic tenor, except that many (though not all) Heldentenors specialize in Wagner, because many of them are actually too heavy or "dark"-sounding to sing much else.

Legato A "fine line" or long phrase sung in one breath, in which the voice floats easily and without strain.

Libretto The words or, literally, "book" of an opera. It should be noted, however, that libretto is not necessarily the same thing as the plot. Different opera composers may use the same general plot-outline but their wordsmiths then come up with sometimes quite different librettos for their works.

Lyric Soprano A middle-sized soprano voice, sometimes capable of producing high notes with a "ringing" sound, but generally noted for a smooth, creamy tone and (more often than not) the ability to "float" soft high notes.

Lyric Tenor A middle-sized tenor voice, practically identical to the *lyric soprano*.

Messa Di Voce The most difficult of vocal "tricks" employed by bel canto singers, this is the ability to start a note softly, smoothly increase the volume, and then reduce the volume again. Most modern singers can't even do it, but the legendary tenor Jussi Björling could not only do it forward but backward—which is to say, he could start loudly, diminish the volume, and then increase it again!

Mezzo-Soprano Literally, a "middle-soprano," or a voice range between that of soprano and contralto. Some mezzos can go up to a high B, but not necessarily high C (though that doesn't stop them from trying!); some can briefly touch some notes in the lower contralto range, though usually they have to "age" the voice to do it without effort or discomfort.

Obbligato An accompanying part, usually only sketched in by the composer, that can be omitted from a performance.

Piano The Italian term for "soft" (in volume). Even softer is "pianissimo."

Polyphony Simultaneous performance of two or more melodic parts.

Recitative Words spoken rapidly on one or two pitches, with one instrument, usually a harpsichord or piano, as accompaniment. Sometimes called sung-speech or *sprechstimme* (in German).

Roulade Vocal ornaments sung to a single syllable.

Scena A section or part of the act of an opera, generally starting with recitatives and then moving into aria(s), duet(s), or larger ensembles. Often, though not always, it involves a chorus in addition to solo singers.

Singspiel German style combining sung passages with spoken interludes in the vernacular.

Soubrette A light soprano, normally able to sing a tone or two higher than lyrics or spintos, and usually able to perform coloratura "tricks." The highest of this type of singer, who can go up to high Es, Fs, Gs, or further, is properly known as a *Soprano leggiero*, and improperly called a "Coloratura Soprano."

Spinto A slightly more brilliant and powerful lyric voice, tenor or soprano, in terms of volume somewhere between lyric and dramatic. Many (but not all) of these singers have a modicum of coloratura ability, or at least are flexible enough to sing a few grace notes and maybe some staccato.

Sprechstimme German for "sung-speech." See *Recitative*.

Staccato Short, clipped notes of varying pitches, sung in rapid sequence and attacked separately or "pinpricked" by the singer. Normally the domain of sopranos only.

Tessitura The "average range" of a certain aria or a complete role. By "average range" I mean the place where most of the notes lie. Verdi was known for raising the tessitura in his operas, while the verismo composers kept almost invariably up in the mid-to-high range.

Tone Production The way a singer's voice is produced, which is to say (in effect) the way it comes out of his or her throat and strikes the listener's ear. The best voices have a smooth, even sound, as free of "throatiness" as possible. Some modern singers "pressure" the voice from above as it comes out, increasing the volume but limiting the tone production and making it less even.

Trill A rapid alternation of notes, usually a full tone apart. The most difficult of these is the perfectly even trill, sung at full volume; many singers soften their voices when they sing trills, produce no more than a vague flutter at any volume level, or give out a "machine-gun" burst of sound. The most perfect trills were possessed by

Adelina Patti, Nellie Melba, John McCormack, and Joan Sutherland.

Tremolo A shaking or quivering tone, also (less charitably) called "wobble."

Verismo A style of opera that flourished in Italy during the late 19th and early 20th centuries. The word itself means "realism"; the plots of such operas concern themselves not with dukes, princes, or czars but the lives and problems of "average people," e.g., Bohemians, gypsies, soldiers, and peasants. Ironically, most of the "verismo" composers deserted these simple folk for (you guessed it) princesses, Mandarins, emperors, and kings as their careers progressed.

Vocal Coloration Changing the timbre of the voice, from lyrical to intense and dramatic, to underscore an opera's libretto.

RECORD LABEL AND
VIDEO CONTACTS

Most of the common commercial labels (RCA, Sony-CBS, DG, London, Philips, Angel-EMI, Telarc, Teldec, Erato, etc.) are available in large record stores coast-to-coast—but not always. If you do not see them in stock, feel free to order them through the store; or, if you wish to deal directly with the companies, you may order them from the addresses (and phone numbers) below. Foreign/imported CDs may be acquired from Chambers Record & Video and other specialty mail-order or retail dealers. The phone numbers and addresses of those companies that deal in the recommended videos are also listed below. And don't be bashful about calling: I've found that getting a video directly from the manufacturer, or a CD from the distributor, is often faster than trying to find a domestic label, or even ordering it!

Allegro Imports
3434 S.E. Milwaukie Ave.
Portland, OR 97202
(503) 232-4213

Angel-EMI
810 Seventh Ave., 4th Floor
New York, NY 10019
(212) 603-4167

Arkadia: *See* Qualiton Imports

Bel Canto/Paramount Home Video:
  See Chambers Record & Video

Bel Canto Society
11 Riverside Dr.
New York, NY 10023
(800) 347-5056

Capriccio
c/o Delta Music
2275 S. Carmelina Ave.
Los Angeles, CA 90064
(213) 826-6151

Chambers Record & Video
61 Bennington Ave.
Freeport, NY 11520
(800) 892-9338

Chandos: *See* Koch International

Club 99: *See* Qualiton Imports

Deutsche Grammophon: *See* Polygram Classics

Erato/Musifrance: *See* Teldec/Erato

Eurodisc: *See* RCA/BMG Classics

Fonit-Cetra: *See* Allegro Imports

Harmonia Mundi: *See* Chambers Record & Video

Hunt Productions: *See* Qualiton Imports

Koch International: *See* Chambers Record & Video

Kultur
121 Hwy. 36
West Long Branch, NJ 07764
(800) 458-5887

Laudis: *See* Chambers Record & Video

Legato Classics: *See* Lyric Distribution

L'Oiseau-Lyre: *See* Polygram Classics

London: *See* Polygram Classics

Lyric Distribution
18 Madison Ave.
Hicksville, NY 11801
(800) 325-9742

Melodram: *See* Qualiton Imports

Music Memoria: *See* Chambers Record & Video

Myto: *See* Qualiton Imports

Nimbus
P.O. Box 7427
Charlottesville, VA 22906
(804) 985-1100

Opal: *See* Chambers Record & Video

Orfeo: *See* Chambers Record & Video

Pearl: *See* Koch International

Philips: *See* Polygram Classics

Polygram Classics
Worldwide Plaza
825 Eighth Ave.
New York, NY 10010
(212) 333-8000

Preiser: *See* Chambers Record & Video

Qualiton Imports
24-02 Fortieth Ave.
Long Island City, NY 11101
(718) 729-3239

RCA/BMG Classics
1133 Ave. of the Americas
New York, NY 10036
(212) 930-4000

Sony Classical/CBS Masterworks
1285 Ave. of the Americas
New York, NY 10019
(212) 445-4763

Standing Room Only: *See* Lyric Distribution

Telarc
23307 Commerce Park Rd.
Cleveland, OH 44122
(216) 464-2313

Teldec-Erato
Elektra/WEA Classics
75 Rockefeller Plaza
New York, NY 10019
(212) 399-6963

Thorn-EMI videos: *See* Bel Canto Society,
   Chambers Record & Video.

VAI
158 Linwood Plaza, Suite 301
Fort Lee, NJ 07024
(800) 477-7146

Veritas: *See* Angel-EMI

V.I.E.W. Video
34 East 23rd St.
New York, NY 10010
(800) 843-9843

Virgin Classics: *See* Angel-EMI

APPENDIX A:

A Basic Opera Library

There are so many complete operas and recitals by individual singers recommended in this volume that I've decided to offer a core listening library for those who feel rather overwhelmed by it all. Those who wish to start here and then dive into the main text of the book will not be disappointed; but bear in mind that in following this list you are on your own unless you refer back to my comments made in earlier sections.

In compiling this list, I shrunk the "basic library" to twenty-two complete operas and eight vocal recitals by various great singers. Both categories have been weighed and chosen carefully. In selecting the complete operas, for instance, I tried to include a few great masterpieces that are not popular favorites, a few popular favorites that are not necessarily masterpieces, with the majority being pretty much both. In selecting the recitals, I tried to stick to electrical recordings so as not to alienate the new listener too much with archaic-sounding orchestras. More importantly, I tried to choose those recitals that presented the widest possible snatches of repertoire outside of the twenty-two complete operas, so that they would supplement rather than duplicate material. Finally, I tried to choose recordings that I felt the neophyte would return to again and again; and if this meant selecting the more generally attractive *Pique Dame* of Tchaikovsky over the more rambling and (to the layman) less tuneful *Boris Godunov* of Mussorgsky, so be it.

Complete Operas

Handel *Giulio Cesare in Egitto*. Janet Baker, Valerie Masterson, Della Jones, James Bowman, Sir Charles Mackerras. Thorn-EMI videotape HTVE-3558.

Gluck *Alceste*. Jessye Norman, Nicolai Gedda, Siegmund Nimsgern, Bernd Weikl, Tom Krause, Serge Baudo. Orfeo C-027823-F (three CDs).

Mozart *Le Nozze di Figaro*. Kiri te Kanawa, Lucia Popp, Frederica von Stade, Samuel Ramey, Thomas Allen, Sir Georg Solti. London 410 150-2/4 LH3/4 (three CDs, four cassettes).

Mozart *Don Giovanni*. Joan Sutherland, Elisabeth Schwarzkopf, Graziella Sciutti, Luigi Alva, Eberhard Wächter, Giuseppe Taddei, Carlo Maria Giulini. Angel CDCC-47260 (3 CDs). *Video alternate*: Wilhelm Furtwängler, VAI 69063.

Rossini *Il Barbiere di Siviglia*. Mercedes Capsir, Dino Borgioli, Riccardo Stracciari, Salvatore Baccaloni, Franco Ghione. Music Memoria 30276/7 (two CDs). Stereo alternate: Agnes Baltsa, Francisco Araiza, Thomas Allen, Robert Lloyd, Neville Marriner. Philips 411 058-2/4 PH3 (three CDs/cassettes).

Rossini *William Tell*. Mirella Freni, Della Jones, Luciano Pavarotti, Sherrill Milnes, Nicolai Ghiaurov, Riccardo Chailly. London 417 154-2 LH4 (four CDs).

Bellini *I Puritani*. Maria Callas, Giuseppe di Stefano, Rolando Panerai, Nicola Rossi-Lemeni, Tullio Serafin. Angel CDCB-47308/4AVB-34065 (two CDs/cassettes).

Donizetti *L'Elisir d'Amore*. Kathleen Battle, Luciano Pavarotti, Leo Nucci, Enzo Dara, James Levine. DG 429 744-1/2/4 (two LPs/CDs/cassettes).

Donizetti *Lucia di Lammermoor*. Anna Moffo, Carlo Bergonzi, Mario Sereni, Ezio Flagello, Georges Prêtre. RCA Victor 6504-2-RG (two CDs).

Flotow *Martha*. Lucia Popp, Doris Soffel, Siegfried Jerusalem, Karl Ridderbusch, Siegmund Nimsgern, Heinz Wallberg. Eurodisc 7789-2-RG (two CDs).

Gounod *Faust*. Renata Scotto, Marion dal Piva, Alfredo Kraus, Lorenzo Saccomani, Nicolai Ghiaurov, Paul Ethuin. Lyric Distribution videotape 1724.

Verdi *Il Trovatore*. Leyla Gencer, Fedora Barbieri, Mario del Monaco, Ettore Bastianini, Fernando Previtali. Lyric Distribution videotape 1961.

Verdi *Aida*. Maria Chiara, Fiorenza Cossotto, Nicola Martinucci, Giuseppe Scandola, Anton Guadagno. Thorn-EMI videotape HTVE-2790.

Verdi *Otello*. Herva Nelli, Ramon Vinay, Giuseppe Valdengo, Nicola Moscona, Arturo Toscanini. RCA Victor 60302-2-RG (two CDs). *Video alternate* (missing *Ora e per sempre addio*): Gabrielle Tucci, Mario del Monaco, Tito Gobbi, Alberto Erede. Lyric Distribution videotape 1439.

Wagner *Der Fliegende Höllander*. Lisbeth Balslev, Robert Schunk, Simon Estes, Matti Salmminen, Woldemar Nelsson. Philips videotape 070506-3; also Philips 416 300-2 PH2 (two CDs).

Wagner *Tristan und Isolde*. Birgit Nilsson, Ruth Hesse, Jon Vickers, Walter Berry, Bengt Rundgren, Karl Böhm. Lyric Distribution videotape 1868. CD alternate: Kirsten Flagstad, Ludwig Surhaus, Wilhelm Furtwängler. Angel CDCD-47321 (four CDs).

Bizet *Carmen*. Julia Migenes-Johnson, Faith Esham, Placido Domingo, Ruggero Raimondi, Lorin Maazel. Columbia videotape (no number); also on Erato 45207-2 ZB (three CDs).

Tchaikovsky *Pique Dame*. Tamara Milashkina, Vladimir Atlantov, Valentina Levko, Mark Ermler. Philips 420 375-2 PH3 (three CDs). *Video alternate*: Milashkina, Atlantov, Elena Obratsouva. Kultur 1164.

Leoncavallo *Pagliacci*. Victoria de los Angeles, Jussi Björling, Leonard Warren, Robert Merrill, Renato Cellini. Angel CDC-49503 (one CD).

Puccini *La Bohème*. Mirella Freni, Elisabeth Harwood, Luciano Pavarotti, Rolando Panerai, Herbert von Karajan. London 421 049-2/4 LH2 (two CDs/cassettes).

Strauss *Salome*. Teresa Stratas, Hanna Schwarz, Astrid Varnay, Wieslaw Ochman, Hans Beirer, Bernd Weikl, Karl Böhm. DG stereo laserdisc 072209-1 NTSC. *CD alternate*: Birgit Nilsson, Grace

Hoffman, Gerhard Stolze, Waldemar Kmentt, Eberhard Wächter, Sir Georg Solti. London 414 414-2 LH2 (two CDs).

Britten *Peter Grimes*. Heather Harper, Elisabeth Bainbridge, Jon Vickers, Norman Bailey, Forbes Robinson, Sir Colin Davis. Thorn-EMI videotape HTVE-3562 (two tapes, VHS).

Vocal Recitals

Lily Pons (Sony Classical/CBS MPK-45694). Arias from *Lakmé*, *Rigoletto*, *I Puritani*, *Il Barbiere di Siviglia*, *Mignon*, and *Dinorah*, plus songs by Delibes, Ponce, Rachmaninov, and Johann Strauss, Jr.

Claudia Muzio (Angel CDH-69790). Excerpts from *Norma*, *La Sonnambula*, *La Forza del Destino*, and *La Traviata* in addition to "verismo" arias from *Adriana Lecouvreur*, *Cavalleria Rusticana*, *La Bohème*, *Mefistofele*, and *Andrea Chénier*.

Kirsten Flagstad (RCA Victor 7915-2-RG). An all-Wagner collection; arias and duets from *Götterdämmerung*, *Lohengrin*, *Parsifal*, *Tristan und Isolde*, and *Die Walküre*.

Ebe Stignani (Preiser 89014). Arias from *Norma*, *La Favorita*, *Linda di Chamounix*, *Orfeo et Eurydice*, *L'Amico Fritz*, *Mignon*, *Semiramide*, *Samson et Dalila*, *Ballo in Maschera*, and *Don Carlos*.

Marcel Wittrisch (Preiser 89024). Arias and duets from *Ernani*, *Les Huguenots*, *Les Pêcheurs de Perles*, *Tales of Hoffmann*, *Cavalleria Rusticana*, *Lakmé*, and *The Barber of Baghdad*, in addition to operas in the complete list.

Lauritz Melchior (Angel CDH-69789). An all-Wagner album; excerpts from *Rienzi*, *Tannhäuser*, *Siegfried*, *Die Walküre*, *Tristan und Isolde*, and *Die Meistersinger*.

Lawrence Tibbett (RCA Victor 7808-2/4-RG [CD/cassettes]). Arias from *Tosca*, *Ballo in Maschera*, *Falstaff*, *Simon Boccanegra*, and *Die Walküre* in addition to excerpts from *Pagliacci*, *Carmen*, and *Faust*.

Feodor Chaliapin (Angel CDH-61009). All of his recordings from *Boris Godunov* as well as excerpts from *A Life for the Czar*, *Russlan und Ludmilla*, *Rusalka*, *The Demon*, *Sadko*, *Aleko*, and *Prince Igor*.

APPENDIX B:

Great Singers on Video

Here are the best home videos featuring legendary singers from the past. In addition to covering many of the singers mentioned in the text, I added two others for the excellence of their respective video-tapes, soprano Eleanor Steber (1914–1990) and tenor Richard Tauber (1892–1948). I've also included a few of the best available performances by such contemporary artists as Kathleen Battle, Kiri te Kanawa, Placido Domingo, and Luciano Pavarotti, though their best work can be found on public television concerts and "Live from the Met" telecasts. Bear in mind that some of these videos are second- or third-generation copies, meaning that the visual quality is not always ideal, but their excellence of performance and superior sound quality (because voices recorded much better on film than on early studio recordings) make them valuable to the collector. I also listed a few movies that may pop up on your local cable TV "nostalgia" channel, which are worth watching and/or taping, but (again) I have not listed everything available by all of these singers, merely a cross-section of their best work.

Kathleen Battle   Her duo recital with Jessye Norman, *Spirituals in Concert*, does not necessarily contain the most representative material by this great artist, but it is beautifully sung (DG NTSC-072249-3 GVG).

Jussi Björling   His 1937 film, *Fram för Framgång* (*Head for Success*), is rather long, silly, and lacking subtitles, but it does contain some extraordinary singing performances (avail. from both Lyric Distribution and the Bel Canto Society); VAI 69101 features him in opera, operetta, and song.

Maria Callas   Her 1958 Paris recital is the best representation of her vocal and acting abilities (Lyric Distribution 1570, Bel Canto Society 1), but the 1959 Hamburg recital has an even better picture and clearer sound (Sony/CBS video).

Feodor Chaliapin   His only visual documents are two different versions (one in French, the other in English) of *Don Quixote* with music by Jacques Ibert; though not really operatic, it is highly recommended as a study of Chaliapin's acting and singing abilities at the age of sixty. Chaliapin is more at ease in the French version (Lyric Distribution 5003, Bel Canto 528), but the English print is ten minutes longer, has a better visual quality, and the advantage of having the dialogue in our native tongue (Lyric Distribution 1487, Bel Canto 28).

Placido Domingo   The excellent *Live from the Met, Vol. 1* (Bel Canto/Paramount Home Video 2373) features him in an extended duet scene (with soprano Mirella Freni) from Verdi's *Don Carlos*.

Kirsten Flagstad   Keep your eyes open for *The Big Broadcast of 1938*: The film is for the most part pretty bad, and of value only to Bob Hope fans, but as far as I know it is the only video clip available of Flagstad—singing *Ho-yo-to-ho!* from Wagner's *Die Walküre*.

Nicolai Gedda   Despite the fact that he continues to sing, the best video of this great tenor in his prime is *Opera Two to Six* (1968, VAI 69090), which partners him with soprano Joan Sutherland and baritone Tito Gobbi.

Beniamino Gigli   There are several available prints of Gigli in films, but the one I particularly recommend is *Solo Per Te (Only for You)*, on Lyric Distribution 5038 and Bel Canto Society 502, which contains extended scenes from *Un Ballo in Maschera* and *Andrea Chénier* with soprano Maria Cebotari and baritone Michael Bohnen.

John McCormack   The great Irish tenor made two films, but the second (in color, from 1938) is almost impossible to find, only features a few songs, and was made when he was past his prime; the 1929 *Song o' My Heart* (VAI 69067) not only contains several Irish songs, but an extended "concert" sequence (filmed in New York's Hippodrome Theater) in which he sings the elegant song *Plaisir d'amour*.

Lauritz Melchior   VAI 69107 features the Heldentenor in arias from *Die Walküre, Die Meistersinger*, and *Der Fliegende Höllander*, plus songs. Also, look for a TV screening of *The Stars Are Singing*, which features him in an excellent performance of *Vesti la giubba* from *Pagliacci*.

Anna Moffo VAI 69114 features the soprano in her prime, singing arias from *La Bohème*, *Madame Butterfly*, *Faust*, and *Pagliacci*, plus assorted songs.

Jessye Norman Her duo recital with Kathleen Battle, *Spirituals in Concert* (DG NTSC-072249-3 GVG), does not really do this great singer full justice; but except for her videotaped performance as Cassandre in *Les Troyens* (see Chapter 5), it is the best that is commercially available to us.

Luciano Pavarotti The famous tenor is best seen (and heard) in excerpts from Verdi's *Un Ballo in Maschera*, on *Live from the Met, Vol. 1* (Bel Canto/Paramount Home Video 2373).

Mado Robin A clip of her singing the "Mad Scene" from *Lucia di Lammermoor*, complete with the high Bb above high C, is on *Legendary Singers on TV* (Bel Canto Society 11), while Lyric Distribution 1454 alternates performance excerpts by the soprano with arias sung by modern-day French coloraturas.

Tito Schipa The tape *Schumann-Heink, Alda, Raisa and Rimini, and Schipa* (Bel Canto Society 9003) features Tito singing the aria from *Martha* and a Spanish song.

Ernestine Schumann-Heink Bel Canto Society 9003 features the great contralto in song.

Eleanor Steber Next to Rosa Ponselle and Jessye Norman, Eleanor Steber had the most perfect and beautiful voice of any American-born soprano. VAI 69102 features arias from *Nozze di Figaro*, *Louise*, and *Forza del Destino*, plus operetta and songs, while VAI 69112 contains arias from *Ernani*, *Madame Butterfly*, *Fledermaus*, and ensembles from *Faust*, *Rigoletto*, and *Lucia di Lammermoor*.

Conchita Supervia The only known surviving film of this great mezzo-soprano is the 1934 *Evensong* (Lyric Distribution 1471, Bel Canto Society 526), but be warned: The majority of this film features the simpering, off-key soprano of Evelyn Laye, who was a "big deal" in England at the time. Supervia only shows up in the last fifteen minutes of the film, singing "Musetta's waltz" from *La Bohème*, plus excerpts from Rossini's *Cenerentola* (Cinderella) and Spanish songs. Her bits are marvelous, but it requires quite a bit of fast-forwarding to get past Laye's whimpering.

Joan Sutherland VAI 69108 contains a half-hour of arias, including excerpts from *Artaxerxes, Semiramide, La Bohème,* and *Les Huguenots*. The famed soprano is also in *Opera Two to Six* (VAI 69090) and *Live from the Met, Vol. 1* (Bel Canto/Paramount 2373) in the sextet from *Lucia di Lammermoor* with tenor Alfredo Kraus and bass Paul Plishka.

Richard Tauber Tauber's voice was less flexible than Wittrisch's, and less far-ranging, but he was a superior stage actor. The aria *E lucevan le stelle* from *Tosca* can be seen in *Great Tenors, Vol. 1* (Bel Canto Society 10). The 1937 British film *Pagliacci* (Lyric Distribution 5081, Bel Canto Society 531; also available from Video Yesteryear) turns the opera into a play, but Tauber sings extended excerpts from the score (in English), including the Prologue (normally given to the baritone) and the "Harlequin's Serenade." The final scene of the opera is given in toto, and Tauber's singing and acting are positively hair-raising!

Kiri te Kanawa The popular New Zealand soprano performs beautifully in *Kiri Sings Mozart* (EMI Classics A5VD-9-91242-3), which includes excerpts from *La Clemenza di Tito, Nozze di Figaro, Die Zauberflöte,* and *Don Giovanni,* with the excellent conducting of Sir Charles Mackerras.

Lawrence Tibbett The 1935 film *Metropolitan* (Bel Canto Society, no number) is practically a nonstop singing festival for Tibbett, including the *Faust* trio (as a bass!) and full arias from *Pagliacci, Il Barbiere di Siviglia,* and *Carmen*.

Marcel Wittrisch The only known clip of him is in *Great Tenors, Vol. 1* (Bel Canto Society 10), in which he sings a German pop song.

INDEX

197

Bonisolli, Franco, 74
Bonynge, Richard, 41, 50, 171
Bori, Lucrezia, 139
Boris Godunov (Mussorgsky), 100, 103,
    112; Bolshoi Opera version of,
    102–3; keynotes in, 102; plot of,
    101–2; recordings of, 102–3
Borthayre, Jean, 107
Botio, Arrigo, 79
Bouilly, Jean Nicolas, 29
Boulez, Pierre, 162, 163
Braun, Victor, 97
Breviario, Giovanni, 43
Britten, Benjamin, 162; as opera
    composer, 157
Brumaire, Jacqueline, 82
Bruson, Renato, 82
Burmeister, Annalies, 91
Burrows, Stuart, 112
Busch, Fritz, 148, 170

C

Caballé, Montserrat, 74
Caccini, Giulio, 6
Caesar's Hour, 132
Caesar, Sid, 132–33
Callas, Maria, 31, 43, 44, 66, 132;
    videos of, 193
Caniglia, Maria, 124
Capecchi, Renato, 41
Capsir, Mercedes, 39
Capuana, Franco, 132
Carmen (Bizet) 59, 112, 115; humorous
    translations of, 116; keynotes in,
    105; plot of, 103–4; recordings of,
    105
Carousel, 97
Carreras, José, 64
Caruso, Enrico, 117–18, 136, 138, 140,
    141, 142
Castrati: in opera, 7–8; popularity of in
    the Baroque era, 14
Cavalleria Rusticana (Mascagni), 120;
    keynotes in, 119; plot of, 118;
    recordings of, 119
Cellini, Renato, 119
Chailly, Riccardo, 41
Chaira, Maria, 78

Chaliapin, Feodor, 64, 99, 136, 139,
    140; videos of, 194
Chicago Civic Opera House, history
    of, 172
Christie, John, 170
Cigna, Gina, 43
Clément, Edmond, 138
Cléofide (Hasse), plot of, 18
Coca, Imogene, 132
Coloratura style, 7
Comeaux, Elisabeth, 162
Corelli, Franco, 31, 124, 132
Corradi, Nelly, 39
Cortubas, Ileana, 115
Cosi Fan Tutte (Mozart), 28
Cossotto, Fiorenza, 44, 50, 78
Covent Garden. *See* Royal Opera
    House, Covent Garden
Crabbe, George, 157

D

Danco, Suzanne, 152
da Ponte, Lorenzo, 24
Dara, Enzo, 36, 46
d'Arnaud, Baculard, 49
Das Rheingold (Wagner), 89; keynotes
    in, 91; plot of, 90–91; recordings of,
    91
Davis, Colin, 28
Dawson, Lynne, 21
de Almedia, Antonio, 64
de Beaumarchais, Pierre Augustin
    Caron, 22
Debussy, Claude, compositions of,
    149–50
Delibes, Léo, 34
del Monaco, Mario, 76, 81, 132
de los Angeles, Victoria, 121–22
de Sabata, Victor, 132
Denize, Nadine, 152
Der Fliegende Höllander (Wagner), 84,
    87; keynotes in, 85–86; plot of, 85;
    recordings of, 86
Der Freischutz (Weber), 64
Der Goldene Klang (The Golden Note),
    98
Dernesch, Helga, 97

L

La Belle Hélène (Offenbach), 108, 115
La Bohème (Puccini), 131; keynotes in, 129–30; plot of, 128–29; recordings of, 130
La Capitole, Toulouse, history of, 168
La Cerentola (Rossini), 41
La Damoiselle élue (Debussy), 149
La Fanciulla del West (Puccini), 132
La Favorita (Donizetti): keynotes in, 50; plot of, 49–50; recordings of, 50–51
La Forza del Destino (Verdi), 79; keynotes in, 76; plot of, 75–76; recordings of, 76–77
La Jolie Fille de Perth (Bizet), 103
La Juive (Halevy), 64
L'Amico Fritz (Mascagni), 125
Lanfranchi, Mario, 74
La Perichole (Offenbach), 108
La Scala, Milan, history of, 169
La Serva Padrona (Pergolesi): keynotes in, 17; plot of, 17; recordings of, 17
La Sonnambula (Bellini), 44
La Traviata (Verdi): keynotes in, 73–74; plot of, 72–73; recordings of, 75
La Vestale (Spontini), 31, 42
Lear, Evelyn, 163
Leech, Richard, 176
Lehmann, Lilli, 166
Lehr, LeRoy, 162
Leinsdorf, Erich, 132
Leitmotif, 89
L'Elisir d'Amore (Donizetti): keynotes in, 46; plot of, 45–46; recordings of, 46
Lemeshev, Sergei, 115
L'enfant prodigue (Debussy), 149
Le Nozze di Figaro (de Beaumarchais), 37
Le Nozze di Figaro (Mozart), 3, 26, 28; keynotes in, 23; plot of, 22–23; recordings of, 23–24
Leoncavallo, Ruggero, 120
Leonore (Beethoven), 29
Leppard, Raymond, 21
Les Huguenots (Meyerbeer): keynotes

in, 55; plot of, 54–55; recordings of, 55–56
Les Pêcheurs de Perles (Bizet), 103, 115
Les Troyens (Berlioz), 12, 61; keynotes in, 63; plot of, 62; recordings of, 63
Les Vêpres Siciliennes (Verdi), 82
Levine, James, 28, 46, 63
L'Incoronazione di Poppea (Monteverdi), 11
L'Italiana in Algeri (Rossini), 37; keynotes in, 36; plot of, 35; recordings of, 36
Litz, Gisela, 59
Lloyd, Robert, 28
Lohengrin (Wagner), 86, 89, 97
Lopardo, Frank, 36
L'Orfeo (Monteverdi): keynotes in, 10; plot of, 10; recordings of, 10–11
Lovecraft, H. P., 108
Lucia di Lammermoor (Donizetti): keynotes in, 48; plot of, 47–48; recordings of, 48–49
Ludwig, Christa, 30, 97
Lully, Jean Baptiste, 8, 16, 54, 135
Lulu (Berg), 154, 162
Lyric bass, 99
Lyric spinto soprano, 66
Lyric spinto tenor, 67

M

Mackerras, Sir Charles, 16, 28
MacNeil, Cornell, 132
Madame Butterfly (Puccini): keynotes in, 131; performance history of, 130–31; plot of, 131; recordings of, 131–32
Maeterlinck, Maurice, 150
Magic Flute, The (Mozart). See Die Zauberflöte
Manon (Massenet), 115, 125–26
Manon Lescaut (Puccini), 125; keynotes in, 127; plot of, 126–27; recordings of, 127
Marriage of Figaro, The. See Le Nozze di Figaro
Marriner, Neville, 28, 39
Martha (Flotow), 7; keynotes in, 57; plot of, 56–57; recordings of, 57